W9-BDR-482

A DISCIPLINE
OF PROGRAMMING

Prentice-Hall
Series in Automatic Computation

MARTIN, *Security, Accuracy, and Privacy in Computer Systems*
MARTIN, *Systems Analysis for Data Transmission*
MARTIN, *Telecommunications and the Computer*
MARTIN, *Teleprocessing Network Organization*
MARTIN AND NORMAN, *The Computerized Society*
MCKEEMAN, et al., *A Compiler Generator*
MEYERS, *Time-Sharing Computation in the Social Sciences*
MINSKY, *Computation: Finite and Infinite Machines*
NIEVERGELT, et al., *Computer Approaches to Mathematical Problems*
PLANE AND MCMILLAN, *Discrete Optimization: Integer Programming and Network Analysis for Management Decisions*
POLIVKA AND PAKIN, *APL: The Language and Its Usage*
PRITSKER AND KIVIAT, *Simulation with GASP II: A FORTRAN-based Simulation Language*
PYLYSHYN, ed., *Perspectives on the Computer Revolution*
RICH, *Internal Sorting Methods Illustrated with PL/1 Programs*
RUDD, *Assembly Language Programming and the IBM 360 and 370 Computers*
SACKMAN AND CITRENBAUM, eds., *On-Line Planning: Towards Creative Problem-Solving*
SALTON, ed., *The SMART Retrieval System: Experiments in Automatic Document Processing*
SAMMET, *Programming Languages: History and Fundamentals*
SCHAEFER, *A Mathematical Theory of Global Program Optimization*
SCHULTZ, *Spline Analysis*
SCHWARZ, et al., *Numerical Analysis of Symmetric Matrices*
SHAH, *Engineering Simulation Using Small Scientific Computers*
SHAW, *The Logical Design of Operating Systems*
SHERMAN, *Techniques in Computer Programming*
SIMON AND SIKLOSSY, eds., *Representation and Meaning: Experiments with Information Processing Systems*
STERBENZ, *Floating-Point Computation*
STOUTEMYER, *PL/1 Programming for Engineering and Science*
STRANG AND FIX, *An Analysis of the Finite Element Method*
STROUD, *Approximate Calculation of Multiple Integrals*
TANENBAUM, *Structured Computer Organization*
TAVISS, ed., *The Computer Impact*
UHR, *Pattern Recognition, Learning, and Thought: Computer-Programmed Models of Higher Mental Processes*
VAN TASSEL, *Computer Security Management*
VARGA, *Matrix Iterative Analysis*
WAITE, *Implementing Software for Non-Numeric Application*
WILKINSON, *Rounding Errors in Algebraic Processes*
WIRTH, *Algorithms + Data Structures = Programs*
WIRTH, *Systematic Programming: An Introduction*
YEH, ed., *Applied Computation Theory: Analysis, Design, Modeling*

A DISCIPLINE
OF PROGRAMMING

EDSGER W. DIJKSTRA

Burroughs Research Fellow,
Professor Extraordinarius,
Technological University, Eindhoven

PRENTICE-HALL, INC.

ENGLEWOOD CLIFFS, N.J.

Library of Congress Cataloging in Publication Data

Dijkstra, Edsger Wybe.
  A discipline of programming.

  1. Electronic digital computers—Programming.
I. Title.
QA76.6.D54   001.6'42   75–40478
ISBN 0–13–215871–X

© 1976 by Prentice-Hall, Inc.
Englewood Cliffs, New Jersey

All rights reserved. No part of this book
may be reproduced in any form or by any means
without permission in writing
from the publisher.

14 15

Printed in the United States of America

PRENTICE-HALL INTERNATIONAL, INC., *London*
PRENTICE-HALL OF AUSTRALIA PTY. LIMITED, *Sydney*
PRENTICE-HALL OF CANADA, LTD., *Toronto*
PRENTICE-HALL OF INDIA PRIVATE LIMITED, *New Delhi*
PRENTICE-HALL OF JAPAN, INC., *Tokyo*
PRENTICE-HALL OF SOUTHEAST ASIA PTE. LTD., *Singapore*

CONTENTS

FOREWORD

In the older intellectual disciplines of poetry, music, art, and science, historians pay tribute to those outstanding practitioners, whose achievements have widened the experience and understanding of their admirers, and have inspired and enhanced the talents of their imitators. Their innovations are based on superb skill in the practice of their craft, combined with an acute insight into the underlying principles. In many cases, their influence is enhanced by their breadth of culture and the power and lucidity of their expression.

This book expounds, in its author's usual cultured style, his radical new insights into the nature of computer programming. From these insights, he has developed a new range of programming methods and notational tools, which are displayed and tested in a host of elegant and efficient examples. This will surely be recognised as one of the outstanding achievements in the development of the intellectual discipline of computer programming.

C.A.R. HOARE

PREFACE

For a long time I have wanted to write a book somewhat along the lines of this one: on the one hand I knew that programs could have a compelling and deep logical beauty, on the other hand I was forced to admit that most programs are presented in a way fit for mechanical execution but, even if of any beauty at all, totally unfit for human appreciation. A second reason for dissatisfaction was that algorithms are often published in the form of finished products, while the majority of the considerations that had played their role during the design process and should justify the eventual shape of the finished program were often hardly mentioned. My original idea was to publish a number of beautiful algorithms in such a way that the reader could appreciate their beauty, and I envisaged doing so by describing the —real or imagined— design process that would each time lead to the program concerned. I have remained true to my original intention in the sense that the long sequence of chapters, in each of which a new problem is tackled and solved, is still the core of this monograph; on the other hand the final book is quite different from what I had foreseen, for the self-imposed task to present these solutions in a natural and convincing manner has been responsible for so much more, that I shall remain grateful forever for having undertaken it.

When starting on a book like this, one is immediately faced with the question: "Which programming language am I going to use?", and this is *not* a mere question of presentation! A most important, but also a most elusive, aspect of any tool is its influence on the habits of those who train themselves in its use. If the tool is a programming language, this influence is —whether we like it or not— an influence on our thinking habits. Having analyzed that influence to the best of my knowledge, I had come to the conclusion that none of the existing programming languages, nor a subset of them, would suit my purpose; on the other hand I knew myself so unready for the design of a new programming language that I had taken a vow not to do so for the next five years, and I had a most distinct feeling that that period had not yet elapsed! (Prior to that, among many other things, this monograph had to be written.) I have tried to resolve this conflict by only designing a mini-language suitable for my purposes, by making only those commitments that seemed unavoidable and sufficiently justified.

This hesitation and self-imposed restriction, when ill-understood, may make this monograph disappointing for many of its potential readers. It will certainly leave all those dissatisfied who identify the difficulty of programming with the difficulty of cunning exploitation of the elaborate and baroque tools known as "higher level programming languages" or —worse!— "programming systems". When they feel cheated because I just ignore all those bells and whistles, I can only answer: "Are you quite sure that all those bells and whistles, all those wonderful facilities of your so-called "powerful" programming languages belong to the solution set rather than to the problem set?". I can only hope that, in spite of my usage of a mini-language, they will study my text; after having done so, they may agree that, even without the bells and the whistles, so rich a subject remains that it is questionable whether the majority of the bells and the whistles should have been introduced in the first place. And to all readers with a pronounced interest in the design of programming languages, I can only express my regret that, as yet, I do not feel able to be much more explicit on that subject; on the other hand I hope that, for the time being, this monograph will inspire them and will enable them to avoid some of the mistakes they might have made without having read it.

During the act of writing —which was a continuous source of surprise and excitement— a text emerged that was rather different from what I had originally in mind. I started with the (understandable) intention to present my program developments with a little bit more formal apparatus than I used to use in my (introductory) lectures, in which semantics used to be introduced intuitively and correctness demonstrations were the usual mixture of rigorous arguments, handwaving, and eloquence. In laying the necessary foundations for such a more formal approach, I had two surprises. The first surprise was that the so-called "predicate transformers" that I had chosen as my vehicle provided a means for directly defining a relation between initial and final state, without any reference to intermediate states as may occur during program execution. I was very grateful for that, as it affords a clear separation between two of the programmer's major concerns, the mathematical correctness concerns (viz. whether the program defines the proper relation between initial and final state—and the predicate transformers give us a formal tool for that investigation without bringing computational processes into the picture) and the engineering concerns about efficiency (of which it is now clear that they are only defined in relation to an implementation). It turned out to be a most helpful discovery that the same program text always admits two rather complementary interpretations, the interpretation as a code for a predicate transformer, which seems the more suitable one for us, versus the interpretation as executable code, an interpretation I prefer to leave to the machines! The second surprise was that the most natural and systematic "codes for predicate transformers" that I could think of would call for nondeterministic implementations when regarded as "executable code". For a while I shuddered at the thought of introducing nondeterminacy already in uniprogramming (the complications it has caused in multiprogramming were only too well known to me!), until I realized that the text interpretation as code for a predicate transformer has its own, independent right of existence. (And in retrospect we may observe that many of the problems multiprogramming has posed in the past are nothing else but the consequence of a prior tendency to attach undue significance to determinacy.) Eventually I came to regard nondeterminacy as the normal situation, determinacy being reduced to a —not even very interesting— special case.

After having laid the foundations, I started with what I had intended to do all the time, viz. solve a long sequence of problems. To do so was an unexpected pleasure. I experienced that the formal apparatus gave me a much firmer grip on what I was doing than I was used to; I had the pleasure of discovering that explicit concerns about termination can be of great heuristic value—to the extent that I came to regret the strong bias towards partial correctness that is still so common. The greatest pleasure, however, was that for the majority of the problems that I had solved before, this time I ended up with a more beautiful solution! This was very encouraging, for I took it as an indication that the methods developed had, indeed, improved my programming ability.

How should this monograph be studied? The best advice I can give is to stop reading as soon as a problem has been described and to try to solve it yourself before reading on. Trying to solve the problem on your own seems the only way in which you can assess how difficult the problem is; it gives you the opportunity to compare your own solution with mine; and it may give you the satisfaction of having discovered yourself a solution that is superior to mine. And, by way of a priori reassurance: be not depressed when you find the text far from easy reading! Those who have studied the manuscript found it quite often difficult (but equally rewarding!); each time, however, that we analyzed their difficulties, we came together to the conclusion that not the text (i.e. the way of presentation), but the subject matter itself was "to blame". The moral of the story can only be that a nontrivial algorithm is just nontrivial, and that its final description in a programming language is highly compact compared to the considerations that justify its design: the shortness of the final text should not mislead us! One of my assistants made the suggestion —which I faithfully transmit, as it could be a valuable one—

that little groups of students should study it together. (Here I must add a parenthetical remark about the "difficulty" of the text. After having devoted a considerable number of years of my scientific life to clarifying the programmer's task, with the aim of making it intellectually better manageable, I found this effort at clarification to my amazement (and annoyance) repeatedly rewarded by the accusation that "I had made programming difficult". But the difficulty has always been there, and only by making it visible can we hope to become able to design programs with a high confidence level, rather than "smearing code", i.e., producing texts with the status of hardly supported conjectures that wait to be killed by the first counterexample. None of the programs in this monograph, needless to say, has been tested on a machine.)

I owe the reader an explanation why I have kept the mini-language so small that it does not even contain procedures and recursion. As each next language extension would have added a few more chapters to the book and, therefore, would have made it correspondingly more expensive, the absence of most possible extensions (such as, for instance, multiprogramming) needs no further justification. Procedures, however, have always occupied such a central position and recursion has been for computing science so much the hallmark of academic respectability, that some explanation is due.

First of all, this monograph has not been written for the novice and, consequently, I expect my readers to be familiar with these concepts. Secondly, this book is not an introductory text on a specific programming language and the absence of these constructs and examples of their use should therefore not be interpreted as my inability or unwillingness to use them, nor as a suggestion that anyone else who can use them well should not do so. The point is that I felt no need for them in order to get my message across, viz. how a carefully chosen separation of concerns is essential for the design of in all respects, high-quality programs: the modest tools of the mini-language gave us already more than enough latitude for nontrivial, yet very satisfactory designs.

The above explanation, although sufficient, is, however, not the full story. In any case I felt obliged to present repetition as a construct in its own right, as such a presentation seemed to me overdue. When programming languages emerged, the "dynamic" nature of the assignment statement did not seem to fit too well into the "static" nature of traditional mathematics. For lack of adequate theory mathematicians did not feel too easy about it, and, because it is the repetitive construct that creates the need for assignment to variables, mathematicians did not feel too easy about repetition either. When programming languages without assignments and without repetition —such as pure LISP— were developed, many felt greatly relieved. They were back on the familiar grounds and saw a glimmer of hope of making programming an activity with a firm and respectable mathematical basis. (Up to this very day there is among the more theoretically inclined computing scientists still a widespread feeling that recursive programs "come more naturally" than repetitive ones.)

For the alternative way out, viz. providing the couple "repetition" and "assignment to a variable" with a sound and workable mathematical basis, we had to wait another ten years. The outcome, as is demonstrated in this monograph, has been that the semantics of a repetitive construct can be defined in terms of a recurrence relation between *predicates*, whereas the semantic definition of general recursion requires a recurrence relation between *predicate transformers*. This shows quite clearly why I regard general recursion as an order of magnitude more complicated than just repetition, and it therefore hurts me to see the semantics of the repetitive construct

"while *B* do *S*"

defined as that of the call

"whiledo(B, S)"

of the recursive procedure (described in ALGOL 60 syntax):

```
procedure whiledo (condition, statement);
begin if condition then begin statement;
                         whiledo (condition, statement) end
end
```

Although correct, it hurts me, for I don't like to crack an egg with a sledgehammer, no matter how effective the sledgehammer is for doing so. For the generation of theoretical computing scientists that became involved in the subject during the sixties, the above recursive definition is often not only "the natural one", but even "the true one". In view of the fact that we cannot even define what a Turing machine is supposed to do without appealing to the notion of repetition, some redressing of the balance seemed indicated.

For the absence of a bibliography I offer neither explanation nor apology.

Acknowledgements. The following people have had a direct influence on this book, either by their willingness to discuss its intended contents or by commenting on (parts of) the finished manuscript: C. Bron, R.M. Burstall, W.H.J. Feijen, C.A.R. Hoare, D.E. Knuth, M. Rem, J.C. Reynolds, D.T. Ross, C.S. Scholten, G. Seegmüller, N. Wirth and M. Woodger. It is a privilege to be able to express in print my gratitude for their cooperation. Furthermore I am greatly indebted to Burroughs Corporation for providing me with the opportunity and necessary facilities, and thankful to my wife for her unfailing support and encouragement.

EDSGER W. DIJKSTRA

Nuenen,
The Netherlands

O EXECUTIONAL ABSTRACTION

Executional abstraction is so basic to the whole notion of "an algorithm" that it is usually taken for granted and left unmentioned. Its purpose is to map different computations upon each other. Or, to put it in another way, it refers to the way in which we can get a specific computation within our intellectual grip by considering it as a member of a large class of different computations; we can then abstract from the mutual differences between the members of that class and, based on the definition of the class as a whole, make assertions applicable to each of its members and therefore also to the specific computation we wanted to consider.

In order to drive home what we mean by "a computation" let me just describe a noncomputational mechanism "producing" —intentionally I avoid the term "computing"— say, the greatest common divisor of *111* and *259*. It consists of two pieces of cardboard, placed on top of each other. The top one displays the text "GCD(*111, 259*)="; in order to let the mechanism produce the answer, we pick up the top one and place it to the left of the bottom one, on which we can now read the text "*37*".

The simplicity of the cardboard mechanism is a great virtue, but it is overshadowed by two drawbacks, a minor one and a major one. The minor one is that the mechanism can, indeed, be used for producing the greatest common divisor of *111* and *259*, but for very little else. The major drawback, however, is that, no matter how carefully we inspect the construction of the mechanism, our confidence that it produces the correct answer can only be based on our faith in the manufacturer: he may have made an error, either in the design of his machine or in the production of our particular copy.

In order to overcome our minor objection we could consider on a huge piece of cardboard a large rectangular array of the grid points with the

1

integer coordinates x and y, satisfying $0 \leq x \leq 500$ and $0 \leq y \leq 500$. For all the points (x, y) with positive coordinates only, i.e. excluding the points on the axes, we can write down at that position the value of GCD(x, y); we propose a two-dimensional table with *250,000* entries. From the point of view of usefulness, this is a great improvement: instead of a mechanism able to supply the greatest common divisor for a single pair of numbers, we now have a "mechanism" able to supply the greatest common divisor for any pair of the *250,000* different pairs of numbers. Great, but we should not get too excited, for what we identified as our second drawback —"Why should we believe that the mechanism produces the correct answer?"— has been multiplied by that same factor of *250,000*: we now have to have a tremendous faith in the manufacturer!

So let us consider a next mechanism. On the same cardboard with the grid points, the only numbers written on it are the values *1* through *500* along both axes. Furthermore the following straight lines are drawn:

1. the vertical lines (with the equation $x = $ constant);
2. the horizontal lines (with the equation $y = $ constant);
3. the diagonals (with the equation $x + y = $ constant);
4. the "answer line" with the equation $x = y$.

In order to operate this machine, we have to follow the following instructions ("play the game with the following rules"). When we wish to find the greatest common divisor of two values X and Y, we place a pebble —also provided by the manufacturer— on the grid point with the coordinates $x = X$ and $y = Y$. As long as the pebble is not lying on the "answer line", we consider the smallest equilateral rectangular triangle with its right angle coinciding with the pebble and one sharp angle (either under or to the left of the pebble) on one of the axes. (Because the pebble is not on the answer line, this smallest triangle will have only one sharp angle on an axis.) The pebble is then moved to the grid point coinciding with the other sharp angle of the triangle. The above move is repeated as long as the pebble has not yet arrived on the answer line. When it has, the x-coordinate (or the y-coordinate) of the final pebble position is the desired answer.

What is involved when we wish to convince ourselves that this machine will produce the correct answer? If (x, y) is any of the *249,500* points not on the answer line and (x', y') is the point to which the pebble will then be moved by one step of the game, then either $x' = x$ and $y' = y - x$ or $x' = x - y$ and $y' = y$. It is not difficult to *prove* that GCD$(x, y) = $ GCD(x', y'). The important point here is that the *same* argument applies equally well to *each* of the *249,500* possible steps! Secondly —and again it is not difficult— we can *prove* for any point (x, y) where $x = y$ (i.e. such that (x, y) is one of the *500* points on the answer line) that GCD$(x, y) = x$. Again the important point is that the *same* argument is applicable to *each* of the *500* points of the answer line. Thirdly —and again this is not difficult— we have to show that for any initial position (X, Y) a finite number of steps will indeed bring the pebble on the answer line, and again the important observation is that the same argument is equally well applicable to any of the *250,000* initial positions (X, Y). Three simple arguments, whose length is independent of the number of grid points: that, in a nutshell, shows what mathematics can do for us! Denoting with (x, y) any of the pebble positions during a game started at position (X, Y), our first theorem allows us to conclude that during the game the relation

$$\text{GCD}(x, y) = \text{GCD}(X, Y)$$

will always hold or —as the jargon says— "is kept invariant". The second theorem then tells us that we may interpret the x-coordinate of the final pebble position as the desired answer and the third theorem tells us that the final position exists (i.e. will be reached in a finite number of steps). And this concludes the analysis of what we could call "our abstract machine".

Our next duty is to verify that the board as supplied by the manufacturer is, indeed, a fair model. For this purpose we have to check the numbering along both axes and we have to check that all the straight lines have been drawn correctly. This is slightly awkward as we have to investigate a number of objects proportional to N if N (in our example *500*) is the length of the side of the square, but it is always better than N^2, the number of possible computations.

An alternative machine would not work with a huge cardboard but with two nine-bit registers, each capable of storing a binary number between *0* and *500*. We could then use one register to store the value of the x-coordinate and the other to store the value of the y-coordinate as they correspond to "the current pebble position". A move then corresponds to decreasing the contents of one register by the contents of the other. We could do the arithmetic ourselves, but of course it is better if the machine could do that for us. If we then want to believe the answer, we should be able to convince ourselves that the machine compares and subtracts correctly. On a smaller scale the history repeats itself: we derive once and for all, i.e. for any pair of n-digit binary numbers, the equations for the binary subtractor and then satisfy ourselves that the physical machine is a fair model of this binary subtractor.

If it is a parallel subtractor, the number of verifications —proportional to the number of components and their interactions— is proportional to $n = \log_2 N$. In a serial machine the trading of time against equipment is carried still one step further.

Let me try, at least for my own illumination, to capture the highlights of our preceding example.

Instead of considering the single problem of how to compute the GCD(*111, 259*), we have generalized the problem and have regarded this as a specific instance of the wider class of problems of how to compute the GCD(*X, Y*). It is worthwhile to point out that we could have generalized the problem of computing GCD(*111, 259*) in a different way: we could have regarded the task as a specific instance of a wider class of tasks, such as the computation of GCD(*111, 259*), SCM(*111, 259*), *111 * 259, 111 + 259, 111/259, 111 − 259, 111²⁵⁹*, the day of the week of the *111*th day of the *259*th year B.C., etc. This would have given rise to a "*111*-and-*259*-processor" and in order to let that produce the originally desired answer, we should have had to give the request "GCD, please" as its input! We have proposed a "GCD-computer" instead, that should be given the number pair "*111, 259*" as its input if it is to produce the originally desired answer, and that is a quite different machine!

In other words, when asked to produce one or more results, it is usual to generalize the problem and to consider these results as specific instances of a wider class. But it is no good just to say that everything is a special instance of something more general! If we want to follow such an approach we have two obligations:

1. We have to be quite specific as to how we generalize, i.e. we have to choose that wider class carefully and to define it explicitly, because our argument has to apply to that whole class.
2. We have to choose ("invent" if you wish) a generalization that is helpful to our purpose.

In our example I certainly prefer the "GCD-computer" above the "*111*-and-*259*-processor" and a comparison between the two will give us a hint as to what characteristics make a generalization "helpful for our purpose". The machine that upon request can produce as answer the value of all sorts of funny functions of *111* and *259* becomes harder to verify as the collection of functions grows. This is in sharp contrast with our "GCD-computer".

The GCD-computer would have been equally bad if it had been a table with *250,000* entries containing the "ready-made" answers. Its unique feature is that it could be given in the form of a compact set of "rules of a game" that, when played according to those rules, will produce the answer.

The tremendous gain is that a single argument applied to these rules allows us to prove the vital assertions about the outcome of any of the games. The price to be paid is that in each of the *250,000* specific applications of these rules, we don't get our answer "immediately": each time the game has to be played according to the rules!

The fact that we could give such a compact formulation of the rules of the game such that a single argument allowed us to draw conclusions about any possible game is intimately tied to the systematic arrangement of the *250,000* grid points. We would have been powerless if the cardboard had shown a shapeless, chaotic cloud of points without a systematic nomenclature! As things are, however, we could divide our pebble into two half-pebbles and move one half-pebble downward until it lies on the horizontal axis and the other half-pebble to the left until it lies on the vertical axis. Instead of coping with one pebble with *250,000* possible positions, we could also deal with two half-pebbles with only *500* possible positions each, i.e. only *1000* positions in toto! Our wealth of *250,000* possible states has been built up by the circumstance that any of the *500* positions of the one half-pebble can be combined with any of the *500* positions of the other half-pebble: the number of positions of the undivided pebble equals the product of the number of positions of the half-pebbles. In the jargon we say that "the total state space is regarded as the Cartesian product of the state spaces of the variables x and y".

The freedom to replace one pebble with a two-dimensional freedom of position by two half-pebbles with a one-dimensional freedom of position is exploited in the suggested two-register machine. From a technical point of view this is very attractive; one only needs to build registers able to distinguish between *500* different cases ("values") and by just combining two such registers, the total number of different cases is squared! This multiplicative rule enables us to distinguish between a huge number of possible total states with the aid of a modest number of components with only a modest number of possible states each. By adding such components the size of the state space grows exponentially but we should bear in mind that we may only do so provided that the argument justifying our whole contraption remains very compact; by the time that the argument grows exponentially as well, there is no point in designing the machine at all!

Note. A perfect illustration of the above can be found in an invention which is now more than ten centuries old: the decimal number system! This has indeed the fascinating property that the number of digits needed only grows proportional to the logarithm of the largest number to be represented. The binary number system is what you get when you ignore that each hand has five fingers. (*End of note.*)

In the above we have dealt with one aspect of multitude, viz. the great number of pebble positions (= possible states). There is an analogous multiplicity, viz. the large number of different games (= computations) that can be played according to our rules of the game: one game for each initial position to be exact. Our rules of the game are very general in the sense that they are applicable to any initial position. But we have insisted upon a compact justification for the rules of the game and this implies that the rules of the game themselves have to be compact. In our example this has been achieved by the following device: instead of enumerating "do this, do that" we have given the rules of the game in terms of the rules for performing "a step" together with a criterion whether "the step" has to be performed another time. (As a matter of fact, the step has to be repeated until a state has been reached in which the step is undefined.) In other words, even a single game is allowed to be generated by repeatedly applying the same "sub-rule".

This is a very powerful device. An algorithm embodies the design of the class of computations that may take place under control of it; thanks to the conditional repetition of "a step" the computations from such a class may greatly differ in length. It explains how a short algorithm can keep a machine busy for a considerable period of time. Alternatively we may see it as a first hint as to why we might need extremely fast machines.

It is a fascinating thought that this chapter could have been written while Euclid was looking over my shoulder.

1 THE ROLE OF PROGRAMMING LANGUAGES

In the chapter "Executional Abstraction" I have given an informal description of various "machines" designed to compute the greatest common divisor of two positive (and not too large) integers. One was in terms of a pebble moving over a cardboard, another was in terms of two half-pebbles, each moving along the axes, and the last one was in terms of two registers, each capable of holding an integer value (up to a certain bound). Physically, these three "machines" are very different; mathematically, however, they are very similar: the major part of the argument that they are capable of computing the greatest common divisor is the same for all three of them. This is because they are only different embodiments of the same set of "rules of the game" and it is really this set of rules that constitute the core of the invention, the invention which is known as "Euclid's algorithm".

In the previous chapter Euclid's algorithm was described verbally in a rather informal way. Yet it was argued that the number of possible computations corresponding to it was so large that we needed a proof of its correctness. As long as an algorithm is only given informally, it is not a very proper object for a formal treatment. For the latter we need a description of the algorithm in some suitable formal notation.

The possible advantages of such a formal notation technique are numerous. Any notation technique implies that whatever is described by it is presented as a specific member of the (often infinite) class of objects describable by it. Our notation technique has, of course, to cater for an elegant and concise description of Euclid's algorithm, but once that has been achieved it will indeed have been presented as a member of a huge class of all sorts of algorithms. And in the description of some of these other algorithms we may expect to find the more interesting applications of our notation technique.

In the case of Euclid's algorithm, one can argue that it is so simple that we can come away with an informal description of it. The power of a formal notation should manifest itself in the achievements we could never do without it!

The second advantage of a formal notation technique is that it enables us to study algorithms as mathematical objects; the formal description of the algorithm then provides the handle for our intellectual grip. It will enable us to prove theorems about classes of algorithms, for instance, because their descriptions share some structural property.

Finally, such a notation technique should enable us to define algorithms so unambiguously that, given an algorithm described by it and given the values for the arguments (the input), there should be no doubt or uncertainty as to what the corresponding answers (the output) should be. It is then conceivable that the computation is carried out by an automaton that, given (the formal description of) the algorithm and the arguments, will produce the answers without further human intervention. Such automata, able to carry out the mutual confrontation of algorithm and argument with each other, have indeed been built. They are called "automatic computers". Algorithms intended for automatic execution by computers are called "programs" and since the late fifties the formal techniques used for program notation are called "programming languages". (The introduction of the term "language" in connection with notation techniques for programs has been a mixed blessing. On the one hand it has been very helpful in as far as existing linguistic theory now provided a natural framework and an established terminology ("grammar", "syntax", "semantics", etc.) for discussion. On the other hand we must observe that the analogy with (now so-called!) "natural languages" has also been very misleading, because natural languages, nonformalized as they are, derive both their weakness and their power from their vagueness and imprecision.)

Historically speaking, this last aspect, viz. the fact that programming languages could be used as a vehicle for instructing existing automatic computers, has for a long time been regarded as their most important property. The efficiency with which existing automatic computers could execute programs written in a certain language became the major quality criterion for that language! As a regrettable result, it is not unusual to find anomalies in existing machines truthfully reflected in programming languages, this at the expense of the intellectual manageability of the programs expressed in such a language (as if programming without such anomalies was not already difficult enough!). In our approach we shall try to redress the balance, and we shall do so by regarding the fact that our algorithms could actually be carried out by a computer as a lucky accidental circumstance that need not occupy a central position in our considerations. (In a recent educational text addressed to the PL/I programmer one can find the strong advice to avoid procedure calls as much as possible "because they make the program so inefficient". In view of the fact that the procedure is one of PL/I's main vehicles for expressing structure, this is a terrible advice, so terrible that I can hardly call the text in question "educational". If you are convinced of the usefulness of the procedure concept and are surrounded by implementations in which the overhead of the procedure mechanism imposes too great a penalty, then blame these inadequate implementations instead of raising them to the level of standards! The balance, indeed, needs redressing!)

I view a programming language primarily as a vehicle for the description of (potentially highly sophisticated) abstract mechanisms. As shown in the chapter "Executional Abstraction", the algorithm's outstanding virtue is the potential compactness of the arguments on which our confidence in the mechanism can be based. Once this compactness is lost, the algorithm has lost much of its "right of existence" and therefore we shall consciously aim at retaining that compactness. Also our choice of programming language shall be aimed at that goal.

2 STATES AND THEIR CHARACTERIZATION

Since many centuries man characterizes natural numbers. I imagine that in prehistoric times, when the notion of "a number" dawned upon our ancestors, they invented individual names for each number they found they wanted to refer to; they must have had names for numbers in very much the same way as we have the names "one, two, three, four, etcetera."

They are truly "names" in the sense that by inspecting the sequence "one, two, three" no rule enables us to derive that the next one will be "four". You really must *know* that. (At an age that I knew perfectly well how to count —in Dutch— I had to *learn* how to count in English, and during a school test no clever inspection of the words "seven" and "nine" would enable me to derive how to spell "eight", let alone how to pronounce it!)

It is obvious that such a nonsystematic nomenclature enables us to distinguish only between a very limited number of different numbers; in order to overcome that limitation each language in the civilized world has introduced a (more or less) systematic nomenclature for the natural numbers and learning to count is mainly discovering the system underlying the nomenclature. When a child has learned how to count up to a thousand, he has not learned those thousand names (in order!) by heart, he knows the rules: comes the moment that the child has discovered how to go from any number to the next and therefore also from "four hundred and thirty-nine" to "four hundred and forty".

The ease of manipulation with numbers is greatly dependent on the nomenclature we have chosen for them. It is much harder to establish that

twelve times a dozen = a gross

eleven plus twelve = twenty-three

XLVII + IV = LI

10

than it is to establish that

$$12 * 12 = 144$$

$$11 + 12 = 23$$

$$47 + 4 = 51$$

because the latter three answers can be generated by a simple set of rules that any eight-year-old child can master.

In mechanical manipulation of numbers, the advantages of the decimal number system are much more pronounced. For centuries already, we have had mechanical adding machines, displaying the answer in a window behind which there are a number of wheels with ten different positions, each wheel showing one decimal digit in each of its positions. (It is no longer a problem to display "00000019", to add 4, and then to display "00000023"; it would be a problem —at least by purely mechanical means— to display "nineteen" and "twenty-three" instead!)

The essential thing about such a wheel is that it has ten different, stable positions. In the jargon this is expressed in a variety of ways. For instance, the wheel is called "a ten-valued variable" and if we want to be more explicit we even enumerate the values: from 0 through 9. Here each "position" of the wheel is identified with a "value" of the variable. The wheel is called "a variable" because, although the positions are stable, the wheel can be turned into another position: the "value" can be changed. (This term is, I am sorry to say, rather misleading in more than one respect. Firstly, such a wheel which is (almost) always in one of its ten positions and therefore (almost) always represents a "value", is a concept widely different from what mathematicians call a "variable", because, as a rule, a mathematical variable represents no specific value at all; if we say that for each whole number n the assertion $n^2 \geq 0$ is true, then this n is a variable of quite a different nature. Secondly, in our context we use the term "variable" for something existing in time, whose value, unless something is done about it, remains constant! The term "changeable constant" would have been better, but we shall not introduce it and shall stick to the by now firmly established tradition.)

Another way in which the jargon tries to capture the essentials of such a wheel that is (almost) always in one of ten different positions or "states" is to associate with the wheel "a state space of ten points". Here each state (position) is associated with "a point" and the collection of these "points" is called —and this is in accordance with mathematical tradition— a "space" or if we want to be more specific "a state space". Instead of saying that the variable has (almost) always one of its possible values one can now express this by saying that the system consisting of this single variable is (almost) always in one of the points of its state space. The state space describes the amount of freedom of the system; it just has nowhere else to go.

So much for a single wheel. Let us now turn our attention to a register with eight of such wheels in a row. Because each of these eight wheels is in one of ten different states, this register, considered as a whole, is in one of 100,000,000 possible, different states, each of which is suitably identified by the number (or rather by the row of eight digits) displayed through the window.

If the state for each of the wheels is given, then the state of the register as a whole is uniquely determined; conversely, from each state of the register as a whole, the state of each individual wheel is determined uniquely. In this case we say (in an earlier chapter we have already used the term) that we get (or build) the state space of the register as a whole by forming the "Cartesian product" of the state spaces of the eight individual wheels. The total number of points in that state space is the product of the number of points in the state spaces from which it has been built (that is why it is called the Cartesian *product*).

Whether such a register is considered as a single variable with 10^8 different possible values, or as a composite variable composed out of eight different ten-valued variables called "wheels" depends on our interest in the thing. If we are only interested in the value displayed, we shall probably regard the register as an unanalyzed entity, whereas the maintenance engineer who has to replace a wheel with a worn tooth will certainly regard the register as a composite object.

We have seen another example of building up a state space as the Cartesian product of much smaller state spaces when we discussed Euclid's algorithm and observed that the position of the pebble somewhere on the board could equally well be identified by two half-pebbles, each somewhere on an axis, that is, by the combination (or more precisely, an ordered pair) of two variables "x" and "y". (The idea of identifying the position of a point in a plane by the values of its x-and y-coordinates comes from Descartes when he developed the analytical geometry, and the Cartesian product is named that way in honour of him.) The pebble on the board has been introduced as a visualization of the fact that an evolving computational process —such as the execution of Euclid's algorithm— can be viewed as the system travelling through its state space. In accordance with this metaphor, the initial state is also referred to as "the starting point".

In this book we shall mainly, or perhaps even exclusively, occupy ourselves with systems whose state space will eventually be regarded as being built up as a Cartesian product. This is certainly not to be interpreted as my suggesting that state spaces built by forming Cartesian products are the one and final answer to all our problems, for I know only too well that this is not true. As we proceed it will become apparent why they are worthy of so much of our attention and, simultaneously, why the concept plays such a central role in many programming languages.

Before proceeding I mention one problem that we shall have to face. When we construct a state space by forming a Cartesian product, it is by no means certain that we shall have good use for all its points. The usual example to illustrate this is characterizing the days of a given year by a pair (month, day), where "month" is a *12*-valued variable (running from "Jan" through "Dec") and "day" a *31*-valued variable (ranging from "*1*" through "*31*"). We have then created a state space with *372* points, while no year has more than *366* days. What do we do with, say, (Jun, *31*)? Either we disallow it, thereby catering for "impossible dates" and thus enabling in a sense the system to contradict itself, or we allow it as an alternative name for one of the "true" days, e.g. equating it to (Jul, *1*). The phenomenon of "unused points of the state space" is bound to arise whenever the number of different possible values between which we want to distinguish happens to be a prime number.

The nomenclature that is automatically introduced when we form a state space as a Cartesian product enables us to identify a single point; for instance, I can now state that my birthday is (May, *11*). Thanks to Descartes, however, we now know of another way of stating this fact: I have my birthday on the date (month, day) whenever they are a solution of the equation

$$(\text{month} = \text{May}) \textbf{ and } (\text{day} = 11)$$

The above equation has only one solution and is therefore a rather complicated way of specifying that single day in the year. The advantage of using an equation, however, is that we can use it to characterize the set of all its solutions, and such a set can be much larger than just a single point. A trivial example would be the definition of Christmas

$$(\text{month} = \text{Dec}) \textbf{ and } ((\text{day} = 25) \textbf{ or } (\text{day} = 26))$$

a more striking example is the definition of the set of days on which my monthly salary is paid

$$(\text{day} = 23)$$

and this, indeed, is a much more compact specification than an enumeration like "(Jan, *23*), (Feb, *23*), (Mar, *23*)," etc.

From the above it is clear that the ease with which we use such equations to characterize sets of states depends on whether the sets we wish to characterize "match" the structure of the state space, i.e., "match" the coordinate system introduced. In the above coordinate system it would, for instance, be somewhat awkward to characterize the set of days that fall on the same day of the week as (Jan, *1*). Many a programmer's decisions have to do with the introduction of state spaces with coordinate systems that are appropriate for his goal and the latter requirement will often lead him to the introduction of state spaces with a number of points many times larger than the number of different possible values he has to distinguish between.

We have seen another example of using an equation to characterize a set of states in our description of the cardboard machine for the computation of GCD(X, Y), viz.

$$x = y$$

characterizing all the points of what we called the "answer line"; it is the set of final states, i.e. the computation stops if and only if a state satisfying the equation $x = y$ has been reached.

Besides the coordinates of the state space, i.e. the variables in terms of whose values the computational process evolves, we have seen in our equations constants (such as "May" or "23"). Besides those, we may also have so-called "free variables" which you may think of as "unspecified constants". We use them specifically to relate different states as they occur at successive stages of the *same* computational process. For instance, during a *specific* execution of Euclid's algorithm with starting point (X, Y), all states (x, y) will satisfy

$$\text{GCD}(x, y) = \text{GCD}(X, Y) \textbf{ and } 0 < x \leq X \textbf{ and } 0 < y \leq Y$$

Here the X and Y are not variables such as x and y. They are "their initial values", they are constants for a specific computation, but unspecified in the sense that we could have started Euclid's algorithm with any point of the grid as initial position of our pebble.

Some final terminology. I shall call such equations "conditions" or "predicates". (I could, and perhaps should, distinguish between them, reserving the term "predicate" for the formal expression denoting the "condition": we could then, for instance, say that the two different predicates "$x = y$" and "$y = x$" denote the same condition. Knowing myself I do not expect to indulge very much in such a mannerism.) I shall use synonymously expressions such as "a state for which a predicate is true" and "a state that satisfies a condition" and "a state in which a condition is satisfied" and "a state in which a condition holds", etc. If a system is certain to arrive at a state satisfying a condition P, we shall say that the system is certain "to establish the truth of P".

Each predicate is assumed to be defined in each point of the state space under consideration: in each point the value of a predicate is either "true" or "false", and the predicate is used to characterize the set of all points for which (or where) the predicate is true.

We call two predicates P and Q equal (in formula: "$P = Q$") when they denote the same condition, i.e. when they characterize the same set of states.

Two predicates will play a special role and we reserve the names "T" and "F" for them.

T is the predicate that is true in all points of the state space concerned: the corresponding set is the universe.

F is the predicate that is false in all points of the state space: it corresponds to the empty set.

3 THE CHARACTERIZATION OF SEMANTICS

We are primarily interested in systems that, when started in an "initial state", will end up in a "final state" which, as a rule, depends on the choice of the initial state. This is a view that is somewhat different from the idea of the finite state automaton that on the one hand absorbs a stream of input characters and on the other hand produces a stream of output characters. To translate that in our picture we must assume that the value of the input (i.e. the argument) is reflected in the choice of the initial state and that the value of the output (i.e. the answer) is reflected in the final state. Our view relieves us from all sorts of peripheral complications.

The first section of this chapter deals almost exclusively with so-called "deterministic machines", whereas the second section (which can be skipped at first reading) deals with so-called "nondeterministic machines". The difference between the two is that for the deterministic machine the happening that will take place upon activation of the mechanism is fully determined by its initial state. When activated twice in identical initial states, identical happenings will take place: the deterministic machine has a fully reproducible behaviour. This is in contrast to the nondeterministic machine, for which activation in a given initial state will give rise to one out of a class of possible happenings, the initial state only fixing the class as a whole.

Now I assume that the design of such a system is a goal-directed activity, in other words that we want to achieve something with the system. For instance, if we want to make a machine capable of computing the greatest common divisor, we could demand of the final state that it satisfies

$$x = \text{GCD}(X, Y) \qquad (1)$$

In the machine we have been envisaging, we shall also have $y = \text{GCD}(X, Y)$

15

because the game terminates when $x = y$, but that is *not* part of our requirement when we decide to accept the final value of x as our "answer".

We call condition (*1*) the (desired) "post-condition"—"post" because it imposes a condition upon the state in which the system must find itself *after* its activity. Note that the post-condition could be satisfied by many of the possible states. In that case we apparently regard each of them as equally satisfactory and there is then no reason to require that the final state be a unique function of the initial state. (As the reader will be aware, it is here that the potential usefulness of a nondeterministic mechanism presents itself.)

In order to use such a system when we want it to produce an answer, say "reach a final state satisfying post-condition (*1*) for a given set of values of X and Y", we should like to know the set of corresponding initial states, more precisely, the set of initial states such that activation will certainly result in a properly terminating happening leaving the system in a final state satisfying the post-condition. If we can bring the system without computational effort into one of these states, we know how to use the system to produce for us the desired answer! To give the example for Euclid's cardboard game: we can guarantee a final state satisfying the postcondition (*1*) for any initial state satisfying

$$GCD(x, y) = GCD(X, Y) \text{ and } 0 < x \leq 500 \text{ and } 0 < y \leq 500 \qquad (2)$$

(The upper limits have been added to do justice to the limited size of the cardboard. If we start with a pair (X, Y) such that $GCD(X, Y) = 713$, then there exists no pair (x, y) satisfying condition (*2*), i.e. for those values of X and Y condition (*2*) reduces to F; and that means that the machine in question cannot be used to compute the $GCD(X, Y)$ for that pair of values of X and Y.)

For many (X, Y) combinations, many states satisfy (*2*). In the case that $0 < X \leq 500$ and $0 < Y \leq 500$, the *trivial* choice is $x = X$ and $y = Y$. It is a choice that can be made without any evaluation of the GCD-function, even without appealing to the fact that the GCD-function is a symmetric function of its arguments.

The condition that characterizes the set of *all* initial states such that activation will certainly result in a properly terminating happening leaving the system in a final state satisfying a given post-condition is called "the weakest pre-condition corresponding to that post-condition". (We call it "weakest", because the weaker a condition, the more states satisfy it and we aim here at characterizing *all* possible starting states that are certain to lead to a desired final state.)

If the system (machine, mechanism) is denoted by "S" and the desired post-condition by "R", then we denote the corresponding weakest pre-condition by

$$wp(S, R)$$

If the initial state satisfies wp(S, R), the mechanism is certain to establish eventually the truth of R. Because wp(S, R) is the weakest pre-condition, we also know that if the initial state does not satisfy wp(S, R), this guarantee cannot be given, i.e. the happening may end in a final state not satisfying R or the happening may even fail to reach a final state at all (as we shall see, either because the system finds itself engaged in an endless task or because the system has got stuck).

We take the point of view that we know the possible performance of the mechanism S sufficiently well, provided that we can derive for any post-condition R the corresponding weakest pre-condition wp(S, R), because then we have captured what the mechanism can do for us; and in the jargon the latter is called "its semantics".

Two remarks are in order. Firstly, the set of possible post-conditions is in general so huge that this knowledge in tabular form (i.e. in a table with an entry for each R wherein we would find the corresponding wp(S, R)) would be utterly unmanageable, and therefore useless. Therefore the definition of the semantics of a mechanism is always given in another way, viz. in the form of a rule describing how for any given post-condition R the corresponding weakest pre-condition wp(S, R) can be derived. For a fixed mechanism S such a rule, which is fed with the predicate R denoting the post-condition and delivers a predicate wp(S, R) denoting the corresponding weakest precondition, is called "a predicate transformer". When we ask for the definition of the semantics of the mechanism S, what we really ask for is its corresponding predicate transformer.

Secondly —and I feel tempted to add "thank goodness"— we are often not interested in the complete semantics of a mechanism. This is because it is our intention to use the mechanism S for a specific purpose only, viz. for establishing the truth of a very specific post-condition R for which it has been designed. And even for that specific post-condition R, we are often not interested in the exact form of wp(S, R); often we are content with a stronger condition P, that is, a condition for which we can show that

$$P \Rightarrow \text{wp}(S, R) \qquad \text{for all states} \qquad (3)$$

holds. (The predicate "$P \Rightarrow Q$" (read "P implies Q") is only false in those points in state space where P holds, but Q does not, and it is true everywhere else. By requiring that "$P \Rightarrow \text{wp}(S, R)$" holds for all states, we just require that wherever P is true, wp(S, R) is true as well: P is a sufficient pre-condition. In terms of sets it means that the set of states characterized by P is a subset of the set of states characterized by wp(S, R).) If for a given P, S, and R relation (3) holds, this can often be proved without explicit formulation —or, if you prefer, "computation" or "derivation"— of the predicate wp(S, R). And this is a good thing, for except in trivial cases we must expect that the explicit formulation of wp(S, R) will defy at least the size of our sheet of paper, our patience, or our (analytical) ingenuity (or any combination of them).

The meaning of wp(S, R) i.e. "the weakest pre-condition for the initial state such that activation will certainly result in a properly terminating happening, leaving the system S in a final state satisfying the post-condition R", allows us to conclude that, considered as a function of the post-condition R, the predicate transformer has a number of properties.

PROPERTY 1. For any mechanism S we have

$$\text{wp}(S, F) = F \tag{4}$$

Suppose that this was not true; under that assumption there would be at least one state satisfying wp(S, F). Take such a state as the initial state for the mechanism S; then, according to our definition, activation would result in a properly terminating happening, leaving the system S in a final state satisfying F. But this is a contradiction, for by definition there are no states satisfying F and thus relation (4) has been proved. Property 1 is also known under the name of the "Law of the Excluded Miracle".

PROPERTY 2. For any mechanism S and any post-conditions Q and R such that

$$Q \Rightarrow R \quad \text{for all states} \tag{5}$$

we also have

$$\text{wp}(S, Q) \Rightarrow \text{wp}(S, R) \quad \text{for all states} \tag{6}$$

Indeed, for any initial state satisfying wp(S, Q) will upon activation establish the truth of Q by definition; on account of (5) it will therefore establish the truth of R as well and as initial state it will therefore satisfy wp(S, R) as well, as expressed in (6). Property 2 is a property of monotonicity.

PROPERTY 3. For any mechanism S and any post-condition Q and R we have

$$(\text{wp}(S, Q) \text{ and } \text{wp}(S, R)) = \text{wp}(S, Q \text{ and } R) \tag{7}$$

In every point of the state space the left-hand side of (7) implies the right-hand side, because for any initial state satisfying both wp(S, Q) and wp(S, R) we have the combined knowledge that a final state will be established satisfying both Q and R. Furthermore, because by definition

$$(Q \text{ and } R) \Rightarrow Q \quad \text{for all states}$$

property 2 allows us to conclude

$$\text{wp}(S, Q \text{ and } R) \Rightarrow \text{wp}(S, Q) \quad \text{for all states}$$

similarly,

$$\text{wp}(S, Q \text{ and } R) \Rightarrow \text{wp}(S, R) \quad \text{for all states}$$

But from $A \Rightarrow B$ and $A \Rightarrow C$, propositional calculus tells us that we may conclude $A \Rightarrow (B$ **and** $C)$; therefore the right-hand side of (7) implies the left-hand side in every point of the state space. Both sides implying each other everywhere, they must be equal and thus property 3 has been proved.

PROPERTY 4. For any mechanism S and any post-conditions Q and R we have

$$(\text{wp}(S, Q) \text{ or } \text{wp}(S, R)) \Rightarrow \text{wp}(S, Q \text{ or } R) \qquad \text{for all states} \qquad (8)$$

Because by definition

$$Q \Rightarrow (Q \text{ or } R) \qquad \text{for all states}$$

property 2 allows us to conclude

$$\text{wp}(S, Q) \Rightarrow \text{wp}(S, Q \text{ or } R) \qquad \text{for all states}$$

similarly,

$$\text{wp}(S, R) \Rightarrow \text{wp}(S, Q \text{ or } R) \qquad \text{for all states}$$

But from $A \Rightarrow C$ and $B \Rightarrow C$, propositional calculus tells us that we may conclude $(A \text{ or } B) \Rightarrow C$, and thus (8) has been proved. In general, the implication in the other direction does not hold: the certainty that a pregnant woman will give birth to a son is nil, similarly the certainty that she will give birth to a daughter is nil, the certainty that she will give birth to a son or a daughter, however, is absolute. For deterministic mechanisms, however, we have the stronger property which follows.

PROPERTY 4'. For any deterministic mechanism S and any post-conditions Q and R we have

$$(\text{wp}(S, Q) \text{ or } \text{wp}(S, R)) = \text{wp}(S, Q \text{ or } R)$$

We have to show the implication to the left. Consider an initial state satisfying $\text{wp}(S, Q \text{ or } R)$; to this initial state corresponds a *unique* final state, satisfying either Q, or R, or both; the initial state therefore must satisfy either $\text{wp}(S, Q)$ or $\text{wp}(S, R)$ or both respectively, i.e. it must satisfy $(\text{wp}(S, Q)$ **or** $\text{wp}(S, R))$. And this proves property 4'.

In this book —and that may turn out to be one of its distinctive features— I shall treat nondeterminacy as the rule and determinacy as the exception: a deterministic machine will be regarded as a special case of the nondeterministic one, as a mechanism for which property 4' holds rather than the somewhat weaker property 4. This decision reflects a drastic change in my own thinking. Back in 1958 I was one of the first to develop the basic software for a machine with an I/O interrupt and the irreproducibility of the behaviour of such a —to all intents and purposes: nondeterministic— machine was a traumatic experience. When the idea of the I/O interrupt was first suggested I was so terrified at the thought of having to build reliable software for such an intractable beast that I delayed the decision to incorporate the feature for at least three months. And even after I had given in (I had been flattered out of my resistance!) I was highly uncomfortable. When the prototype was becoming kind of operational I had my worst fears fully confirmed: a bug in the program could evoke the erratic behaviour so strongly suggestive of an irreproducible machine error. And secondly —and that was in the time that for deterministic machines we still believed in "debugging"— it was right from the start quite obvious that program testing was quite ineffective as a means for raising the confidence level.

For many years thereafter I have regarded the irreproducibility of the behaviour of the nondeterministic machine as an added complication that should be avoided whenever possible. Interrupts were nothing but a curse inflicted by the hardware engineers upon the poor software makers! Out of this fear of mine the discipline for "harmoniously cooperating sequential processes" has been born. In spite of its success I was still afraid, for our solutions —although proved to be correct— seemed ad hoc solutions to the problem of "taming" (that is the way we felt about it!) special forms of nondeterminacy. The background of my fear was the absence of a general methodology.

Two circumstances have changed the scene since then. The one is the insight that, even in the case of fully deterministic machines, program testing is hardly helpful. As I have now said many times and written in many places: program testing can be quite effective for showing the presence of bugs, but is hopelessly inadequate for showing their absence. The other one is the discovery that in the meantime it has emerged that any design discipline must do justice to the fact that the design of a mechanism that is to have a purpose must be a goal-directed activity. In our special case it means that we can expect our post-condition to be the starting point of our design considerations. In a sense we shall be "working backwards". In doing so we shall find that the implication of property 4 is the essential part; for the equality of property 4' we shall have very little use.

Once the mathematical equipment needed for the design of nondeterministic mechanisms achieving a purpose has been developed, the nondeterministic machine is no longer frightening. On the contrary! We shall learn to appreciate it, even as a valuable stepping stone in the design of an ultimately fully deterministic mechanism.

(The remainder of this chapter can be skipped at first reading.) We have stated our position that we know the possible performance of the mechanism S sufficiently well, provided that we know how its associated predicate transformer wp(S, R) acts upon any post-condition R. If we also know that the mechanism is deterministic, the knowledge of this predicate transformer fixes its possible behaviour completely. For a deterministic mechanism S

and some post-condition R each initial state falls in one of three disjoint sets, according to the following, mutually exclusive, possibilities:

(a) Activation of S will lead to a final state satisfying R.
(b) Activation of S will lead to a final state satisfying **non** R.
(c) Activation of S will not lead to a final state, i.e. the activity will fail to terminate properly.

The first set is characterized by wp(S, R), the second set by wp(S, **non** R), their union by

$$(\text{wp}(S, R) \textbf{ or } \text{wp}(S, \textbf{non } R)) = \text{wp}(S, R \textbf{ or non } R) = \text{wp}(S, T)$$

and therefore the third set is characterized by **non** wp(S, T).

To give the complete semantic characterization of a nondeterministic system requires more. With respect to a given post-condition R we have again the three possible types of happenings as listed above under (a), (b), and (c). But in the case of a nondeterministic system an initial state need not lead to a unique happening, which by definition is one out of the three mutually exclusive categories; for each initial state the possible happenings may now belong to two or even to all three categories.

In order to describe them we can use the notion of "a liberal pre-condition". Earlier we considered pre-conditions such that it was guaranteed that "the right result", i.e. a final state satisfying R, would be reached. A liberal pre-condition is weaker: it only guarantees that the system won't produce the wrong result, i.e. will not reach a final state not satisfying R, but non-termination is left as an alternative. Also for liberal pre-conditions we can introduce the concept of "the weakest liberal pre-condition"; let us denote it by wlp(S, R). Then the initial state space is, in principle, subdivided into seven mutually exclusive regions, none of which need to be empty. (Seven, because from three objects one can make seven nonempty selections.) They are all easily characterized by three predicates, viz. wlp(S, R), wlp(S, **non** R), and wp(S, T).

(a)   wp(S, R) = (wlp(S, R) **and** wp(S, T))
      Activation will establish the truth of R.
(b)   wp(S, **non** R) = (wlp(S, **non** R) **and** wp(S, T))
      Activation will establish the truth of **non** R.
(c)   wlp(S, F) = (wlp(S, R) **and** wlp(S, **non** R))
      Activation will fail to lead to a properly terminating activity.
(ab) wp(S, T) **and non** wlp (S, R) **and non** wlp(S, **non** R)
      Activation will lead to a terminating activity, but the initial state does not determine whether the final state will satisfy R or not.

(ac)   wlp(S, R) **and non** wp(S, T)
If activation leads to a final state, that final state will satisfy R, but the initial state does not determine whether the activity will terminate or not.

(bc)   wlp(S, **non** R) **and non**wp(S, T)
If activation leads to a final state, that final state will not satisfy R, but the initial state does not determine whether the activity will terminate or not.

(abc) **non** (wlp(S, R) or wlp(S, **non** R) or wp(S, T))
The initial state does not determine, whether activation will lead to a terminating activity, nor whether in the case of termination, R will be satisfied or not.

The last four possibilities only exist for nondeterministic machines.

From the definition of wlp(S, R) it follows that

$$\text{wlp}(S, T) = T$$

it is also clear that

$$(\text{wlp}(S, F) \text{ and } \text{wp}(S, T)) = F$$

If it were not, there would be an initial state for which both termination and nontermination could be guaranteed.

Figure *3.1* gives a pictorial representation of the initial state space with the insides of the rectangles satisfying wlp(S, R), wlp(S, **non** R) and wp(S, T) respectively.

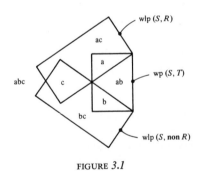

FIGURE *3.1*

The above analysis has been given for completeness' sake and also because in practice the notion of a liberal pre-condition is a quite useful one. If one implements, for instance, a programming language, one will not prove that the implementation executes any correct program correctly; one should be happy and content with the assertion that no correct program will be processed incorrectly without warning—provided, of course, that the class of programs that indeed will be processed correctly is sufficiently large to make the implementation of any interest.

For the time being, however, we shall pay no attention to the concept of the liberal pre-condition and shall confine ourselves to the characterization of initial states that guarantee that the right result will be produced. Once this tool has been developed, we shall consider how it can be bent into one allowing us to talk about liberal pre-conditions to the extent we are interested in them.

4 THE SEMANTIC CHARACTERIZATION OF A PROGRAMMING LANGUAGE

In the previous chapter we have taken the position that we know the semantics of a mechanism S sufficiently well if we know its "predicate transformer", i.e. a rule telling us how to derive for any post-condition R the corresponding weakest pre-condition, which we have denoted by "wp(S, R)", for the initial state such that attempted activation will lead to a properly terminating activity that leaves the system in a final state satisfying R. The question is: how does one derive wp(S, R) for given S and R?

So much, for the time being, about a single, specific mechanism S. A program written in a well-defined programming language can be regarded as a mechanism, a mechanism that we know sufficiently well provided that we know the corresponding predicate transformer. But a programming language is only useful provided that we can use it for the formulation of many different programs and for all of them we should like to know their corresponding predicate transformers.

Any such program is defined by its text as written in that well-defined programming language and that text should therefore be our starting point. But now we see suddenly two completely different roles for such a program text! On the one hand the program text is to be interpreted by a *machine* whenever we wish the program to be executed automatically, whenever we wish a specific computation to be performed for us. On the other hand the program text should tell *us* how to construct the corresponding predicate transformer, how to accomplish the predicate transformation that will derive wp(S, R) for any given post-condition R that has caught our fancy. This observation tells us what we mean by "a well-defined programming language" as far as *we* are concerned. While the semantics of a specific mechanism (program) are given by its predicate transformer, we consider the semantic characterization of a programming language given by the set of rules that associate the corresponding predicate transformer with each program written in that language. From that point of view we can regard the program as "a code" for a predicate transformer.

If one so desires one can approach the problem of programming language design from out of that corner. In such an approach the —rather formal— starting point is that the rules for constructing predicate transformers must be such that whatever can be constructed by applying them must be a predicate transformer enjoying the properties *1* through *4* from the previous chapter "The Characterization of Semantics", for if they don't, you are just massaging predicates in a way such that they can no longer be interpreted as postconditions and corresponding weakest preconditions respectively.

Two very simple predicate transformers that satisfy the required properties immediately present themselves.

There is, to begin with, the identity transformation, i.e. the mechanism S such that for any post-condition R we have $wp(S, R) = R$. This mechanism is known to and beloved by all programmers: they know it as "the empty statement" and in their program text they often denote it by writing nothing at a place in the text where syntactically a statement is required. This is not a particularly good convention (a compiler only "sees" it by *not* seeing a statement that should be there) and we shall give it a name, say "*skip*". The semantics of the statement named "*skip*" are therefore given by:

$$wp(skip, R) = R \quad \text{for any post-condition } R$$

(As everybody does, I shall use the term "statement" because it has found its firm place in the jargon; when people suggested that "command" was perhaps a more appropriate term, it was already too late!)

Note. Those who think it a waste of characters to introduce an explicit name such as "*skip*" for the empty statement while "nothing" expresses its semantics so eloquently, should realize that the decimal number system was only possible thanks to the introduction of the character "*0*" for the concept zero. (*End of note.*)

Before going on I would not like to miss the opportunity of pointing out that in the meantime we have defined a programming language! Admittedly it is a rather rudimentary one: it is a one-statement language in which only one mechanism can be defined and the only thing that mechanism can do for us is "leaving things as they are" (or "doing nothing", but on account of the negation that is a dangerous use of language; see next paragraph).

The next simple predicate transformer is the one which leads to a constant weakest pre-condition that does not depend on the post-condition R at all. As constant predicates we have two, T and F. A mechanism S such that $wp(S, R) = T$ for all R cannot exist, for it would violate the Law of the Excluded Miracle; a mechanism S such that $wp(S, R) = F$ for all R has, however, a predicate transformer that satisfies all the necessary properties. We shall also give this statement a name, say "*abort*". The semantics of the statement named "*abort*" are therefore given by

$$\text{wp}(abort, R) = F \quad \text{for any post-condition } R$$

This one cannot even "do nothing" in the sense of "leaving things as they are"; it really cannot do a thing. If we take $R = T$, i.e. imposing beyond its existence no further requirement upon the final state, even then there is no corresponding initial state. When evoked, the mechanism named "*abort*" will therefore fail to reach a final state: its attempted activation is interpreted as a symptom of failure. (It need not concern us here (and not even later!) that later we shall present frameworks of statements that contain the semantic equivalents of "*skip*" and "*abort*" as special cases.)

Now we have a (still very rudimentary!) two-statement programming language in which we can define two mechanisms, one doing nothing and the other always failing. Since the publication of the famous "Report on the Algorithmic Language ALGOL *60*" in *1960*, no self-respecting computing scientist can reach this stage without giving a formal definition of the syntax of his language thus far developed in the notational technique called "BNF" (short for "Backus-Naur-Form"), viz.:

$$\langle statement \rangle :: = skip \,|\, abort$$

(To be read as: "An element of the syntactic category called "statement" (that is what the funny brackets " $\langle$ " and " $\rangle$ " stand for) is defined as (that is what "::=" stands for) "*skip*" or (that is what the vertical bar "|" stands for) "*abort*".". Great! But don't worry; more impressive applications of BNF as notational technique will follow in due time!)

A class of definitely more interesting predicate transformers is based upon substitution, i.e. replacing all occurrences of a variable in the formal expression for the post-condition R by (the same) "something else". If in a predicate R all occurrences of the variable x are replaced by some expression (E), then we denote the result of this transformation by $R_{E \to x}$. Now we can consider for given x and E a mechanism such that for all post-conditions R we have $\text{wp}(S, R) = R_{E \to x}$, where x is a "coordinate variable" of our state space and E is an expression of the appropriate type.

Note. Such a transformation by substitution satisfies the properties *1* through *4* from the previous chapter. We shall not try to demonstrate this and leave it to the reader's taste whether he will regard this as a trivial or as a deep mathematical result. (*End of note.*)

The above pattern introduces a whole class of predicate transformers, a whole class of mechanisms. They are denoted by a statement that is called "an assignment statement" and such a statement has to specify three things:

1. the identity of the variable to be replaced;

2. the fact that substitution is the corresponding rule for predicate transformation;

3. the expression which is to replace every occurrence of the variable to be replaced in the post-condition.

If the variable x is to be replaced by the expression (E), the usual way to write such a statement is:

$$x := E$$

(where the so-called assignment operator ":=" should be read as "becomes"). This can be summarized by defining

$$wp("x := E", R) = R_{E \to x} \quad \text{for any post-condition } R$$

which for any coordinate variable x and any expression E of the appropriate type can, if we so desire, be viewed as the semantic definition of the assignment operator.

Revelling, as we do, in the use of BNF we can extend our formal syntax to read:

$$\langle \text{statement} \rangle ::= skip \,|\, abort \,|\, \langle \text{assignment statement} \rangle$$
$$\langle \text{assignment statement} \rangle ::= \langle \text{variable} \rangle := \langle \text{expression} \rangle$$

where the last line should be read as "An element of the syntactic category called "assignment statement" is defined as an element of the syntactic category called "variable", followed by the assignment operator ":=", followed by an element of the syntactic category called "expression".".

Before proceeding it seems wise to verify that our formal definition of the semantics of the assignment statement indeed captures our intuitive understanding of the assignment statement—if we have one! Let us consider a state space with the two integer coordinate variables "a" and "b". Then

$$wp("a := 7", a = 7) = \{7 = 7\}$$

and because the boolean expression at the right-hand side is true for all values of a and b, i.e. for all points in the state space, we can simplify to

$$wp("a := 7", a = 7) = T$$

i.e., each initial state will guarantee that the assignment "$a := 7$" will establish the truth of "$a = 7$". Similarly

$$wp("a := 7", a = 6) = \{7 = 6\}$$

and because the boolean expression is false for all values of a and b, we find

$$wp("a := 7", a = 6) = F$$

This means that there is no initial state for which we can guarantee that the assignment "$a := 7$" establishes the truth of "$a = 6$". (This is in accordance with our previous result that all initial states would establish the final truth of "$a = 7$" and therefore the final falsity of "$a \neq 7$".) Also

$$\text{wp}(\text{"}a := 7\text{"}, \, b = b0) = \{b = b0\}$$

i.e. if we wish to guarantee that after the assignment "$a := 7$" the variable b has some value $b0$, then b should have that value already at the initial state. In other words, all variables other than "a" are not tampered with, they keep the value they had; the assignment "$a := 7$" moves the point in state space corresponding to the current system state parallel to the a-axis such that "$a = 7$" finally holds.

Instead of choosing a constant for the expression E, we could also have a function of the initial state. This is illustrated in the following examples:

$$\text{wp}(\text{"}a := 2 * b + 1\text{"}, \, a = 13) = \{2 * b + 1 = 13\} = \{b = 6\}$$
$$\text{wp}(\text{"}a := a + 1\text{"}, \, a > 10) = \{a + 1 > 10\} = \{a > 9\}$$
$$\text{wp}(\text{"}a := a - b\text{"}, \, a > b) = \{a - b > b\} = \{a > 2 * b\}$$

There is a slight complication if we allow the expression E to be a partial function of the initial state, i.e. such that its attempted evaluation with an initial state that lies outside its domain will not lead to a properly terminating activity; if we wish to cater to that situation as well, we must sharpen our definition of the semantics of the assignment operator and write

$$\text{wp}(\text{"}x := E\text{"}, \, R) = \{D(E) \textbf{ cand } R_{E \to x}\}$$

Here the predicate $D(E)$ means "in the domain of E"; the boolean expression "$B1$ **cand** $B2$" (the so-called "conditional conjunction") has the same value as "$B1$ **and** $B2$" where both operands are defined, but is also defined to have the value "false" where $B1$ is "false", the latter regardless of the question whether $B2$ is defined. Usually the condition $D(E)$ is not mentioned explicitly, either because it is $= T$ or because we have seen to it that the assignment statement will never be activated in initial states outside the domain of E.

A natural extension of the assignment statement, beloved by some programmers, is the so-called "concurrent assignment". Here a number of *different* variables can be substituted simultaneously; the concurrent assignment statement is denoted by a list of the different variables to be substituted (mutually separated by commas) at the left-hand side of the assignment operator and an equally long list of expressions (also mutually separated by commas) at its right-hand side. Thus one is allowed to write

$$x1, x2 := E1, E2$$
$$x1, x2, x3 := E1, E2, E3$$

Note that the ith variable from the left-hand list is to be replaced by the *i*th expression from the right-hand list, such that, for instance, for given *x1*, *x2*, *E1*, and *E2*

$$x1, x2 := E1, E2$$

is semantically equivalent with

$$x2, x1 := E2, E1$$

The concurrent assignment allows us to prescribe that the two variables *x* and *y* interchange their values by means of

$$x, y := y, x$$

an operation that is awkward to describe otherwise. This, the fact that it is easily implemented, and the fact that it allows us to avoid some over-specification, are the reasons for its popularity. If the lists become long, the resulting program becomes very hard to read.

The true BNF addict will extend his syntax by providing two alternative forms for the assignment statement, viz.:

⟨assignment statement⟩ ::= ⟨variable⟩ := ⟨expression⟩|

⟨variable⟩, ⟨assignment statement⟩, ⟨expression⟩

This is a so-called "recursive definition", because one of the alternative forms for a syntactic unit called "assignment statement" (viz. the second one) contains as one of its components again the same syntactic unit called "assignment statement", i.e., the syntactic unit we are defining! At first sight such a cyclic definition seems frightening, but upon closer inspection we can convince ourselves that, at least from a syntactic point of view, there is nothing wrong with it. For instance, because according to the first alternative

$$x2 := E1$$

is an instance of an assignment statement, the formula

$$x1, x2 := E1, E2$$

admits a parsing of the form

$$x1, ⟨\text{assignment statement}⟩, E2$$

and is therefore, according to the second alternative, also an assignment statement. From a semantic point of view, however, it is a horror because it suggests that *E2* is associated with *x1* instead of with *x2*.

Compared with the two-statement language with only "*skip*" and "*abort*" our language with the assignment statement is considerably richer: there is no upper bound anymore on the number of different instances of the syntactic unit "assignment statement". Yet it is clearly insufficient for our purpose; we need the ability to build more sophisticated programs, more elaborate mechanisms. For the construction of potentially elaborate mechanisms we follow the pattern that can be described recursively by

⟨mechanism⟩ ::= ⟨primitive mechanism⟩|

⟨proper composition of ⟨mechanism⟩'s⟩

For this pattern to be of any use at all, two conditions must be satisfied: we must have "primitive mechanisms" to start with and, secondly, we must know how to "compose properly". The statements introduced thus far can be taken as the primitive mechanisms, and it is with the act of properly composing a new mechanism out of given ones that the remainder of this chapter is concerned. The new mechanism, in its turn, can act as part of a still larger composite object.

Whenever an object has been composed of parts, we can view the resulting object in two ways. Either we view it as "an unanalyzed whole" having its properties more or less by magic (or by faith or postulate); in this view only its properties are relevant, it is irrelevant how it has been composed from which parts. In this view any two mechanisms having the same properties are equivalent. Alternatively we view it as "a composite object" such that we can understand why it has the properties stated. Then we regard the parts as "little" unanalyzed wholes of which only the properties count. The latter view makes clear what we mean by "composition". The composition must define how the properties of the whole follow from the properties of the parts.

After these general remarks we return to our specific mechanisms, whose properties we consider captured by their predicate transformers. More specifically, given two mechanisms $S1$ and $S2$, whose predicate transformers are known, can we think of a rule for deriving a new predicate transformer from the two given ones? If so, we can regard this resulting predicate transformer as describing the properties of a composite object, built in a special way from the parts $S1$ and $S2$.

One of the simplest ways of deriving a new function from two given ones is the so-called "functional composition", i.e. supplying the value of the one as argument to the other. It is tradition to denote the composite object corresponding to that predicate transformer by "$S1; S2$" and we define

$$\text{wp}(\text{``}S1; S2\text{''}, R) = \text{wp}(S1, \text{wp}(S2, R))$$

which, if we so desire, can be viewed as the semantic definition of the semicolon.

Note. From the fact that the predicate transformers for $S1$ and $S2$ enjoy the properties *1* through *4* of the previous chapter, we can derive that also the predicate transformer for "$S1; S2$" as defined above has these four properties. For instance, because for $S1$ and $S2$ the Law of the Excluded Miracle holds:

$$\text{wp}(S1, F) = F \quad \text{and} \quad \text{wp}(S2, F) = F$$

we conclude, by substituting F for R in the above definition,

$$wp(\text{``}S1; S2\text{''}, F) = wp(S1, wp(S2, F))$$
$$= wp(S1, F)$$
$$= F$$

The verification that the other three properties hold as well is left as an exercise for the reader. (*End of Note.*)

Before proceeding we shall convince ourselves that our formal definition of the semantics of the semicolon captures our intuitive understanding of it (if we have one!), viz. that the composite mechanism "$S1; S2$" can be implemented by the rule "first activate $S1$ and upon termination of this activity, activate $S2$". Indeed, in our definition of $wp(\text{``}S1; S2\text{''}, R)$ we supply R —the post-condition for the composite mechanism— as the post-condition to the predicate transformer for $S2$ and that reflects that the total activity of "$S1; S2$" can end with the activity of $S2$; the corresponding weakest pre-condition for $S2$, viz. $wp(S2, R)$, is supplied as post-condition to the predicate transformer for $S1$, i.e. we apparently identify the initial state for $S2$ with the final state for $S1$. But this is exactly mirrored when the activity of $S1$ is followed in time by the activation of $S2$.

Let us, just to be sure, consider an example. Let "$S1; S2$" be

$$\text{``}a := a + b; b := a * b\text{''}$$

and let our post-condition be some predicate $R(a, b)$. In that case

$$wp(S2, R(a, b)) = wp(\text{``}b := a * b\text{''}, R(a, b))$$
$$= R(a, a * b)$$

and

$$wp(\text{``}S1; S2\text{''}, R(a, b)) = wp(S1, wp(S2, R(a, b)))$$
$$= wp(S1, R(a, a * b))$$
$$= wp(\text{``}a := a + b\text{''}, R(a, a * b))$$
$$= R(a + b, (a + b) * b)$$

i.e., we can guarantee a relation R between the final values of a and b, provided initially the same relation holds between $a + b$ and $(a + b) * b$ respectively.

Finally, because functional composition is associative, it does not matter whether we parse "$S1; S2; S3$" as either "$[S1; S2]; S3$" or "$S1; [S2; S3]$", i.e. we are indeed entitled to regard the semicolon as a concatenation symbol and there is no ambiguity when we write down a statement list of the form "$S1; S2; S3; \ldots; Sn$" and we shall freely do so when the opportunity presents itself.

EXERCISE

Verify that

$$\text{"}x1:= E1;\ x2:= E2\text{"} \quad \text{and} \quad \text{"}x2:= E2;\ x1:= E1\text{"}$$

are semantically equivalent if the variable $x1$ does not occur in the expression $E2$ while, also, the variable $x2$ does not occur in the expression $E1$. As a matter of fact, they are then both semantically equivalent to the concurrent assignment "$x1, x2:= E1, E2$". (This equivalence is one of the arguments for promoting the concurrent assignment; its use enables us to avoid sequential overspecification and, even more, in the concurrent assignment it is clear that the two expressions $E1$ and $E2$ could be evaluated concurrently, a fact that for some implementation techniques could be of interest. Besides that we have the perhaps more interesting possibility that "$x1, x2:= E1, E2$" is semantically equivalent neither to "$x1:= E1;\ x2:= E2$" nor to "$x2:= E2;\ x1:= E1$".)   (*End of Exercise.*)

Before the introduction of the semicolon we could only write single-statement programs; with the aid of the semicolon we can write programs as a concatenation of n ($n > 0$) statements: "$S1;\ S2;\ S3;\ \ldots;\ Sn$". Intermediate nontermination excluded, the execution of such a program always implies the time-succession of n statement executions, first $S1$, then $S2$, etc. until Sn. From our example of the cardboard game implementing Euclid's algorithm we know, however, that we must be able to describe a wider class of "rules of the game": each game will exist of a succession of moves, where each move is either "$x:= x - y$" or "$y:= y - x$", but the way in which these moves alternate in time and even their total number will differ from game to game; it depends on the initial position of the pebble, it depends on the initial state of the system. If the semicolon is our only means for composing a new whole of given parts, we are unable to express this and we must therefore look for something new.

As long as the semicolon is the only connective we have, the one and only circumstance under which one of the constituent mechanisms Si ($i > 1$) is activated is proper termination of the (lexicographically) preceding one. In order to achieve the flexibility we need, it must be possible to make the activation of a (sub)mechanism co-dependent on the current state of the system. For this purpose we introduce —in two steps— the notion of a "guarded command", the syntax for which is given by:

$\langle$guarding head$\rangle$ ::= $\langle$boolean expression$\rangle \rightarrow \langle$statement$\rangle$

$\langle$guarded command$\rangle$ ::= $\langle$guarding head$\rangle$ {; $\langle$statement$\rangle$}

where the braces "{" and "}" should be read as: "followed by zero or more instances of the enclosed".

(An alternative syntax for a guarded command would have been:

$\langle$statement list$\rangle$ ::= $\langle$statement$\rangle${;$\langle$statement$\rangle$}

$\langle$guarded command$\rangle$ ::= $\langle$boolean expression$\rangle \rightarrow \langle$statement list$\rangle$

but for reasons that need not concern us now, I prefer the syntax that introduces the concept of the guarding head.)

In this connection the boolean expression preceding the arrow is called "a guard". The idea is that the statement list following the arrow will only be executed provided initially the corresponding guard is true. The guard enables us to prevent execution of a statement list under those initial circumstances under which execution would be undesirable or, if partial operations are involved, impossible.

The truth of the guard is a necessary initial condition for the execution of the guarded command as a whole; it is, of course, not sufficient, because in some way or another —we shall meet two of them— it must also potentially be "its turn". That is why a guarded command is not considered as a statement: a statement is irrevocably executed when its turn has arrived, the guarded command can be used as a building block for a statement. More precisely: we shall propose two different ways of composing a statement of a set of guarded commands.

After some reflection it is quite natural to consider a set of guarded commands. Suppose that we are requested to construct a mechanism such that, if the initial state satisfies Q, the final state will satisfy R. Suppose furthermore that we cannot find a single statement list that will do the job in all cases. (If there existed such a statement list, we should use just that one and there would be no need for guarded commands.) We may, however, be able to find a number of statement lists, each of which will do the job for a subset of possible initial states. To each of these statement lists we can attach as guard a boolean expression characterizing the subset for which it is adequate and when we have enough sufficiently tolerant guards such that the truth of Q implies the truth of at least one guard, we have for each initial state satisfying Q a mechanism that will bring the system in a state satisfying R, viz. one of the guarded commands whose guard is initially true.

In order to express this we define first

⟨guarded command set⟩ ::= ⟨guarded command⟩{▯⟨guarded command⟩}

where the symbol "▯" (pronounce "bar") acts as a separator between otherwise unordered alternatives. One of the ways to form a statement from a guarded command set is by embracing it by the bracket pair "**if** ... **fi**", i.e. our syntax for the syntactic category called "statement" is extended with a next form:

⟨statement⟩ ::= **if** ⟨guarded command set⟩ **fi**

It indicates a special way in which we can combine a number of guarded commands into a new mechanism. We can view the activity that will take place when this mechanism is activated as follows. One of the guarded commands whose guard is true is selected and its statement list is activated.

Before we proceed to give a formal definition of the semantics of our new construct, three remarks are in order.

1. It is assumed that all guards are defined; if not, i.e. if the evaluation of a guard may lead to a not properly terminating activity, then the whole construct is allowed to fail to terminate properly.

2. In general our construct will give rise to nondeterminacy, viz. for each initial state for which more than one guard is true, because it is left undefined which of the corresponding statement lists will then be selected for activation. No nondeterminacy is introduced if any two guards exclude each other.

3. If the initial state is such that none of the guards is true, we are faced with an initial state to which none of the alternatives and therefore neither the construct as a whole does cater. Activation in such an initial state will lead to abortion.

Note. If we allow the empty guarded command set as well, the statement "**if fi**" is therefore semantically equivalent with our earlier statement "*abort*". (*End of note.*)

(In the following formal definition of the weakest pre-condition for the **if-fi**-construct we shall restrict ourselves to the case that all the guards are total functions. If this is not the case, the expression should be pre-fixed, with a **cand**, by the additional requirement that the initial state lies in the domain of all the guards.)

Let "IF" be the name of the statement

$$\textbf{if } B_1 \rightarrow SL_1 \,\mathbb{0}\, B_2 \rightarrow SL_2 \,\mathbb{0}\, \ldots \,\mathbb{0}\, B_n \rightarrow SL_n \textbf{ fi}$$

then for any post-condition R

$$\text{wp(IF, } R) = (\textbf{E }j: 1 \leq j \leq n: B_j) \textbf{ and}$$
$$(\textbf{A }j: 1 \leq j \leq n: B_j \Rightarrow \text{wp}(SL_j, R))$$

This formula should be read as follows: wp(IF, R) is true for every point in state space where there exists at least one j in the range $1 \leq j \leq n$ such that B_j is true and where furthermore for all j in the range $1 \leq j \leq n$ such that B_j is true, wp(SL_j, R) is true as well. Using the "..." as we have done in the definition of IF itself, we could have given the alternative form

$$\text{wp(IF, } R) = (B_1 \textbf{ or } B_2 \textbf{ or } \ldots \textbf{ or } B_n) \textbf{ and}$$
$$(B_1 \Rightarrow \text{wp}(SL_1, R)) \textbf{ and}$$
$$(B_2 \Rightarrow \text{wp}(SL_2, R)) \textbf{ and } \ldots \textbf{ and}$$
$$(B_n \Rightarrow \text{wp}(SL_n, R))$$

It is not too difficult to understand these formulae. The requirement that at least one of the guards is true reflects abortion in the case that all guards are false. Furthermore we require for each initial state satisfying wp(IF, R) that $B_j \Rightarrow \text{wp}(SL_j, R)$ for all j. For those values of j for which B_j is false, this implication is true regardless of the value of wp(SL_j, R), i.e. for those values of j, apparently it does not matter what SL_j would do. Our implementation reflects this by not selecting for activation an SL_j with an initially false guard B_j. For those values of j for which B_j is true, this implication can only be true if wp(SL_j, R) is true as well. As our formal definition requires the truth of the implication for all values of j, our implementation is indeed free to choose when more than one guard is true.

The **if-fi**-construct is only one of the two ways in which we can build a statement from a guarded command set. In the **if-fi**-construct, a state in which all guards are false leads to abortion; in our second form we allow the state in which no guards are true to lead to proper termination, and because then no statement list is activated, it is only natural that it will then be semantically equivalent to the empty statement; the counterpart of this permission to terminate properly when no guard is true, however, is that the activity is not allowed to terminate as long as one of the guards is true. That is, upon activation the guards are inspected. The activity terminates if there are no true guards; if there are true guards one of the corresponding statement lists is activated and upon its termination the implementation starts all over again inspecting the guards. This second construct is denoted by embracing the guarded command list by the bracket pair "do . . . od".

·The formal definition of the weakest pre-condition for the **do-od**-construct is more complicated than the one for the **if-fi**-construct; as a matter of fact the first one is expressed in terms of the second one. We shall first give the formal definition and then its explanation. Let "DO" be the name of the statement

$$\textbf{do } B_1 \rightarrow SL_1 \mathbin{[\!]} B_2 \rightarrow SL_2 \mathbin{[\!]} \dots \mathbin{[\!]} B_n \rightarrow SL_n \textbf{ od}$$

and let "IF" be the name of the statement formed by embracing the same guarded command set by the bracket pair "**if** . . . **fi**". The conditions $H_k(R)$ are given by

$$H_0(R) = R \textbf{ and non } (\textbf{E } j: 1 \leq j \leq n: B_j)$$

and for $k > 0$:

$$H_k(R) = \text{wp(IF, } H_{k-1}(R)) \textbf{ or } H_0(R)$$

then

$$\text{wp(DO, } R) = (\textbf{E } k: k \geq 0: H_k(R))$$

Here the intuitive understanding of $H_k(R)$ is: the weakest precondition such that the **do-od**-construct will terminate after at most k selections of a guarded command, leaving the system in a final state satisfying the postcondition R.

For $k = 0$ it is required that the **do-od**-construct will terminate without selecting any guarded command, i.e. there may not exist a true guard, as is expressed by the second term; and the initial truth of R is then clearly the necessary and sufficient additional condition for the final truth of R, as is expressed by the first term.

For $k > 0$ we have to distinguish two cases: either none of the guards is true, but then R must hold and this leads to the second term; or at least one of the guards is true, but what then happens starts as if the statement "IF" is activated once (in an initial state not leading to immediate abortion due to lack of true guards). But after that execution, in which one guarded command has been selected, we must be sure to arrive in a state such that at most $k - 1$ further selections are needed to ensure termination in a final state satisfying R. According to our definition, this post-condition for the statement "IF" is $H_{k-1}(R)$.

The last line, defining wp(DO, R) expresses that there must exist a value of k such that at most k selections will be needed to ensure termination in a final state satisfying the post-condition R.

Note. If we allow the empty guarded command set as well, the statement "**do od**" is therefore semantically equivalent with our earlier statement "*skip*". (*End of note.*)

5 TWO THEOREMS

In this chapter we derive two theorems concerning the statements we build from guarded command sets. The minor theorem concerns the alternative **if-fi**-construct, the major one the repetitive **do-od**-construct. In this chapter we shall discuss the constructs derived from the guarded command set

$$B_1 \rightarrow SL_1 \,\square\, B_2 \rightarrow SL_2 \,\square\, \ldots \,\square\, B_n \rightarrow SL_n$$

We shall denote by "IF" and "DO" respectively the statements constructed by embracing the above guarded command set by the bracket pairs "**if . . . fi**" and "**do . . . od**" respectively. We shall furthermore use the abbreviation

$$BB = (\mathbf{E}\, j\colon 1 \leq j \leq n\colon B_j)$$

THEOREM

The basic theorem for the alternative construct.

Using the notational conventions just described, we can formulate the basic theorem for the alternative construct:

Let the alternative construct IF and a predicate pair Q and R be such that

$$Q \Rightarrow BB \tag{1}$$

and

$$(\mathbf{A}\, j\colon 1 \leq j \leq n\colon (Q \text{ and } B_j) \Rightarrow \mathrm{wp}(SL_j, R)) \tag{2}$$

both hold for all states, then

$$Q \Rightarrow \mathrm{wp}(\mathrm{IF}, R) \tag{3}$$

holds for all states as well.

Because by definition

$$\mathrm{wp}(\mathrm{IF},\ R) = BB \text{ and } (\mathbf{A}\, j\colon 1 \leq j \leq n\colon B_j \Rightarrow \mathrm{wp}(SL_j, R))$$

37

and Q implies on account of (1) the first term on the right-hand side, (3) is proved if on account of (2) we can conclude that

$$Q \Rightarrow (\mathbf{A} j: 1 \leq j \leq n: B_j \Rightarrow \mathrm{wp}(SL_j, R)) \qquad (4)$$

holds for all states. For any state for which Q is false, (4) is true by definition of the implication. For any state for which Q is true and for any j we distinguish two cases: either B_j is false, but then $B_j \Rightarrow \mathrm{wp}(SL_j, R)$ is true by definition of the implication, or B_j is true, but then on account of (2), $\mathrm{wp}(SL_j, R)$ is true and therefore $B_j \Rightarrow \mathrm{wp}(SL_j, R)$ is true as well. As a result (4) and therefore (3) has been proved.

Note. In the special case of binary choice ($n = 2$) and $B_2 = \mathbf{non}\ B_1$, we have $BB = T$ and the weakest pre-condition reduces to

$$(B_1 \Rightarrow \mathrm{wp}(SL_1, R))\ \mathbf{and}\ (\mathbf{non}\ B_1 \Rightarrow \mathrm{wp}(SL_2, R)) =$$
$$(\mathbf{non}\ B_1\ \mathbf{or}\ \mathrm{wp}(SL_1, R))\ \mathbf{and}\ (B_1\ \mathbf{or}\ \mathrm{wp}(SL_2, R)) =$$
$$(B_1\ \mathbf{and}\ \mathrm{wp}(SL_1, R))\ \mathbf{or}\ (\mathbf{non}\ B_1\ \mathbf{and}\ \mathrm{wp}(SL_2, R)) \qquad (5)$$

The last reduction is possible because of the four cross-terms $B_1\ \mathbf{and\ non}$ $B_1 = F$ and can be omitted, while $\mathrm{wp}(SL_1, R)\ \mathbf{and}\ \mathrm{wp}(SL_2, R)$ can be omitted as well: in every state such that it is true, exactly one of the two terms of (5) must be true and thus it can be omitted from that disjunction. Formula (5) is closely related to the way in which C.A.R. Hoare has given the semantics for the **if-then-else** of ALGOL *60*. Because here $BB = T$ and is implied by everything, we can conclude (3) on the weaker assumption

$$((Q\ \mathbf{and}\ B_1) \Rightarrow \mathrm{wp}(SL_1, R))\ \mathbf{and}\ ((Q\ \mathbf{and\ non}\ B_1) \Rightarrow \mathrm{wp}(SL_2, R)).$$

(*End of Note.*)

The theorem for the alternative construct is of special importance in the case that the predicate pair Q and R can be written as

$$R = P$$
$$Q = P\ \mathbf{and}\ BB$$

In that case the antecedent (1) is fulfilled automatically while the antecedent (2) reduces —because $(BB\ \mathbf{and}\ B_j) = B_j$— to

$$(\mathbf{A} j: 1 \leq j \leq n: (P\ \mathbf{and}\ B_j) \Rightarrow \mathrm{wp}(SL_j, P)) \qquad (6)$$

from which we can conclude, on account of (3)

$$(P\ \mathbf{and}\ BB) \Rightarrow \mathrm{wp}(\mathrm{IF}, P) \qquad \text{for all states} \qquad (7)$$

a relation that will form the antecedent for our next theorem.

THEOREM

The basic theorem for the repetitive construct.

Let a guarded command set with its derived alternative construct IF and a predicate P be such that

$$(P \text{ and } BB) \Rightarrow \text{wp(IF, } P) \tag{7}$$

holds for all states; then for the corresponding repetitive construct DO we can conclude that

$$(P \text{ and } \text{wp(DO, } T)) \Rightarrow \text{wp(DO, } P \text{ and non } BB) \tag{8}$$

for all states.

This theorem is also referred to as the "Fundamental Invariance Theorem for Loops" and it is intuitively not difficult to understand. Our antecedent (7) tells us that if P holds initially and one of the guarded commands is selected for execution, then after its execution, P is still true. In other words, the guards ensure that the execution of the corresponding statement lists will not destroy the validity of P when initially valid. No matter how often a guarded command of the set is selected, P will therefore hold at each new inspection of the guards. Upon completion of the whole repetitive construct, when none of the guards is true, we shall therefore end in a final state satisfying P **and non** BB. The question is: will it terminate properly? Yes, it will, provided that wp(DO, T) holds initially as well; as any state satisfies T, wp(DO, T) is by definition the weakest pre-condition for the initial state such that activation of the statement DO will lead to a properly terminating activity.

The formal proof of the basic theorem for the repetitive construct relies on the formal definition of its semantics (see the previous chapter) from which we derive

$$H_0(T) = \textbf{non } BB \tag{9}$$

for $k > 0$:
$$H_k(T) = \text{wp(IF, } H_{k-1}(T)) \textbf{ or non } BB \tag{10}$$
$$H_0(P \textbf{ and non } BB) = P \textbf{ and non } BB \tag{11}$$

for $k > 0$:
$$H_k(P \textbf{ and non } BB) = \text{wp(IF, } H_{k-1}(P \textbf{ and non } BB)) \textbf{ or }$$
$$P \textbf{ and non } BB \tag{12}$$

We start by proving via mathematical induction that the antecedent (7) guarantees that

for $k \geq 0$:
$$(P \textbf{ and } H_k(T)) \Rightarrow H_k(P \textbf{ and non } BB) \tag{13}$$

for all states.

Relations (9) and (11) tell us that (13) holds for $k = 0$. We shall show that relation (13) can be proved for $k = K$ ($K > 0$) on the assumption that (13) holds for $k = K - 1$.

$$
\begin{aligned}
P \textbf{ and } H_K(T) &= P \textbf{ and } \text{wp(IF, } H_{K-1}(T)) \textbf{ or } P \textbf{ and non } BB \\
&= P \textbf{ and } BB \textbf{ and } \text{wp(IF, } H_{K-1}(T)) \textbf{ or } P \textbf{ and non } BB \\
&\Rightarrow \text{wp(IF, } P) \textbf{ and } \text{wp(IF, } H_{K-1}(T)) \textbf{ or } P \textbf{ and non } BB \\
&= \text{wp(IF, } P \textbf{ and } H_{K-1}(T)) \textbf{ or } P \textbf{ and non } BB \\
&\Rightarrow \text{wp(IF, } H_{K-1}(P \textbf{ and non } BB)) \textbf{ or } P \textbf{ and non } BB \\
&= H_K(P \textbf{ and non } BB)
\end{aligned}
$$

The equality in the first line follows from (*10*), the equality in the second line follows from the fact that any wp(IF, R) $\Rightarrow$ *BB*, the implication in the third line follows from (*7*), the equality in the fourth line from property *3* for predicate transformers, the implication of the fifth line follows from property *2* for predicate transformers and (*13*) assumed for $k = K - 1$, and the last line follows from (*12*). Thus (*13*) has now been proved for $k = K$ and therefore for all $k \geq 0$.

Finally, for any point in state space we have —thanks to (*13*)—

$$P \text{ and } \text{wp(DO, } T) = (\text{E } k\colon k \geq 0\colon P \text{ and } H_k(T))$$
$$\Rightarrow (\text{E } k\colon k \geq 0\colon H_k(P \text{ and non } BB))$$
$$= \text{wp(DO, } P \text{ and non } BB)$$

and thus (*8*), the basic theorem for the repetitive construct, has been proved. The basic theorem for the repetitive construct derives its extreme usefulness from the fact that neither in the antecedent nor in the consequent the actual number of times a guarded command has been selected is mentioned. As a result it allows assertions even in those cases in which this number is not determined by the initial state.

6 ON THE DESIGN OF PROPERLY TERMINATING CONSTRUCTS

The basic theorem for the repetitive construct asserts for a condition P that is kept invariantly true that

$$(P \text{ and } \text{wp}(DO, T)) \Rightarrow \text{wp}(DO, P \text{ and non } BB)$$

Here the term $\text{wp}(DO, T)$ is the weakest pre-condition such that the repetitive construct will terminate. Given an arbitrary construct DO it is in general very hard —if not impossible— to determine $\text{wp}(DO, T)$; I therefore suggest to design our repetitive constructs with the requirement of termination consciously in mind, i.e. to choose an appropriate proof for termination and to make the program in such a way that it satisfies the assumptions of the proof.

Let, again, P be the relation that is kept invariant, i.e.

$$(P \text{ and } BB) \Rightarrow \text{wp}(IF, P) \qquad \text{for all states,} \qquad (1)$$

let furthermore t be a finite integer function of the current state such that

$$(P \text{ and } BB) \Rightarrow (t > 0) \qquad \text{for all states} \qquad (2)$$

and furthermore, for any value $t0$ and for all states

$$(P \text{ and } BB \text{ and } t \leq t0 + 1) \Rightarrow \text{wp}(IF, t \leq t0) \qquad (3)$$

Then we shall prove that

$$P \Rightarrow \text{wp}(DO, T) \qquad \text{for all states} \qquad (4)$$

from which, together with the basic theorem for repetition we can conclude that we have for all states

$$P \Rightarrow \text{wp}(DO, P \text{ and non } BB) \qquad (5)$$

We show this by proving first via mathematical induction that

$$(P \text{ and } t \leq k) \Rightarrow H_k(T) \qquad \text{for all states} \qquad (6)$$

holds for all $k \geq 0$. We first establish the truth of (6) for $k = 0$. As $H_0(T) =$ **non** BB, we have to show that

$$(P \text{ and } t \leq 0) \Rightarrow \textbf{non } BB \qquad \text{for all states} \qquad (7)$$

But (7) is no other expression than (2): both are equal to

$$\textbf{non } P \textbf{ or non } BB \textbf{ or } (t > 0)$$

and thus (6) holds for $k = 0$.

We now assume that (6) holds for $k = K$; then

$$(P \textbf{ and } BB \textbf{ and } t \leq K + 1) \Rightarrow \text{wp(IF, } P \text{ and } t \leq K)$$
$$\Rightarrow \text{wp(IF, } H_K(T));$$
$$(P \textbf{ and non } BB \textbf{ and } t \leq K + 1) \Rightarrow \textbf{non } BB$$
$$= H_0(T)$$

And these two implications can be combined (from $A \Rightarrow C$ and $B \Rightarrow D$ we may conclude that $(A \textbf{ or } B) \Rightarrow (C \textbf{ or } D)$ holds):

$$(P \textbf{ and } t \leq K + 1) \Rightarrow \text{wp(IF, } H_K(T)) \textbf{ or } H_0(T) = H_{K+1}(T)$$

and thus the truth of (6) has been established for all $k \geq 0$. Becuase t is a finite function, we have

$$(\textbf{E } k\colon k \geq 0\colon t \leq k)$$

and

$$P \Rightarrow (\textbf{E } k\colon k \geq 0\colon P \text{ and } t \leq k)$$
$$\Rightarrow (\textbf{E } k\colon k \geq 0\colon H_k(T))$$
$$= \text{wp(DO, } T)$$

and thus (4) has been proved.

Intuitively the theorem is quite clear. On the one hand P will remain true and therefore $t \geq 0$ will remain true as well; on the other hand relation (3) expresses that each selection of a guarded command will cause an effective decrease of t by at least 1. An unbounded number of selections of a guarded command would decrease t below any limit, which would lead to a contradiction.

The applicability of this theorem relies upon the validity of (2) and (3). Relation (2) is rather straightforward, relation (3) is more tricky. Our basic theorem for the alternative construct with

$$Q = (P \textbf{ and } BB \textbf{ and } t \leq t0 + 1)$$
$$R = (t \leq t0)$$

—the occurrence of the free variable $t0$ in both predicates is the reason why we have talked about "a predicate pair"— tells us, that we can conclude that (3) holds if

$$(\mathbf{A}\, j\colon 1 \leq j \leq n\colon (P \text{ and } B_j \text{ and } t \leq t0 + 1) \Rightarrow \text{wp}(SL_j, t \leq t0))$$

In other words, we have to prove for each guarded command that the selection will cause an effective decrease of t. Bearing in mind that t is a function of the current state, we can consider

$$\text{wp}(SL_j, t \leq t0) \qquad (8)$$

This is a predicate involving, besides the coordinate variables of the state space, also the free variable $t0$. Up till now we have regarded such a predicate as a predicate characterizing a subset of states. For any given state, however, we can also regard it as a condition imposed upon $t0$. Let $t0 = tmin$ be the minimum solution for $t0$ of equation (8); we can then interpret the value $tmin$ as the lowest upper bound for the final value of t. Remembering that, just as t itself, $tmin$ also is a function of the current state, the predicate

$$tmin \leq t - 1$$

can be interpreted as the weakest pre-condition such that execution of SL_j is guaranteed to decrease the value of t by at least 1. Let us denote this precondition, where —we repeat— the second argument t is an integer valued function of the current state, by

$$\text{wdec}(SL_j, t);$$

then the invariance of P and the effective decrease of t is guaranteed if we have for all j:

$$(P \text{ and } B_j) \Rightarrow (\text{wp}(SL_j, P) \text{ and } \text{wdec}(SL_j, t)) \qquad (9)$$

A usually practical way for finding a suitable B_j is the following. Equation (9) is of the type

$$(P \text{ and } Q) \Rightarrow R$$

where a —practically computable!— Q must be found for given P and R. We observe that

1. $Q = R$ is a solution.
2. If $Q = (Q1 \text{ and } Q2)$ is a solution and $P \Rightarrow Q2$, then $Q1$ is a solution as well.
3. If $Q = (Q1 \text{ or } Q2)$ is a solution and $P \Rightarrow \textbf{non } Q2$ (or, what amounts to the same thing: $(P \text{ and } Q2) = F$), then $Q1$ is a solution as well.
4. If Q is a solution and $Q1 \Rightarrow Q$, then $Q1$ is a solution as well.

Note 1. If, in doing so, we arrive at a candidate Q for B_j such that $P \Rightarrow \textbf{non } Q$, this candidate can further be simplified (according to step

(3) from above, because for every Q we have $Q = $ (false **or** Q)) to $Q = $ false; this means that the guarded command under consideration is no good, it can be omitted from the set because it will never be selected. (*End of Note 1.*)

Note 2. It is often practical to split equation (9) into the two equations

$$(P \text{ and } B_j) \Rightarrow \text{wp}(SL_j, P) \tag{9a}$$

and

$$(P \text{ and } B_j) \Rightarrow \text{wdec}(SL_j, t) \tag{9b}$$

and deal with them separately. Thus one separates the two concerns: (9a) is concerned with what remains invariant, while (9b) is concerned with what ensures progress. If, while dealing with an equation (9a) we arrive at a B_j, such that $P \Rightarrow B_j$, then it is certain that that condition will *not* satisfy (9b), because with such a B_j the invariance of P would ensure nontermination.   (*End of Note 2.*)

Thus we can make a mechanism DO, such that

$$P \Rightarrow \text{wp}(\text{DO}, P \text{ and non } BB)$$

our B_j's must be strong enough so as to satisfy the implications (9) and as a result the now guaranteed post-condition P **and non** BB might be too weak to imply the desired post-condition R. In that case we have not solved our problem yet and we should consider other possibilities.

7 EUCLID'S ALGORITHM REVISITED

At the risk of boring my readers I shall now devote yet another chapter to Euclid's algorithm. I expect that in the meantime some of my readers will already have coded it in the form

$$x, y := X, Y;$$
$$\textbf{do } x \neq y \rightarrow \textbf{if } x > y \rightarrow x := x - y$$
$$\qquad\qquad \textbf{l } y > x \rightarrow y := y - x$$
$$\qquad \textbf{fi}$$
$$\textbf{od};$$
$$print(x)$$

where the guard of the repetitive construct ensures that the alternative construct will not lead to abortion. Others will have discovered that the algorithm can be coded more simply as follows:

$$x, y := X, Y;$$
$$\textbf{do } x > y \rightarrow x := x - y$$
$$\quad \textbf{l } y > x \rightarrow y := y - x$$
$$\textbf{od};$$
$$print(x)$$

Let us now try to forget the cardboard game and let us try to invent Euclid's algorithm for the greatest common divisor of two positive numbers X and Y afresh. When confronted with such a problem, there are in principle always two ways open to us.

The one way is to try to follow the definition of the required answer as closely as possible. Presumably we could form a table of the divisors of X;

45

this table would only contain a finite number of entries, among which would be *1* as the smallest and *X* as the largest entry. (If $X = 1$, smallest and largest entry will coincide.) We could then also form a similar table of the divisors of *Y*. From those two tables we could form a table of the numbers occurring in both of them; this then is the table of the *common* divisors of *X* and *Y* and is certainly nonempty, because it will contain the entry *1*. From this third table we therefore can select (because it is also finite!) the maximum entry and that would be the *greatest* common divisor.

Sometimes following the definition closely, as sketched above, is the best thing we can do. There is, however, an alternative approach to be tried if we know (or can find) properties of the function to be computed. It may be that we know so many properties that they together determine the function and we may try to construct the answer by exploiting those properties.

In the case of the greatest common divisor we observe, for instance, that, because the divisors of $-x$ are the same as those for *x* itself, the GCD(*x*, *y*) is also defined for negative arguments and not changed if we change the sign of arguments. It is also defined when just one of the arguments is $=0$; that argument has an infinite table of divisors (and we should therefore not try to construct that table!), but because the other argument ($\neq 0$) has a finite table of divisors, the table of common divisors is still nonempty and finite. So we come to the conclusion that GCD(*x*, *y*) is defined for each pair (*x*, *y*) such that $(x, y) \neq (0, 0)$. Furthermore, on account of the symmetry of the notion "common", the greatest common divisor of two numbers is a symmetric function of its two arguments. A little more reasoning can convince us of the fact that the greatest common divisor of two arguments is unchanged if we replace one of them by their sum or difference. Collecting our knowledge we can write down:

for $(x, y) \neq (0, 0)$

(a) GCD(*x*, *y*) = GCD(*y*, *x*).
(b) GCD(*x*, *y*) = GCD($-x$, *y*).
(c) GCD(*x*, *y*) = GCD($x + y$, *y*) = GCD($x - y$, *y*), etc.
(d) GCD(*x*, *y*) = *abs*(*x*) if $x = y$.

Let us suppose for the sake of argument that the above four properties represent our only knowledge about the GCD-function. Do they suffice? You see, the first three relations express the greatest common divisor of *x* and *y* in that of another pair, but the last one expresses it directly in terms of *x*. And this is strongly suggestive of an algorithm that, to start with, establishes the truth of

$$P = (GCD(X, Y) = GCD(x, y))$$

(this is trivially achieved by the assignment "*x, y := X, Y*"), whereafter we "massage" the value pair (x, y) in such ways, that according to (a), (b) or (c) relation P is kept invariant. If we can manage this massaging process so as to reach a state satisfying $x = y$, then, according to (d), we have found our answer by taking the absolute value of x.

Because our ultimate goal is to establish under invariance of P the truth of $x = y$ we could try as monotonically decreasing function $t = abs(x - y)$.

In order to simplify our analysis —always a laudable goal!— we observe that, when starting with nonnegative values for x and y, there is nothing to be gained by introducing a negative value: if the assignment $x := E$ would have established $x < 0$, the assignment $x := -E$ would never have given rise to a larger final value of t (because $y \geq 0$). We therefore sharpen our relation P to be kept invariant:

$$P = (P1 \text{ and } P2)$$

with

$$P1 = (\text{GCD}(X, Y) = \text{GCD}(x, y))$$

and

$$P2 = (x \geq 0 \text{ and } y \geq 0)$$

This means that we have lost all usage for the operations $x := -x$ and $y := -y$, the massagings permissible on account of property (b). We are left with

from (a): $x, y := y, x$

from (c): $x := x + y \qquad y := y + x$

$\qquad\qquad\qquad x := x - y \qquad y := y - x$

$\qquad\qquad\qquad x := y - x \qquad y := x - y$

Let us deal with them in turn and start with $x, y := y, x$:

$$\text{wp}(``x, y := y, x", abs(x - y) \leq t0) = (abs(y - x) \leq t0)$$

therefore

$$tmin(x, y) = abs(y - x)$$

hence

$$\text{wdec}(``x, y := y, x", abs(x - y)) = (abs(y - x) \leq abs(x - y) - 1) = F.$$

And here —for those who would not believe it without a formal derivation— we haved proved (or, if you prefer, discovered) by means of our calculus that the massaging operation $x, y := y, x$ is no good because it fails to cause an effective decrease of our t as chosen.

The next trial is $x := x + y$ and we find, again applying the calculus of the preceding chapters:

$$\text{wp}(``x := x + y", abs(x - y) \leq t0) = (abs(x) \leq t0)$$

$$tmin(x, y) = abs(x) = x \qquad \text{(we confine ourselves to states satisfying } P)$$

$$\text{wdec}(\text{"}x := x + y\text{"}, abs(x - y)) = (tmin(x, y) \le t(x, y) - 1)$$
$$= (x \le abs(x - y) - 1)$$
$$= (x + 1 \le abs(x - y))$$
$$= (x + 1 \le x - y \text{ or } x + 1 \le y - x)$$

Because P implies the negation of the first term and furthermore $P \Rightarrow$ wp("$x := x + y$", P), the equation for our guard

$$(P \text{ and } B_j) \Rightarrow (\text{wp}(SL_j, P) \text{ and } \text{wdec}(SL_j, t))$$

is satisfied by the last term and we have found our first and —for reasons of symmetry also— our second guarded command:

$$x + 1 \le y - x \to x := x + y$$

and

$$y + 1 \le x - y \to y := y + x$$

Similarly we find (the formal manipulations are left as an exercise for the industrious reader)

$$1 \le y \text{ and } 3 * y \le 2 * x - 1 \to x := x - y$$

and

$$1 \le x \text{ and } 3 * x \le 2 * y - 1 \to y := y - x$$

and

$$x + 1 \le y - x \to x := y - x$$

and

$$y + 1 \le x - y \to y := x - y$$

Investigating what we have got, we must come to the sad conclusion that, in the manner mentioned at the close of our previous chapter, we have failed to solve our problem: P **and non** BB does not imply $x = y$. (For instance, for $(x, y) = (5, 7)$ all the guards are false.) The moral of the story is, of course, that our six steps do not always provide a path from initial state to final state, such that $abs(x - y)$ is monotonically decreasing. So we must try "other possibilities".

To start with, we observe that there is no harm in making P2 a little stronger

$$P2 = (x > 0 \text{ and } y > 0)$$

for the initial values of x and y satisfy it and, also, there is no point in generating a value $= 0$, for this value can only be generated by subtraction in a state where $x = y$ and then the final state has already been reached. But this is only a minor modification; the major modification must come from a new function t and I suggest to take a t that is only bounded from below thanks to the invariant relation P. An obvious example is

$$t = x + y$$

We find for the concurrent assignment

$$\text{wdec}(``x, y := y, x", x + y) = F$$

so the concurrent assignment is rejected.

We find for the assignment $x := x + y$

$$\text{wdec}(``x := x + y", x + y) = (y < 0)$$

an expression the truth of which is excluded by the truth of the invariant relation P and therefore (together with $y := y + x$) also this is rejected.

For the next assignment $x := x - y$, however, we find

$$\text{wdec}(``x := x - y", x + y) = (y > 0)$$

a condition that is implied by P (that I have strengthened for this reason). Full of hope we investigate

$$\text{wp}(``x := x - y", P) = (\text{GCD}(X, Y) = \text{GCD}(x - y, y) \text{ and}$$
$$x - y > 0 \text{ and } y > 0)$$

the outermost terms can be dropped as they are implied by P and we are left with the middle one; thus we find

$$x > y \rightarrow x := x - y$$

and

$$y > x \rightarrow y := y - x$$

and now we could stop the investigation, for when both guards have become false, our desired relation $x = y$ holds. When we would proceed we would find a third and a fourth alternative:

$$x > y - x \text{ and } y > x \rightarrow x := y - x$$

and

$$y > x - y \text{ and } x > y \rightarrow y := x - y$$

but it is not clear what could be gained by their inclusion.

EXERCISES

1. Investigate for the same P the choice $t = max(x, y)$.

2. Investigate for the same P the choice $t = x + 2 * y$.

3. Prove that for $X > 0$ and $Y > 0$ the following program, operating on four variables

```
x, y, u, v: = X, Y, Y, X;
do x > y → x, v: = x − y, v + u
▯ y > x → y, u: = y − x, u + v
od;
print((x + y)/2); print((u + v)/2)
```

prints the greatest common divisor of X and Y, followed by their smallest common multiple. (*End of exercises.*)

Finally, if our little algorithm is activated with a pair (X, Y) that does not satisfy our assumption $X > 0$ **and** $Y > 0$, unpleasant things will happen: if $(X, Y) = (0, 0)$, it will produce the erroneous result zero, and if one of the arguments is negative, activation will set an endless activity in motion. This can be prevented by writing

> **if** $X > 0$ **and** $Y > 0 \rightarrow$
>
> $\quad x, y := X, Y;$
>
> $\quad$ **do** $x > y \rightarrow x := x - y \,[\!]\, y > x \rightarrow y := y - x$ **od**;
>
> $\quad print(x)$
>
> **fi**

By providing only one alternative in the alternative construct we have clearly expressed the conditions under which this little program is expected to work. In this form it is a well-protected and rather self-contained piece with the more pleasant property that attempted activation outside its domain will lead to immediate abortion.

8 THE FORMAL TREATMENT OF SOME SMALL EXAMPLES

In this chapter I shall give the formal development of a series of small programs solving simple problems. This chapter should **not** be interpreted as my suggestion that these programs must or should be developed in such a way: such a suggestion would be somewhat ridiculous. I expect most of my readers to be familiar with most of the examples and, if not, they can probably write down a program, hardly aware of having to think about it.

The development, therefore, is given for quite other reasons. One reason is to make ourselves more familiar with the formalism as far as it has been developed up till now. A second reason is to convince ourselves that, in principle at least, the formalism is able to make explicit and quite rigorous what is often justified with a lot of hand-waving. A third reason is precisely that most of us are so familiar with them that we have forgotten how, a long time ago, we have convinced ourselves of their correctness: in this respect this chapter resembles the beginning lessons in plane geometry that are traditionally devoted to proving the obvious. Fourthly, we may occasionally get a little surprise and discover that a little familiar problem is not so familiar after all. Finally it may shed some light on the feasibility, the difficulties, and the possibilities of automatic program composition or mechanical assistance in the programming process. This could be of importance even if we do not have the slightest interest in automatic program composition, for it may give us a better appreciation of the role that our inventive powers may or have to play.

In my examples I shall state requirements of the form "for fixed x, y, . . ."; this is an abbreviation for "for any values $x0, y0,$ . . . a post-condition of the form $x = x0$ **and** $y = y0$ **and** . . . should give rise to a pre-condition implying $x = x0$ **and** $y = y0$ **and** . . .". We shall guarantee this by treating such quantities as "temporary constants"; they will not occur to the left of an assigment statement.

First example.

Establish for fixed x and y the relation $R(m)$:

$$(m = x \text{ or } m = y) \text{ and } m \geq x \text{ and } m \geq y$$

For general values of x and y the relation $m = x$ can only be established by the assignment $m := x$; as a consequence $(m = x \text{ or } m = y)$ can only be established by activating either $m := x$ or $m := y$. In flow-chart form:

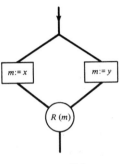

FIGURE *8-1*

The point is that at the entry the good choice must be made so as to guarantee that upon completion $R(m)$ holds. For this purpose we "push the post-condition through the alternatives":

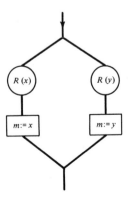

FIGURE *8-2*

and we have derived the guards! As

$$R(x) = ((x = x \text{ or } x = y) \text{ and } x \geq x \text{ and } x \geq y) = (x \geq y)$$

and

$$R(y) = ((y = x \text{ or } y = y) \text{ and } y \geq x \text{ and } y \geq y) = (y \geq x)$$

we arrive at our solution:

$$\text{if } x \geq y \rightarrow m := x \, \Box \, y \geq x \rightarrow m := y \text{ fi}$$

Because $(x \geq y \text{ or } y \geq x) = T$, the program will never abort (and in passing we have given an existence proof: for any values x and y there exists an m satisfying $R(m)$). Because $(x \geq y \text{ and } y \geq x) \neq F$, our program is not necessarily deterministic. If initially $x = y$, it is undetermined which of the two assignments will be selected for execution; this nondeterminacy is fully correct, because we have shown that the choice does not matter.

Note. If the function "*max*" had been an available primitive, we could have coded $m := max(x, y)$ because $R(max(x, y)) = T$. (*End of note.*)

The program we have derived is not very impressive; on the other hand we observe that in the process of deriving the program from our post-condition, next to nothing has been left to our invention.

Second example.

For a fixed value of n $(n > 0)$ a function $f(i)$ is given for $0 \leq i < n$. Establish the truth of R:

$$0 \leq k < n \text{ and } (A \, i: 0 \leq i < n: f(k) \geq f(i))$$

Because our program must work for any positive value of n it is hard to see how R can be established without a loop; we are therefore looking for a relation P that is easily established to start with and such that eventually $(P \text{ and non } BB) \Rightarrow R$. In search of P we are therefore looking for a relation weaker than R; in other words, we want a generalization of our final state. A standard way of generalizing a relation is the replacement of a constant by a variable —possibly with a restricted range— and here my experience suggests that we replace the constant n by a new variable, j say, and take for P:

$$0 \leq k < j \leq n \text{ and } (A \, i: 0 \leq i < j: f(k) \geq f(i))$$

where the condition $j \leq n$ has been added in order to do justice to the finite domain of the function f. Then, with such a generalization, we have trivially

$$(P \text{ and } j = n) \Rightarrow R$$

In order to verify whether this choice of P can be used, we must have an easy way of establishing it to start with. Well, because

$$(k = 0 \text{ and } j = 1) \Rightarrow P$$

we venture the following structure for our program (comments are added between braces).

$k, j := 0, 1$ {P has been established};
do $j \neq n \longrightarrow$ a step towards $j = n$ under invariance of P **od**
{R has been established}

Again my experience suggests to choose as monotonically decreasing function t of the current state $t = (n - j)$, which, indeed, is such that $P \Rightarrow (t \geq 0)$. In order to ensure this monotonic decrease of t, I propose to subject j to an increase by 1 and we can develop

$\text{wp}(\text{``}j := j + 1\text{''}, P) =$
$\quad 0 \leq k < j + 1 \leq n \text{ and } (\text{A } i: 0 \leq i < j + 1: f(k) \geq f(i)) =$
$\quad 0 \leq k < j + 1 \leq n \text{ and } (\text{A } i: 0 \leq i < j: f(k) \geq f(i)) \text{ and } f(k) \geq f(j)$

The first two terms are implied by P and $j \neq n$ (for $(j \leq n$ and $j \neq n) \Rightarrow (j + 1 \leq n)$ and this is the reason why we decided to increase j only by 1). Therefore

$$(P \text{ and } j \neq n \text{ and } f(k) \geq f(j)) \Rightarrow \text{wp}(\text{``}j := j + 1\text{''}, P)$$

and we can take the last condition as guard. The program

$k, j := 0, 1;$
$\quad$**do** $j \neq n \longrightarrow$ **if** $f(k) \geq f(j) \longrightarrow j := j + 1$ **fi od**

will indeed give the correct answer when it terminates properly. Proper termination, however, is not guaranteed, because the alternative construct might lead to abortion —and it will certainly do so if $k = 0$ does not satisfy R. If $f(k) \geq f(j)$ does not hold, we can make it hold by the assignment $k := j$ and therefore our next investigation is

$\text{wp}(\text{``}k, j := j, j + 1\text{''}, P) =$
$\quad 0 \leq j < j + 1 \leq n \text{ and } (\text{A } i: 0 \leq i < j + 1: f(j) \geq f(i)) =$
$\quad 0 \leq j < j + 1 \leq n \text{ and } (\text{A } i: 0 \leq i < j: f(j) \geq f(i))$

To our great relief we see that

$$(P \text{ and } j \neq n \text{ and } f(k) \leq f(j)) \Rightarrow \text{wp}(\text{``}k, j := j, j + 1\text{''}, P)$$

and the following program will do the job without the danger of abortion:

$k, j := 0, 1;$
$\quad$**do** $j \neq n \longrightarrow$ **if** $f(k) \geq f(j) \longrightarrow j := j + 1$
$\qquad\qquad\qquad \blacksquare \; f(k) \leq f(j) \longrightarrow k, j := j, j + 1$ **fi od**

A few remarks are in order. The first one is that, as the guards of the alternative construct do not necessarily exclude each other, the program harbours the same kind of internal nondeterminacy as the first example. Externally it may display this nondeterminacy as well. The function f could be such that the final value of k is not unique; in that case our program can deliver any acceptable value!

The second remark is that having developed a correct program does not mean that we are through with the problem. Programming is as much a mathematical discipline as an engineering discipline; correctness is as much our concern as, say, efficiency. Under the assumptio that the computation of a value of the function f for a given argument is a relatively time-consuming operation, a good engineer should observe that in all probability this program will often ask for many re-computations of $f(k)$ for the same value of k. If this is the case, the trading of some storage space against some computation time is indicated. The effort to make our program more time-efficient, however, should never be an excuse to make a mess of it. (This is obvious, but I state it explicitly because so much messiness is so often defended by an appeal to efficiency considerations. However upon closer inspection the defense is always invalid: it must be, for a mess is never defensible.) The orderly technique for trading storage space versus computation time is the introduction of one or more redundant variables, the value of which can be used because some relation is kept invariant. In this example the observation of the possibly frequent re-computation of $f(k)$ for the same value of k suggests the introduction of a further variable, *max* say, and to extend the invariant relation with the further term

$$max = f(k)$$

This relation must be established upon initialization of k and be kept invariant —by explicit assignment to *max*— upon modification of k. We arrive at the following program

$$k, j, max := 0, 1, f(0);$$
$$\textbf{do } j \neq n \rightarrow \textbf{if } max \geq f(j) \rightarrow j := j + 1$$
$$\textbf{‖ } max \leq f(j) \rightarrow k, j, max := j, j + 1, f(j) \textbf{ fi od}$$

This program is probably much more efficient than our previous version. If it is, a good engineer does not stop here, because he will now observe that for the same value of j he might order a number of times the computation of $f(j)$. It is suggested to introduce a further variable, h say (short for "help"), and to keep

$$h = f(j)$$

invariant. This, however, is something that we cannot do on the same global level as with our previous term: the value $j = n$ is not excluded and for that value $f(j)$ is not necessarily defined. The relation $h = f(j)$ is therefore re-established every time $j \neq n$ has just been checked; upon completion of the outer guarded command —"just before the **od**" so to speak— we have $h = f(j - 1)$ but we don't bother and leave it at that.

$$k, j, max := 0, 1, f(0);$$
$$\textbf{do } j \neq n \rightarrow h := f(j);$$
$$\quad \textbf{if } max \geq h \rightarrow j := j + 1$$
$$\quad \textbf{‖ } max \leq h \rightarrow k, j, max := j, j + 1, h \textbf{ fi od}$$

A final remark is not so much concerned with our solution as with our considerations. We have had our mathematical concerns, we have had our engineering concerns, and we have accomplished a certain amount of separation between them, now focussing our attention on this aspect and then on that aspect. While such a separation of concerns is absolutely essential when dealing with more complicated problems, I must stress that focussing one's attention on one aspect does not mean completely ignoring the others. In the more mathematical part of the design activity we should not head for a mathematically correct program that is so badly engineered that it is beyond salvation. Similarly, while "trading" we should not introduce errors through sloppiness, we should do it carefully and systematically; also, although the mathematical analysis as such has been completed, we should still understand enough about the problem to judge whether our considered changes are significant improvements.

Note. Prior to my getting used to these formal developments I would always have used "$j < n$" as the guard for this repetitive construct, a habit I still have to unlearn, for in a case like this, the guard "$j \neq n$" is certainly to be preferred. The reason for the preference is twofold. The guard "$j \neq n$" allows us to conclude $j = n$ upon termination without an appeal to the invariant relation P and thus simplifies the argument about what the whole construct achieves for us compared with the guard "$j < n$". Much more important, however, is that the guard "$j \neq n$" makes termination dependent upon (part of) the invariant relation, viz. $j \leq n$, and is therefore to be preferred for reasons of robustness. If the addition $j := j + 1$ would erroneously increase j too much and would establish $j > n$, then the guard "$j < n$" would give no alarm, while the guard "$j \neq n$" would at least prevent proper termination. Even without taking machine malfunctioning into account, this argument seems valid. Let a sequence $x_0, x_1, x_2, \ldots$ be given by a value for x_0 and for $i > 0$ by $x_i = f(x_{i-1})$, where f is some computable function and let us carefully and correctly keep the relation $X = x_i$ invariant. Suppose that we have in a program a monotonically increasing variable n such that for some values of n we are interested in x_n. Provided $n \geq i$, we can always establish $X = x_n$ by

$$\textbf{do } i \neq n \rightarrow i, X := i + 1, f(X) \textbf{ od}$$

If —due perhaps to a later change in the program with the result that it is no longer guaranteed that n can only increase as the computation proceeds— the relation $n \geq i$ does not necessarily hold, the above construct would (luckily!) fail to terminate, while the use of the terminating

$$\textbf{do } i < n \rightarrow i, X := i + 1, f(X) \textbf{ od}$$

would have failed to establish the relation $X = x_n$. The moral of the story is that, all other things being equal, we should choose our guards as weak as possible. (*End of note.*)

Third example.

For fixed a $(a \geq 0)$ and d $(d > 0)$ it is requested to establish R:

$$0 \leq r < d \text{ and } d \,|\, (a - r)$$

(Here the vertical bar " $|$ " is to be read as "is a divisor of".) In other words we are requested to compute the smallest nonnegative remainder r that is left after division of a by d. In order that the problem be a problem, we have to restrict ourselves to addition and subtraction as the only arithmetic operations. Because the term $d \,|\, (a - r)$ is satisfied by $r = a$, an initialization that, on account of $a \geq 0$, also satisfies $0 \leq r$, it is suggested to choose as invariant relation P:

$$0 \leq r \text{ and } d \,|\, (a - r)$$

For the function t, the decrease of which should ensure termination, we choose r itself. Because the massaging of r must be such that the relation $d \,|\, (a - r)$ is kept invariant, r may only be changed by a multiple of d, for instance d itself. Thus we find ourselves invited to evaluate

$$\text{wp}(\text{``} r := r - d \text{''}, P) \text{ and } \text{wdec}(\text{``} r := r - d \text{''}, r) =$$
$$0 \leq r - d \text{ and } d \,|\, (a - r + d) \text{ and } d > 0$$

Because the term $d > 0$ could have been added to the invariant relation P, only the first term is then not implied; we find the corresponding guard "$r \geq d$" and the tentative program:

$$\begin{aligned} &\textbf{if } a \geq 0 \textbf{ and } d > 0 \rightarrow \\ &\quad r := a; \\ &\quad \textbf{do } r \geq d \rightarrow r := r - d \textbf{ od} \\ &\textbf{fi} \end{aligned}$$

Upon completion the truth of P **and non** $r \geq d$ has been established, a relation that implies R and thus the problem has been solved.

Suppose now that in addition it would have been required to assign to q such a value that finally we also have

$$a = d * q + r$$

in other words it is requested to compute the quotient as well, then we can try to add this term to our invariant relation. Because

$$(a = d * q + r) \Rightarrow (a = d * (q + 1) + (r - d))$$

we are led to the program:

$$\textbf{if } a \geq 0 \textbf{ and } d > 0 \rightarrow$$
$$q, r := 0, a;$$
$$\textbf{do } r \geq d \rightarrow q, r := q + 1, r - d \textbf{ od}$$
fi

The above programs are, of course, very time-consuming if the quotient is large. Can we speed it up? The obvious way to do that is to decrease r by larger multiples of d. Introducing for this purpose a new variable, dd say, the relation to be established and kept invariant is

$$d \mid dd \textbf{ and } dd \geq d$$

We can speed up our first program by replacing "$r := r - d$" by a possibly repeated decrease of r by dd, while dd, initially $= d$, is allowed to grow rather rapidly, e.g. by doubling it each time. So we are led to consider the following program

$$\textbf{if } a \geq 0 \textbf{ and } d > 0 \rightarrow$$
$$r := a;$$
$$\textbf{do } r \geq d \rightarrow$$
$$dd := d;$$
$$\textbf{do } r \geq dd \rightarrow r := r - dd; dd := dd + dd \textbf{ od}$$
$$\textbf{od}$$
fi

The relation $0 \leq r$ and $d \mid (a - r)$ is clearly kept invariant and therefore this program establishes R if it terminates properly, but does it? Of course it does, because the inner loop, that terminates on account of $dd > 0$, is only activated with initial states satisfying $r \geq dd$ and therefore the decrease $r := r - dd$ is performed at least once for every repetition of the outer loop.

But the above reasoning —although convincing enough!— is a very informal one and because this chapter is called "a formal treatment" we can try to formulate and prove the theorem to which we have appealed intuitively.

With the usual meanings of IF, DO and BB, let P be the relation that is kept invariant, i.e.

$$(P \textbf{ and } BB) \Rightarrow \text{wp(IF, } P) \qquad \text{for all states} \qquad (1)$$

and furthermore let t be an integer function such that for any value of $t0$ and for all states

$$(P \textbf{ and } BB \textbf{ and } t \leq t0 + 1) \Rightarrow \text{wp(IF, } t \leq t0) \qquad (2)$$

or, in an equivalent formulation,

$$(P \textbf{ and } BB) \Rightarrow \text{wdec(IF, } t) \qquad \text{for all states,} \qquad (3)$$

then for any value of $t0$ and for all states

$$(P \textbf{ and } BB \textbf{ and } \text{wp(DO, } T) \textbf{ and } t \leq t0 + 1) \Rightarrow \text{wp(DO, } t \leq t0) \qquad (4)$$

or, in an equivalent formulation,

$$(P \text{ and } BB \text{ and } \text{wp}(DO, T)) \Rightarrow \text{wdec}(DO, t) \qquad (5)$$

In words: if the relation P that is kept invariant guarantees that each selected guarded command causes an effective decrease of t, then the repetitive construct will cause an effective decrease of t if it terminates properly after at least one execution of a guarded command. The theorem is so obvious that it would be a shame if it were difficult to prove, but luckily it is not. We shall show that from (1) and (2) follows that for any value $t0$ and all states

$$(P \text{ and } BB \text{ and } H_k(T) \text{ and } t \leq t0 + 1) \Rightarrow H_k(t \leq t0) \qquad (6)$$

for all $k \geq 0$. It holds for $k = 0$, because $(BB \text{ and } H_0(T)) = F$, and we have to derive from the assumption that (6) holds for $k = K$ that it holds for $k = K + 1$ as well.

$(P \text{ and } BB \text{ and } H_{K+1}(T) \text{ and } t \leq t0 + 1)$
$\quad \Rightarrow \text{wp}(IF, P) \text{ and } \text{wp}(IF, H_K(T)) \text{ and } \text{wp}(IF, t \leq t0)$
$\quad = \text{wp}(IF, P \text{ and } H_K(T) \text{ and } t \leq t0)$
$\quad \Rightarrow \text{wp}(IF, (P \text{ and } BB \text{ and } H_K(T) \text{ and } t \leq t0 + 1) \text{ or}(t \leq t0 \text{ and non } BB))$
$\quad \Rightarrow \text{wp}(IF, H_K(t \leq t0) \text{ or } H_0(t \leq t0))$
$\quad = \text{wp}(IF, H_K(t \leq t0))$
$\quad \Rightarrow \text{wp}(IF, H_K(t \leq t0)) \text{ or } H_0(t \leq t0)$
$\quad = H_{K+1}(t \leq t0)$

The first implication follows from (1), the definition of $H_{K+1}(T)$, and (2); the equality in the third line is obvious; the implication in the fourth line is derived by taking the conjunction with $(BB \text{ or non } BB)$ and then weakening both terms; the implication in the fifth line follows from (6) for $k = K$ and the definition of $H_0(t \leq t0)$; the rest is straightforward. Thus relation (6) has been proved for all $k \geq 0$ and from that results (4) and (5) follow immediately.

EXERCISE

Modify also our second program in such a way that it computes the quotient as well and give a formal correctness proof for your program. (*End of exercise*)

Let us assume next that there is a small number, 3 say, by which we are allowed to multiply and to divide and that these operations are sufficiently fast so that they are attractive to use. We shall denote the product by "$m * 3$" —or by "$3 * m$"— and the quotient by "$m / 3$"; the latter expression will only be called for evaluation provided initially $3 \mid m$ holds. (We are working with integer numbers, aren't we?)

Again we try to establish the desired relation R by means of a repetitive construct, for which the invariant relation P is derived by replacing a constant by a variable. Replacing the constant d by the variable dd whose values will be restricted to $d *$ (a power of 3), we come to the invariant relation P:

$$0 \leq r < dd \text{ and } dd \mid (a - r) \text{ and } (\textbf{E } i: i \geq 0: dd = d * 3^i)$$

We shall establish the relation and then try to reach, while keeping it invariant, a state satisfying $d = dd$.

In order to establish it, we need a further repetitive construct: first we establish

$$0 \leq r \text{ and } dd \mid (a - r) \text{ and } (\textbf{E } i: i \geq 0: dd = d * 3^i)$$

and then let dd grow until it is large enough and $r < dd$ is satisfied as well. The following program would do:

```
if a ≥ 0 and d > 0 →
    r, dd:= a, d;
    do r ≥ dd → dd:= dd * 3 od;
    do dd ≠ d → dd:= dd / 3;
                do r ≥ dd → r:= r − dd od
    od
fi
```

EXERCISE

Modify also the above program in such a way that it computes the quotient as well and give a formal correctness proof for your program. This proof has to demonstrate that whenever $dd/3$ is computed, originally $3 \mid dd$ holds. (*End of exercise.*)

The above program exhibits a quite common characteristic. On the outer level we have two repetitive constructs in succession; when we have two or more repetitive constructs on the same level in succession, the guarded commands of the later ones tend to be more elaborate than those of the earlier ones. (This is known as "Dijkstra's Law", which does not always hold.) The reason for this tendency is clear: each repetitive construct adds its "**and non BB**" to the relation it keeps invariant and that additional relation has to be kept invariant by the next one as well. But for the inner loop, the second one is exactly the inverse of the first one; but it is precisely the function of the added statement

$$\textbf{do } r \geq dd \rightarrow r:= r − dd \textbf{ od}$$

to restore the potentially destroyed relation $r < dd$, i.e. the achievement of the first loop.

Fourth example.

For fixed *Q1*, *Q2*, *Q3*, and *Q4* it is requested to establish *R* where *R* is given as *R1* **and** *R2* with

R1:   The sequence of values $(q1, q2, q3, q4)$ is a permutation
      of the sequence of values $(Q1, Q2, Q3, Q4)$

R2: $q1 \leq q2 \leq q3 \leq q4$

Taking *R1* as relation *P* to be kept invariant a possible solution is

$$q1, q2, q3, q4 := Q1, Q2, Q3, Q4;$$
$$\textbf{do } q1 > q2 \rightarrow q1, q2 := q2, q1$$
$$\mathbin{\|} q2 > q3 \rightarrow q2, q3 := q3, q2$$
$$\mathbin{\|} q3 > q4 \rightarrow q3, q4 := q4, q3$$
$$\textbf{od}$$

The first assignment obviously establishes *P* and no guarded command destroys it. Upon termination we have **non** *BB*, and that is relation *R2*. The way in which people convince themselves that it does terminate depends largely on their background: a mathematician might observe that the number of inversions decreases, an operations researcher will interpret it as maximizing $q1 + 2*q2 + 3*q3 + 4*q4$, and I, as a physicist, just "see" the center of gravity moving in the one direction (to the right, to be quite precise). The program is remarkable in the sense that, whatever we would have chosen for the guards, never would there be the danger of destroying relation *P*: the guards are in this example a pure consequence of the requirement of termination.

Note.   Observe that we could have added other alternatives such as

$$q1 > q3 \rightarrow q1, q3 := q3, q1$$

as well; they cannot be used to replace one of the given three.

(End of note.)

It is a nice example of the kind of clarity that our nondeterminacy has made possible to achieve; needless to say, however, I do not recommend to sort a large number of values in an analogous manner.

Fifth example.

We are requested to design a program approximating a square root; more precisely: for fixed n $(n \geq 0)$ the program should establish

R: $\qquad\qquad\qquad a^2 \leq n \textbf{ and } (a + 1)^2 > n$

One way of weakening this relation is to drop one of the terms of the conjunction, e.g. the last one, and focus upon

P: $\qquad\qquad\qquad a^2 \leq n$

a relation that is obviously satisfied by $a = 0$, so that the initialization need not bother us. We observe that if the second term is not satisfied this is due to the fact that a is too small and we could therefore consider the statement "$a := a + 1$". Formally we find

$$\text{wp}(\text{"}a := a + 1\text{"}, P) = ((a + 1)^2 \leq n)$$

Taking this condition as —the only!— guard, we have (P **and non** BB) $= R$ and therefore we are invited to consider the program

> **if** $n \geq 0 \rightarrow$
> $a := 0$ {P has been established};
>   **do** $(a + 1)^2 \leq n \rightarrow a := a + 1$ {P has not been destroyed} **od**
>   {R has been established}
> **fi** {R has been established}

all under the assumption that the program terminates, which is what it does thanks to the fact that the square of a nonnegative number is a monotonically increasing function: we can take for t the function $n - a^2$.

This program is not very surprising; it is not very efficient either: for large values of n it could be rather time-consuming. Another way of generalizing R is by the introduction of another variable (b say—and again restricting its range) that is to replace part of R, for instance

P: $\qquad\qquad a^2 \leq n$ **and** $b^2 > n$ **and** $0 \leq a < b$

By the way this has been chosen it has the pleasant property that

$$(P \text{ and } (a + 1 = b)) \Rightarrow R$$

Thus we are led to consider a program of the form (from now on omitting the **if** $n \geq 0 \rightarrow \dots$ **fi**)

> $a, b := 0, n + 1$ {P has been established};
> **do** $a + 1 \neq b \rightarrow$ decrease $b - a$ under invariance of P **od**
> {R has been established}

Each time the guarded command is executed let d be the amount by which the difference $b - a$ is decreased. Decreasing this difference can be done by either decreasing b or increasing a or both. Without loss of generality we can restrict ourselves to such steps in which either a or b is changed, but not both: if a is too small and b is too large and in one step only b is decreased, then a can be increased in a next step. This consideration leads to a program of the following form.

> $a, b := 0, n + 1$ {P has been established};
> **do** $a + 1 \neq b \rightarrow$
> $d := \dots$ {d has a suitable value and P is still valid};
>   **if** $\dots \rightarrow a := a + d$ {P has not been destroyed}
>   ▯ $\dots \rightarrow b := b - d$ {P has not been destroyed}
>   **fi** {P has not been destroyed}
> **od** {R has been established}

Now

$$\text{wp}(\text{``}a := a + d\text{''}, P) = ((a + d)^2 \leq n \text{ and } b^2 > n)$$

which, because P implies the second term, leads to the first term as our first guard; the second guard is derived similarly and our next form is

> $a, b := 0, n + 1;$
> **do** $a + 1 \neq b \rightarrow d := \ldots;$
>   **if** $(a + d)^2 \leq n \rightarrow a := a + d$
>   ▯ $(b - d)^2 > n \rightarrow b := b - d$
>   **fi** $\{P$ has not been destroyed$\}$
> **od** $\{R$ has been established$\}$

We are still left with a suitable choice for d. Because we have chosen $b - a$ (actually, $b - a - 1$) as our function t, effective decrease implies that d must satisfy $d > 0$. Furthermore the following alternative construct may not lead to abortion, i.e. at least one of the guards must be true. That is, the negation of the first, $(a + d)^2 > n$, must imply the other, $(b - d)^2 > n$; this is guaranteed if

$$a + d \leq b - d$$

or

$$2 * d \leq b - a$$

Besides a lower bound we have also found an upper bound for d. We could choose $d = 1$, but the larger d is, the faster the program, and therefore we propose:

> $a, b := 0, n + 1;$
> **do** $a + 1 \neq b \rightarrow d := (b - a)\textbf{div } 2;$
>   **if** $(a + d)^2 \leq n \rightarrow a := a + d$
>   ▯ $(b - d)^2 > n \rightarrow b := b - d$
>   **fi**
> **od**

where n **div** 2 is given by $n/2$ if $2 | n$ and by $(n - 1)/2$ if $2 | (n - 1)$.

The use of the operator **div** suggests that we should see what happens if we impose upon ourselves the restriction that whenever d is computed, $b - a$ should be even. Introducing $c = b - a$ and eliminating the b, we get the invariant relation

P: $a^2 \leq n \text{ and } (a + c)^2 > n \text{ and } (\textbf{E } i: i \geq 0: c = 2^i)$

and the program (in which the roles of c and d have coincided)

$$a, c:= 0, 1; \textbf{do } c^2 \leq n \rightarrow c:= 2 * c \textbf{ od};$$
$$\textbf{do } c \neq 1 \rightarrow c:= c \,/\, 2;$$
$$\textbf{if } (a + c)^2 \leq n \rightarrow a:= a + c$$
$$\textbf{\text[} (a + c)^2 > n \rightarrow skip$$
$$\textbf{fi}$$
$$\textbf{od}$$

Note. This program is very much like the last program for the third example, the computation of the remainder under the assumption that we could multiply and divide by *3*. The alternative construct in our above program could have been replaced by

$$\textbf{do } (a + c)^2 \leq n \rightarrow a:= a + c \textbf{ od}$$

If the condition for the remainder $0 \leq r < d$ would have been rewritten as $r < d$ **and** $(r + d) \geq d$, the similarity would be even more striking. (*End of note.*)

Under admission of the danger of beating this little example to death, I would like to submit the last version to yet another transformation. We have written the program under the assumption that squaring a number is among the repertoire of available operations; but suppose it is not and suppose that multiplying and dividing by (small) powers of *2* are the only (semi-)multiplicative operations at our disposal. Then our last program as it stands is no good, i.e. it is no good if we assume that the values of the variables as directly manipulated by the machine are to be equated to the values of the variables *a* and *c* if this computation were performed "in abstracto". To put it in another way: we can consider *a* and *c* as abstract variables whose values are represented —according to a convention more complicated than just identity— by the values of other variables that are in fact manipulated by the machine. Instead of directly manipulating *a* and *c*, we can let the machine manipulate *p*, *q*, and *r*, such that

$$p = a * c$$
$$q = c^2$$
$$r = n - a^2$$

It is a coordinate transformation and to each path through our (a,c)-space corresponds a path through our (p,q,r)-space. This is not always true the other way round, for the values of *p*, *q*, and *r* are not independent: in terms of *p*, *q*, and *r* we have redundancy and therefore the potential to trade some storage space against not only computation time but even against the need to square! (The transformation from a point in (a,c)-space to a point in (p,q,r)-space has quite clearly been constructed with that objective in mind.) We can now try to translate all boolean expressions and moves in (a,c)-space into the corresponding boolean expressions and moves in (p,q,r)-space. If this can be done in terms of the permissible operations there, we have been successful. The transformation suggested is indeed adequate and the following program is the result (the variable h has been introduced for a very local optimization):

$$p, q, r := 0, 1, n; \textbf{do } q \leq n \rightarrow q := q * 4 \textbf{ od};$$
$$\textbf{do } q \neq 1 \rightarrow q := q/4; h := p + q; p := p/2 \ \{h = 2 * p + q\};$$
$$\textbf{if } r \geq h \rightarrow p, r := p + q, r - h$$
$$\textnormal{\textbar}\ r < h \rightarrow skip$$
$$\textbf{fi}$$

$$\textbf{od } \{p \text{ has the value desired for } a\}$$

This fifth example has been included because it relates —in an embellished form— a true design history. When the youngest of our two dogs was only a few months old I walked with both of them one evening. At the time, I was preparing my lectures for the next morning, when I would have to address students with only a few weeks exposure to programming, and I wanted a simple problem such that I could "massage" the solutions. During that one-hour walk the first, third, and fourth programs were developed in that order, but for the fact that the correct introduction of h in the last program was something I could only manage with the aid of pencil and paper after I had returned home. The second program, the one manipulating a and b, which here has been presented as a stepping stone to our third solution, was only discovered a few weeks later—be it in a less elegant form than presented here. A second reason for its inclusion is the relation between the third and the fourth program: with respect to the latter one the other one represents our first example of so-called "representational abstraction".

Sixth example.

For fixed X ($X > 1$) and Y ($Y \geq 0$) the program should establish

R: $z = X^Y$

under the —obvious— assumption that exponentiation is not among the available repertoire. This problem can be solved with the aid of an "abstract variable", h say; we shall do it with a loop, for which the invariant relation is

P: $h * z = X^Y$

and our (equally "abstract") program could be

$$h, z := X^Y, 1 \ \{P \text{ has been established}\};$$
$$\textbf{do } h \neq 1 \rightarrow \text{squeeze } h \text{ under invariance of } P \textbf{ od}$$
$$\{R \text{ has been established}\}$$

The last conclusion is justified because $(P \textbf{ and } h = 1) \Rightarrow R$. The above program will terminate under the assumption that a finite number of applications of the operation "squeeze" will have established $h = 1$. The problem, of course, is that we are not allowed to represent the value of h by that of a concrete variable directly manipulated by the machine; if we were allowed to do that, we could have assigned the value of X^Y immediately to z, not bothering about introducing h at all. The trick is that we can introduce two — at this level, concrete— variables, x and y say, to represent the current value of h and our first assignment suggests as convention for this representation

$$h = x^y$$

The condition "$h \neq 1$" then translates into "$y \neq 0$" and our next task is to discover an implementable operation "squeeze". Because the product $h * z$ must remain invariant under squeezing, we should divide h by the same value by which z is multiplied. In view of the way in which h is represented, the current value of x is the most natural candidate. Without any further problems we arrive at the translation of our abstract program

> $x, y, z := X, Y, 1\{P$ has been established$\}$;
> **do** $y \neq 0 \rightarrow y, z := y - 1, z * x$ $\{P$ has not been destroyed$\}$ **od**
> $\{R$ has been established$\}$

Looking at this program we realize that the number of times control goes through the loop equals the original value Y and we can ask ourselves whether we can speed things up. Well, the guarded command has now the task to bring y down to zero; without changing the *value* of h, we can investigate whether we can change the *representation* of that value, in the hope of decreasing the value of y. We are just going to try to exploit the fact that the concrete representation of a value of h as given by x^y is by no means unique. If y is even, we can halve y and square x, and this will not change h at all. Just before the squeezing operation we insert the transformation towards the most attractive representation of h and here is the next program:

> $x, y, z := X, Y, 1$;
> **do** $y \neq 0 \rightarrow$ **do** $2 \mid y \rightarrow x, y := x * x, y/2$ **od**;
> $y, z := y - 1, z * x$
> **od** $\{R$ has been established$\}$

There exists one value that can be halved indefinitely without becoming odd and that is the value 0; in other words: the outer guard ensures that the inner repetition terminates.

I have included this example for various reasons. The discovery that a mere insertion of what on the abstract level acts like an empty statement could change an algorithm invoking a number of operations proportional to Y into one invoking a number of operations only proportional to $\log(Y)$ startled me when I made it. This discovery was a direct consequence of my forcing myself to think in terms of a single abstract variable. The exponentiation program I knew was the following:

$x, y, z := X, Y, 1;$
do $y \neq 0 \rightarrow$ **if non** $2 \, |y \rightarrow y, z := y - 1, z * x \, [\![\, 2 \, |y \rightarrow$ *skip* **fi**;
$\qquad\qquad x, y := x * x, y/2$
od

This latter program is very well known; it is a program that many of us have discovered independently of each other. Because the last squaring of x when y has reached the value 0 is clearly superfluous, this program has often been cited as supporting the need for what were called "intermediate exits". In view of our second program I come to the conclusion that this support is weak.

Seventh example.

For a fixed value of n ($n \geq 0$) a function $f(i)$ is given for $0 \leq i < n$. Assign to the boolean variable "*allsix*" the value such that eventually

R: $allsix = (\text{A } i : 0 \leq i < n : f(i) = 6)$

holds. (This example shows some similarity to the second example of this chapter. Note, however, that in this example, $n = 0$ is allowed as well. In that case the range for i for the all-quantifier "A" is empty and $allsix = true$ should hold.) Analogous to what we did in the second example the invariant relation

P: $(allsix = (\text{A } i : 0 \leq i < j : f(i) = 6))$ **and** $0 \leq j \leq n$

suggests itself, because it is easily established for $j = 0$, while $(P$ **and** $j = n)$ $\Rightarrow R$. The only thing to do is to investigate how to increase j under invariance of P. We therefore derive

$\text{wp}("j := j + 1", P) =$
$(allsix = (\text{A } i : 0 \leq i < j + 1 : f(i) = 6))$ **and** $0 \leq j + 1 \leq n$

The last term is implied by P **and** $j \neq n$; it presents no problem because we had already decided that $j \neq n$ as a guard is weak enough to conclude R upon termination. The weakest pre-condition such that the assignment

$\qquad\qquad$ $allsix := allsix$ **and** $f(j) = 6$

will establish the other term, is

$\qquad$ $(allsix$ **and** $f(j) = 6) = (\text{A } i : 0 \leq i < j + 1 : f(i) = 6)$

a condition that is implied by P. We thus arrive at the program

$\qquad\qquad$ $allsix, j := true, 0;$
$\qquad\qquad$ **do** $j \neq n \rightarrow allsix := allsix$ **and** $f(j) = 6;$
$\qquad\qquad\qquad\qquad$ $j := j + 1$
$\qquad\qquad$ **od**

(In the guarded command we have not used the concurrent assignment for no particular reason.)

By the time that we read this program —or perhaps sooner— we should get the uneasy feeling that as soon as a function value $\neq 6$ has been found, there is not much point in going on. And indeed, although $(P \text{ and } j = n) \Rightarrow R$, we could have used the weaker

$$(P \text{ and } (j = n \text{ or non } allsix)) \Rightarrow R$$

leading to the stronger guard "$j \neq n$ and $allsix$" and to the program

> $allsix, j := true, 0;$
> $\textbf{do } j \neq n \textbf{ and } allsix \longrightarrow allsix, j := f(j) = 6, j + 1 \textbf{ od}$

(Note the simplification of the assignment to $allsix$, a simplification that is justified by the stronger guard.)

EXERCISE

Give for the same problem the correctness proof for

> $\textbf{if } n = 0 \longrightarrow allsix := true$
> $\textbf{[} n > 0 \longrightarrow j := 0;$
> $\qquad \textbf{do } j \neq n - 1 \textbf{ and } f(j) = 6 \longrightarrow j := j + 1 \textbf{ od};$
> $\qquad allsix := f(j) = 6$
> **fi**

and also for the still more tricky program (that does away with the need to invoke the function f from more than one place in the program)

> $j := 0;$
> $\textbf{do } j \neq n \textbf{ cand } f(j) = 6 \longrightarrow j := j + 1 \textbf{ od};$
> $allsix := j = n$

(Here the conditional conjunction operator "**cand**" has been used in order to do justice to the fact that $f(n)$ need not be defined.) The last program is one that some people like very much. (*End of exercise.*)

Eighth example.

Before I can state our next problem, I must first give some definitions and a theorem. Let $p = (p_0, p_1, \ldots, p_{n-1})$ be a permutation of n $(n > 1)$ different values p_i $(0 \leq i < n)$, i.e. $(i \neq j) \Rightarrow (p_i \neq p_j)$. Let $q = (q_0, q_1, \ldots, q_{n-1})$ be a different permutation of the same set of n values. By definition "permutation p precedes q in the alphabetic order" if and only if for the minimum value of k such that $p_k \neq q_k$ we have $p_k < q_k$.

The so-called "alphabetic index$_n$" of a permutation of n different values is the ordinal number given to it when we number the $n!$ possible permutations arranged in alphabetic order from 0 through $n! - 1$. For instance, for $n = 3$ and the set of values 2, 4, and 7 we have

$$\text{index}_3(2, 4, 7) = 0$$
$$\text{index}_3(2, 7, 4) = 1$$
$$\text{index}_3(4, 2, 7) = 2$$
$$\text{index}_3(4, 7, 2) = 3$$
$$\text{index}_3(7, 2, 4) = 4$$
$$\text{index}_3(7, 4, 2) = 5$$

Let $(p_0\S\, p_1\S \ldots \S p_{n-1})$ denote the permutation of the n different values in monotonically increasing order, i.e. $\text{index}_n((p_0\S\, p_1\S \ldots \S p_{n-1})) = 0$. (For example, $(4\S\, 7\S\, 2) = (2, 4, 7)$ but also $(7\S\, 2\S\, 4) = (2, 4, 7)$.)

With the above notation we can formulate the following theorem for $n > 1$:

$$\text{index}_n(p_0, p_1, \ldots, p_{n-1}) =$$
$$\text{index}_n(p_0, (p_1\S\, p_2\S \ldots \S p_{n-1})) + \text{index}_{n-1}(p_1, p_2, \ldots, p_{n-1})$$

(for example, $\text{index}_3(4, 7, 2) = \text{index}_3(4, 2, 7) + \text{index}_2(7, 2) = 2 + 1 = 3$). In words: the index_n of a permutation of n different values is the index_n of the alphabetically first one with the same leftmost value increased by the index_{n-1} of the permutation of the remaining rightmost $n - 1$ values. As a corollary: from

$$p_{n-k} < p_{n-k+1} < \ldots < p_{n-1}$$

follows that $\text{index}_n(p_0, p_1, \ldots, p_{n-1})$ is a multiple of $k!$ and vice versa.

After these preliminaries, we can now describe our problem. We have a row of n positions ($n > 1$) numbered in the order from left to right from 0 through $n - 1$; in each position lies a card with a value written on it such that no two different cards show the same value.

When at any moment c_i ($0 \leq i < n$) denotes the value on the card in position i, we have initially

$$c_0 < c_1 < \ldots < c_{n-1}$$

(i.e. the cards lie sorted in the order of increasing value). For given value of r ($0 \leq r < n!$) we have to rearrange the cards such that

R: $\qquad\qquad\qquad \text{index}_n(c_0, c_1, \ldots, c_{n-1}) = r$

The only way in which our mechanism can interfere with the cards is via the execution of the statement

$$cardswap(i, j) \qquad \text{with } 0 \leq i, j < n$$

that will interchange the cards in positions i and j if $i \neq j$ (and will do nothing if $i = j$).

In order to perform this transformation we must find a class of states — all satisfying a suitable condition $P1$— such that both initial and final states are specific instances of that class. Introducing a new variable, s say, an obvious candidate for $P1$ is

$$\text{index}_n(c_0, c_1, \ldots, c_{n-1}) = s$$

as this is easily established initially (viz. by "$s := 0$") and $(P1 \text{ and } s = r) \Rightarrow R$.

Again we ask whether we can think of restricting the range of s and in view of its initial value we might try

$P1$: $\text{index}_n(c_0, c_1, \ldots, c_{n-1}) = s \text{ and } 0 \leq s \leq r$

which would lead to a program of the form

    $s := 0$ {$P1$ has been established};
    do $s \neq r \rightarrow$ {$P1$ **and** $s < r$}
            increase s by a suitable amount under
            invariance of $P1$ {$P1$ still holds}
    od {R has been established}

Our next concern is what to choose for "a suitable amount". Because our increase of s must be accompanied by a rearrangement of the cards in order to keep $P1$ invariant, it seems wise to investigate whether we can find conditions under which a single *cardswap* corresponds to a known increase of s. For a value of k satisfying $1 \leq k < n$, let

$$c_{n-k} < c_{n-k+1} < \ldots < c_{n-1}$$

hold; this assumption is equivalent with the assumption $k! | s$ (read "$k!$ divides s"). Let $i = n - k - 1$, i.e. c_i is the value on the card to the immediate left of this sequence. Furthermore let $c_i < c_{n-1}$ and let c_j be for j in the range $n - k \leq j < n$ the minimum value such that $c_i < c_j$ (i.e. c_j is the smallest value to the right of c_i exceeding the latter). In that case the operation *cardswap*(i, j) leaves the rightmost k values in the same monotonic order and our theorem about permutations and their indices tells us that $k!$ is the corresponding increase of s. It also tells us that when, besides $k! | s$, we have

$$s \leq r < s + k!$$

c_0 through c_{n-k-1} have attained their final value.

I therefore suggest we strengthen our original invariant relation $P1$ with the additional relation $P2$ (fixing the function of a new variable k),

$P2$: $1 \leq k \leq n \text{ and } k! | s \text{ and } r < s + k!$

which means that the rightmost k cards show still monotonically increasing values, while the leftmost $n - k$ cards are in their final positions. We have decided upon the "major steps" in which we shall walk towards our destination.

In order to find "the suitable amount" for a major step, the machine first determines the largest smaller value of k for which $r < s + k!$ no longer holds (c_i with $i = n - k - 1$ is then too small, but values to the left of it are all OK) and then increases s by the minimum multiple of $k!$ needed to make $r < s + k!$ hold again; this is done in "minor steps" of $k!$ at a time, simultaneously increasing c_i with cards to the right of it. In the following program we introduce the additional variable $kfac$, satisfying

P3: $kfac = k!$

and for the second inner repetition i and j, such that $i = n - k - 1$ and either $j = n$ or $i < j < n$ and $c_j > c_i$ and $c_{j-1} \leq c_i$.

> $s := 0$ {P1 has been established};
> $kfac, k := 1, 1$ {P3 has been established as well};
> **do** $k \neq n \rightarrow kfac, k := kfac *(k + 1), k + 1$ **od**
>   {P2 has been established as well};
> **do** $s \neq r \rightarrow$ {$s < r$, i.e. at least one and therefore
>   at least two cards have not reached their
>   final position}
>   **do** $r < s + kfac \rightarrow kfac, k := kfac/k, k - 1$ **od**
>   {P1 and P3 have been kept true, but in P2
>   the last term is replaced by
> $s + kfac \leq r < s + (k + 1)* kfac$};
> $i, j := n - k - 1, n - k$;
>   **do** $s + kfac \leq r \rightarrow$ {$n - k \leq j < n$}
> $s := s + kfac$; $cardswap(i, j)$; $j := j + 1$
>   **od** {P2 has been restored again: P1 **and** P2 **and** P3}
> **od**{R has been established}

EXERCISE

Convince yourself of the fact that also the following rather similar program would have done the job:

> $s := 0$; $kfac, k := 1, 1$;
> **do** $k \neq n \rightarrow kfac, k := kfac *(k + 1), k + 1$ **od**;
> **do** $k \neq 1 \rightarrow$
> $kfac, k := kfac/k, k - 1$;
> $i, j := n - k - 1, n - k$;
>   **do** $s + kfac \leq r \rightarrow$
> $s := s + kfac$; $cardswap(i, j)$; $j := j + 1$
>   **od**
> **od**

(Hint: the monotonically decreasing function $t \geq 0$ for the outer repetition is $t = r - s + k - 1$.) (*End of exercise.*)

9 ON NONDETERMINACY BEING BOUNDED

This is again a very formal chapter. In the chapter "The Characterization of Semantics" we have mentioned four properties that wp(S, R), for any S considered as a function of R, should have if its interpretation as the weakest pre-condition for establishing R is to be feasible. (For nondeterministic mechanisms the fourth property was a direct consequence of the second one.)

In the next chapter, "The Semantic Characterization of a Programming Language", we have given ways for constructing new predicate transformers, pointing out that these constructions should lead only to predicate transformers having the aforementioned properties (i.e. if the whole exercise is to continue to make sense). For every basic statement ("*skip*", "*abort*", and the assignment statements) one has to *verify* that they enjoy the said properties; for every way of building up new statements from component statements (semicolon, alternative, and repetitive constructs) one has to show that the resulting composite statements enjoy those properties as well, in which demonstration one may assume that the component statements enjoy them. We verified this up to and including the Law of the Excluded Miracle for the semicolon, leaving the rest of the verifications as an exercise to the reader. We leave it at that: in this chapter we shall prove a deeper property of our mechanisms, this time verifying it explicitly for the alternative and repetitive constructs as well. (And the structure of the latter verifications can be taken as an example for the omitted ones.) It is also known as the "Property of Continuity".

PROPERTY 5. For any mechanism S and any infinite sequence of predicates $C_0, C_1, C_2, \ldots$ such that

for $\qquad\qquad r \geq 0: \quad C_r \Rightarrow C_{r+1} \qquad$ for all states $\qquad\qquad (1)$

72

we have for all states

$$\text{wp}(S, (\mathbf{E}\, r: r \geq 0: C_r)) = (\mathbf{E}\, s: s \geq 0: \text{wp}(S, C_s)) \qquad (2)$$

For the statements "*skip*" and "*abort*" and for the assignment statements, the truth of (2) is a direct consequence of their definitions, assumption (1) not even being necessary. For the semicolon we derive

$$\text{wp}(``S1;\, S2", (\mathbf{E}\, r: r \geq 0: C_r)) =$$

(by definition of the semantics of the semicolon)

$$\text{wp}(S1, \text{wp}(S2, (\mathbf{E}\, r: r \geq 0: C_r))) =$$

(because property 5 is assumed to hold for S2)

$$\text{wp}(S1, (\mathbf{E}\, r': r' \geq 0: \text{wp}(S2, C_{r'}))) =$$

(because S2 is assumed to enjoy property 2, so that $\text{wp}(S2, C_r) \Rightarrow$ $\text{wp}(S2, C_{r'+1})$ and S1 is assumed to enjoy property 5)

$$(\mathbf{E}\, s: s \geq 0: \text{wp}(S1, \text{wp}(S2, C_s))) =$$

(by definition of the semantics of the semicolon)

$$(\mathbf{E}\, s: s \geq 0: \text{wp}(``S1;\, S2", C_s)) \qquad \text{Q.E.D.}$$

For the alternative construct we prove (2) in two steps. The easy step is that the right-hand side of (2) implies its left-hand side. For, consider an arbitrary point X in state space, such that the right-hand side of (2) holds, i.e. there exists a nonnegative value, s' say, such that in point X the relation $\text{wp}(S, C_{s'})$ holds. But because $C_{s'} \Rightarrow (\mathbf{E}\, r: r \geq 0: C_r)$ and any S enjoys property 2, we conclude that

$$\text{wp}(S, (\mathbf{E}\, r: r \geq 0: C_r))$$

holds in point X as well. As X was an arbitrary state satisfying the right-hand side of (2), the latter implies the left-hand side of (2). For this argument, antecedent (1) has not been used, but we need it for proving the implication in the other direction.

$$\text{wp}(\text{IF}, (\mathbf{E}\, r: r \geq 0: C_r)) =$$

(by definition of the semantics of the alternative construct)

$$BB \text{ and } (\mathbf{A}\, j: 1 \leq j \leq n: B_j \Rightarrow \text{wp}(SL_j, (\mathbf{E}\, r: r \geq 0: C_r))) =$$

(because the individual SL_j are assumed to enjoy property 5)

$$BB \text{ and } (\mathbf{A}\, j: 1 \leq j \leq n: B_j \Rightarrow (\mathbf{E}\, s: s \geq 0: \text{wp}(SL_j, C_s))) \qquad (3)$$

Consider an arbitrary state X for which (3) is true, and let j' be a value for j such that $B_{j'}(X) = true$; then we have in point X

$$(\mathbf{E}\, s: s \geq 0: \text{wp}(SL_{j'}, C_s)) \qquad (4)$$

Because of (1) and the fact that $SL_{j'}$ enjoys property 2, we conclude that

$$\text{wp}(SL_{j'}, C_s) \Rightarrow \text{wp}(SL_{j'}, C_{s+1})$$

and thus we conclude from (4) that in point X we also have

$$(\mathbf{E}\ s': s' \geq 0: (\mathbf{A}\ s: s \geq s': \text{wp}(SL_{j'}, C_s))) \tag{5}$$

Let $s' = s'(j')$ be the minimum value satisfying (5). We now define *smax* as the maximum value of $s'(j')$ taken over the (at most n, and therefore the maximum exists!) values j' for which $B_{j'}(X) = true$. In point X then holds on account of (3) and (5)

$$BB\ \textbf{and}\ (\mathbf{A}\ j: 1 \leq j \leq n: B_j \Rightarrow \text{wp}(SL_j, C_{smax})) =$$

(by definition of the semantics of the alternative construct)

$$\text{wp}(IF, C_{smax})$$

But the truth of the latter relation in state X implies that there also

$$(\mathbf{E}\ s: s \geq 0: \text{wp}(IF, C_s))$$

but as X was an arbitrary state satisfying (3), for $S = IF$ the fact that the left-hand side of (2) implies its right-hand side as well has been proved, and thus the alternative construct enjoys property 5 as well. Note the essential role played by the antecedent (1) and the fact that a guarded command set is a *finite* set of guarded commands.

Property 5 is proved for the repetitive construct by mathematical induction.

Base: Property 5 holds for H_0.

$$H_0(\mathbf{E}\ r: r \geq 0: C_r) =$$
$$(\mathbf{E}\ r: r \geq 0: C_r)\ \textbf{and non}\ BB =$$
$$(\mathbf{E}\ s: s \geq 0: C_s\ \textbf{and non}\ BB) =$$
$$(\mathbf{E}\ s: s \geq 0: H_0(C_s)) \qquad\qquad \text{Q.E.D.}$$

Induction step: From the assumption that property 5 holds for H_k and H_0 it follows that it holds for H_{k+1}.

$$H_{k+1}(\mathbf{E}\ r: r \geq 0: C_r) =$$

(by virtue of the definition of H_{k+1})

$$\text{wp}(IF, H_k(\mathbf{E}\ r: r \geq 0: C_r))\ \textbf{or}\ H_0\ (\mathbf{E}\ r: r \geq 0: C_r) =$$

(because property 5 is assumed to hold for H_k and for H_0)

$$\text{wp}(IF, (\mathbf{E}\ r': r' \geq 0: H_k(C_{r'})))\ \textbf{or}\ (\mathbf{E}\ s: s \geq 0: H_0(C_s)) =$$

(because property 5 holds for the alternative construct and property 2 is enjoyed by H_k)

$$(\mathbf{E}\ s: s \geq 0 : \mathrm{wp}(\mathrm{IF}, H_k(C_s))) \text{ or } (\mathbf{E}\ s: s \geq 0 : H_0(C_s)) =$$
$$(\mathbf{E}\ s: s \geq 0 : \mathrm{wp}(\mathrm{IF}, H_k(C_s)) \text{ or } H_0(C_s)) =$$
(by virtue of the definition of H_{k+1})
$$(\mathbf{E}\ s: s \geq 0 : H_{k+1}(C_s)) \qquad\qquad \text{Q.E.D.}$$

From base and induction step we conclude that property 5 holds for all H_k, and hence
$$\mathrm{wp}(\mathrm{DO}, (\mathbf{E}\ r: r \geq 0 : C_r)) =$$
(by definition of the semantics of the repetitive construct)
$$(\mathbf{E}\ k: k \geq 0 : H_k(\mathbf{E}\ r: r \geq 0 : C_r)) =$$
(because property 5 holds for all H_k)
$$(\mathbf{E}\ k: k \geq 0 : (\mathbf{E}\ s: s \geq 0 : H_k(C_s))) =$$
(because this expresses the existence of a (k, s)-pair)
$$(\mathbf{E}\ s: s \geq 0 : (\mathbf{E}\ k: k \geq 0 : H_k(C_s))) =$$
(by definition of the semantics of the repetitive construct)
$$(\mathbf{E}\ s: s \geq 0 : \mathrm{wp}(\mathrm{DO}, C_s)) \qquad\qquad \text{Q.E.D.}$$

Property 5 is of importance on account of the semantics of the repetitive construct
$$\mathrm{wp}(\mathrm{DO}, R) = (\mathbf{E}\ k: k \geq 0 : H_k(R))$$
such a pre-condition could be the post-condition for another statement. Because
$$\text{for} \qquad k \geq 0: \qquad H_k(R) \Rightarrow H_{k+1}(R) \qquad \text{for all states}$$
(this is easily proved by mathematical induction), the conditions under which property 5 is relevant, are satisfied. We can, for instance, prove that in all initial states in which BB holds
$$\mathbf{do}\ B_1 \rightarrow SL_1\ \mathbb{I}\ B_2 \rightarrow SL_2\ \mathbb{I} \dots \mathbb{I}\ B_n \rightarrow SL_n\ \mathbf{od}$$
is equivalent to
$$\mathbf{if}\ B_1 \rightarrow SL_1\ \mathbb{I}\ B_2 \rightarrow SL_2\ \mathbb{I} \dots \mathbb{I}\ B_n \rightarrow SL_n\ \mathbf{fi};$$
$$\mathbf{do}\ B_1 \rightarrow SL_1\ \mathbb{I}\ B_2 \rightarrow SL_2\ \mathbb{I} \dots \mathbb{I}\ B_n \rightarrow SL_n\ \mathbf{od}$$
(In initial states in which BB does not hold, the first program would have acted as "*skip*", the second one as "*abort*".) That is, we have to prove that
$$(BB \textbf{ and } \mathrm{wp}(\mathrm{DO}, R)) = (BB \textbf{ and } \mathrm{wp}(\mathrm{IF}, \mathrm{wp}(\mathrm{DO}, R)))$$
$$BB \textbf{ and } \mathrm{wp}(\mathrm{IF}, \mathrm{wp}(\mathrm{DO}, R)) =$$
(on account of the semantics of the repetitive construct)
$$BB \textbf{ and } \mathrm{wp}(\mathrm{IF}, (\mathbf{E}\ k: k \geq 0 : H_k(R))) =$$

(because property 5 holds for IF)

$$BB \text{ and } (E \, s: s \geq 0: \text{wp}(\text{IF}, H_s(R))) =$$

(because $(BB \text{ and } H_0(R)) = F$)

$$BB \text{ and } (E \, s: s \geq 0: \text{wp}(\text{IF}, H_s(R)) \text{ or } H_0(R)) =$$

(on account of the recurrence relation for the $H_k(R)$)

$$BB \text{ and } (E \, s: s \geq 0: H_{s+1}(R)) =$$

(because $(BB \text{ and } H_0(R)) = F$)

$$BB \text{ and } (E \, k: k \geq 0: H_k(R)) =$$

(on account of the semantics of the repetitive construct)

$$BB \text{ and wp}(\text{DO}, R) \qquad\qquad \text{Q.E.D.}$$

Finally, we would like to draw attention to a very different consequence of the fact that all our mechanisms enjoy property 5. We could try to make the program S: "set x to any positive integer" with the properties:

(a) $\text{wp}(S, x > 0) = T$.
(b) $(A \, s: s \geq 0: \text{wp}(S, 0 < x < s) = F)$

Here property (a) expresses the requirement that activation of S is guaranteed to terminate with x equal to some positive value, property (b) expresses that S is a mechanism of unbounded nondeterminacy, i.e. that no a priori upper bound for the final value of x can be given. For such a program S, we could, however, derive now:

$$
\begin{aligned}
T &= \text{wp}(S, x > 0) \\
&= \text{wp}(S, (E \, r: r \geq 0: 0 < x < r)) \\
&= (E \, s: s \geq 0: \text{wp}(S, 0 < x < s)) \\
&= (E \, s: s \geq 0: F) \\
&= F
\end{aligned}
$$

This, however, is a contradiction: for the mechanism S "set x to any positive integer" *no* program exists!

As a result, any effort to write a program for "set x to any positive integer" must fail. For instance, we could consider:

```
go on:= true; x:= 1;
do go on → x:= x + 1
 ▯ go on → go on:= false
od
```

This construct will continue to increase x as long as the first alternative is chosen; as soon as the second alternative has been chosen once, it terminates immediately. Upon termination x may indeed be "any positive integer" in the sense that we cannot think of a positive value X such that termination with $x = X$ is impossible. But termination is not guaranteed either! We can enforce termination: with N some large, positive constant we can write

$$go\ on := true; x := 1;$$
$$\textbf{do}\ go\ on\ \textbf{and}\ x < N \longrightarrow x := x + 1$$
$$\textcolor{black}{[\!]}\ go\ on \longrightarrow go\ on := false$$
$$\textbf{od}$$

but then property (b) is no longer satisfied.

The nonexistence of a program for "set x to any positive integer" is reassuring in more than one sense. For, if such a program could exist, our definition of the semantics of the repetitive construct would have been subject to doubt, to say the least. With

S:
$$\textbf{do}\ x > 0 \longrightarrow x := x - 1$$
$$[\!]\ x < 0 \longrightarrow \text{"set } x \text{ to any positive integer"}$$
$$\textbf{od}$$

our formalism for the repetitive construct gives $wp(S, T) = (x \geq 0)$, while I expect most of my readers to conclude that under the assumption of the existence of "set x to any positive integer" for $x < 0$ termination would be guaranteed as well. But then the interpretation of $wp(S, T)$ as the *weakest* pre-condition guaranteeing termination would no longer be justified. However, when we substitute our first would-be implementation:

S:
$$\textbf{do}\ x > 0 \longrightarrow x := x - 1$$
$$[\!]\ x < 0 \longrightarrow go\ on := true; x := 1;$$
$$\qquad \textbf{do}\ go\ on \longrightarrow x := x + 1$$
$$\qquad [\!]\ go\ on \longrightarrow go\ on := false$$
$$\qquad \textbf{od}$$
$$\textbf{od}$$

$wp(S, T) = (x \geq 0)$ is fully correct, both intuitively and formally.

The second reason for reassurance is of a rather different nature. A mechanism of unbounded nondeterminacy yet guaranteed to terminate would be able to make within a finite time a choice out of infinitely many possibilities: if such a mechanism could be formulated in our programming language, that very fact would present an insurmountable barrier to the possibility of the implementation of that programming language.

Acknowledgement. I would like to express my great indebtedness to John C. Reynolds for drawing my attention to the central role of property 5 and to the fact that the nonexistence of a mechanism "set x to any positive integer" is essential for the intuitive justification of the semantics of the repetitive construct. He is, of course, in no way to be held responsible for any of the above. (*End of acknowledgement.*)

10 AN ESSAY ON THE NOTION: "THE SCOPE OF VARIABLES"

Before embarking on what the notion "the scope of a variable" could or should mean, it seems wise to pose a preliminary question first, viz. "Why did we introduce variables in the first place?". This preliminary question is not as empty as it might seem to someone with programming experience only. For instance, in the design of sequential circuitry, it is not unusual to design, initially, a finite-state automaton in which the different possible states of the automaton to be built are just numbered "$0, 1, 2, \ldots$" in the order in which the designer becomes aware of the desirability of their inclusion. As the design proceeds, the designer builds up a so-called "transition table", tabulating for each state the successor state as function of the incoming symbol to be processed. He recalls, only when the transition table has been completed, that he has only binary variables (he calls them "flip-flops") at his disposal and that, if the number of states is, say, between 33 and 64 (bounds included) he needs at least six of them. Those six binary variables span a state space of 64 points and the designer is free in his choice how to identify the different states of his finite-state automaton with points in the 64-point state space. That this choice is not irrelevant becomes clear as soon as we realize that a state transition of the finite-state automaton has to be translated in combinations of boolean variables being operated upon under control of boolean values. To circuit designers this choice is known as the "state assignment problem" and technical constraints or optimization goals may make it a hairy one—so hairy, as a matter of fact, that one may be tempted to challenge the adequacy of the design methodology evoking it. A critical discussion of circuit design methodologies, however, lies beyond the limits of my competence and therefore falls outside the scope of this monograph; we only mentioned it in order to show that there exist design traditions in which, apparently, the introduction of "variables" right at the start does not come naturally.

For two reasons the programmer lives in another world than the circuit designer, particularly the old-fashioned circuit designer. There has been a time that technical considerations exerted a very strong pressure towards minimization of the number of flip-flops used and to use more than six flip-flops to build a finite-state machine with at most *64* states was at that time regarded, if not as a crime, at least as a failure. At any rate, flip-flops being expensive, the circuit designer confined his attention to the design of (sub)-mechanisms of which the number of possible states were extremely modest compared with the number of internal states of the mechanisms programmers are now invited to consider. The programmer lives in a world where the bits are cheaper and this has two consequences: firstly his mechanisms may have many times more internal states, secondly he can allow larger portions of his state space to remain "unused". The second reason why the programmer's world differs from that of the circuit designer is that the larger number of times that (groups of) bits change translates into a longer computation time: the cheapest thing a programmer can prescribe is leaving large sections of the store unaffected!

Comparing the programmer's world with that of the circuit designer, who, initially, just "names" his states by ordinal number of introduction, we immediately see why the programmer wishes to introduce, right at the start, variables that he regards as Cartesian coordinates of a state space of as many dimensions as he feels bound to introduce: the number of different states to be introduced is so incredibly large that a nonsystematic terminology would make the design utterly unmanageable. Whether (and, if so, how!) the design can be kept "manageable" by introducing variables —by way of "nomenclature"— is, of course, the crucial question.

The basic mechanism for changing the state is the assignment statement, redefining (until further notice, that is the next assignment to it) the value of *one* variable. In state space it is a movement parallel to one of the coordinate axes. This can be embellished, leading to the concurrent assignment; from a small number of assignment statements we can form a program component, but such a program component will always affect a modest number of variables. The net effect of such a program component can be understood in terms of a movement in the subspace spanned by the few variables that are affected by it (if you wish, in terms of the projection upon that subspace). As such, it is absolutely independent of all other variables in the system: we can "understand" it without taking any of the other variables into account, even without being aware of their existence. The possibility of this separation, which is also referred to as "factorization", is not surprising in view of the fact that our total state space has been built up as a Cartesian "product" in the first place. The important thing to observe is that this separation, vital for our ability to cope (mentally) with the program as a whole, is the more vital the larger the total number of variables involved. The question is whether (and, if so, how) such "separations" should be reflected more explicitly in our program texts.

Our first "autocoders" (the later ones of which were denoted by misnomers such as "automatic programming systems" or —even worse— "high level programming languages") certainly did not cater to such possibilities. They were conceived at a time when it was the general opinion that it was our program's purpose to instruct our machines, in contrast to the situation of today in which more and more people are leaning towards the opinion that it is our machines' purpose to execute our programs. In those early days it was quite usual to find all sorts of machine properties directly reflected in the write-up of our programs. For instance, because machines had so-called "jump instructions", our programs used "go to statements". Similarly, because machines had constant size stores, computations were regarded as evolving in a state space with a constant number of dimensions, i.e. manipulating the values of a constant set of variables. Similarly, because in a random access store each storage location is equally well accessible, the programmer was allowed to refer at any place in the program text to any variable of the program.

This was all right in the old days when, due to the limited storage sizes, program texts were short and the number of different variables referred to was small. With growing size and sophistication, however, such homogeneity becomes, as a virtue, subject to doubt. From the point of view of flexibility and general applicability the random access store is of course a splendid invention, but comes the moment that we must realize that each flexibility, each generality of our tools requires a discipline for its exploitation. That moment has come. Let us tackle the "free accessibility" first.

In FORTRAN's first version there were two types of variables, integer variables and floating point variables, and the first letter of their name decided —according to a fixed convention— the type, and any occurrence of a variable name anywhere in the program text implied at run time the permanent existence of a variable with that name. In practice this proved to be very unsafe: if in a program operating on a variable named "TEST" a single misspelling occurred, erroneously referring to "TETS" instead of to "TEST", no warning could be generated; another variable called "TETS" would be introduced. In ALGOL 60 the idea of so-called "declarations" was introduced and as far as catching such silly misspellings was concerned, this proved to be an extremely valuable form of redundancy. The basic idea of the explicit declaration of variables is that statements may only refer to variables that have been explicitly declared to exist: an erroneous reference to a variable by the name of "TETS" is then caught automatically if no variable with the name "TETS" has been declared. The declarations of ALGOL 60 served a second purpose besides enumerating the "vocabulary" of names of variables permissible in statements; they also coupled each introduced name to a specific type, thereby abolishing the original FORTRAN convention that the type was determined by the first letter of the name. As people tended more and more to choose names of mnemonic significance, this greater freedom of nomenclature was greatly appreciated.

A greater departure from FORTRAN was ALGOL 60's so-called "block concept" that was used to limit the so-called "textual scope" of the declarations. A "block" in ALGOL 60 extends from an opening bracket "**begin**" to the corresponding closing bracket "**end**" and this bracket pair marks the boundaries of a textual level of nomenclature. Following the opening bracket "**begin**" one or more new names are declared (in the case of more than one name they must all be different) to mean something and those names with those new meanings are said to be "local" to that block: all usage of those names with those new meanings must occur in statements between the preceding "**begin**" and the corresponding "**end**". If our whole program is just one single block, every variable is accessible from everywhere in the text and the protection against misspellings (as referred to in the previous paragraph) is the only gain. A block, however, is one of the possible forms of a statement and therefore blocks may occur nested inside each other and this gives a certain amount of protection because variables local to an inner block are inaccessible from outside.

The ALGOL 60 scope rules protect the local variables of an inner block from outside interference; in the other direction, however, they provide no protection whatsoever. From the interior of an inner block everything outside is in principle accessible, i.e. everything also accessible in the textually embracing block. I said "in principle", for there is one exception, an exception that in those days was regarded as a great invention but that, upon closer scrutiny 15 years later, looks more like a logical patch. The exception is the so-called "re-declared identifier". If at the head of an inner block a declaration occurs for a name —ALGOL 60 calls them "identifiers"— which (accidentally) has already a meaning in the embracing block, then this outside meaning of that name is textually dormant in the inner block, whose local declaration for that same meaning overrules the outside one. The idea behind this "priority of innermost declarations" was that the composer of an inner block needs only to be aware of the global names in the surrounding context to which he is actually referring, but that any other global names should not restrict him in the freedom of the choice of his own names with local significance only. The fact that this convention smoothly catered to the embedding of inner blocks within a "growing" environment (e.g. user programs implicitly embedded in an implementation-supplied outermost block containing the standard procedure library) has for a long time been regarded as a sufficient justification for the convention of priority of innermost declarations. The fact that at that time it had been recently discovered how a one-pass assembler could use a stack for coping with textually nested different meanings of the same name, may have had something to do with its adoption.

From the user's point of view, however, the convention is less attractive, for it makes the variables declared in his outermost block extremely vulnerable. If he discovers to his dismay that the value of one of these variables has been tampered with in an unintended and as yet unexplained way, he is in principle obliged to read all the code of all the inner blocks, including the ones that should not refer to the variable at all—for precisely there such a reference would be erroneous! Under the assumption that the programmer does not need to refer everywhere to anything he seems to be better served by more explicit means for restricting the textual scope of names than the more or less accidental re-declaration.

A first step in this direction, which maintains the notion of textually nested contexts is the following. For each block we postulate for its level (i.e. its text with the exception of its inner blocks) a textual context, i.e. a constant nomenclature in which all names have a unique meaning. The names occurring in a block's textual context are either "global", i.e. inherited with their meaning from the immediate surroundings, or "local", i.e. with its meaning only pertinent to the text of this block. The suggestion is to enumerate after the block's opening bracket (with the appropriate separators) the names that together form its textual context, for instance first the global names (if any) and then the local names (if any); obviously all these names must be different.

Confession.   The above suggestion was only written down after long hesitations, during which I considered alternatives that would enable the programmer to introduce in a block one or more local names without also being obliged to *enumerate* all the global names the block would inherit, i.e. alternatives that would indicate (with the same compactness) the change of nomenclature of the ALGOL *60* block (without "re-declaration of identifiers"), i.e. a pure extension of the nomenclature. This would give the programmer the possibility to indicate contraction of the nomenclature, i.e. limited inheritance from the immediate surroundings, but not the obligation. And for some time I thought that this would be a nice, nonpaternalistic attitude for a language designer; I also felt that this would make my scope rules more palatable, because I feared that many a programmer would object to explicit enumeration of the inheritance whenever he felt like introducing a local variable. This continued until I got very cross with myself: too many language designs have been spoiled by fear of nonacceptance and I know of only one programmer who is going to program in this language and that is myself! And I am enough of a puritan to oblige myself to indicate the inheritance explicitly. Even stronger: not only will my inner blocks refer only to global variables explicitly inherited, but also the inheritance will not mention any global variables not referred to. The inheritance will give a complete description of the block's possible interference with the state space valid in its surroundings, no more and no less! When I discovered that I had allowed my desire "to please my public" —which, I think, is an honourable one— to influence not only the way of presentation, but also the subject matter itself, I was frightened, cross with, and ashamed of myself. (*End of confession.*)

Besides having a name, variables have the unique property of being able to have a value that may be changed. This immediately raises the question "What will be the value of a local variable upon block entry?". Various answers have been chosen. ALGOL *60* postulates that upon block entry the values of its local variables are "undefined", i.e. any effort to evaluate their value prior to an assignment to them is regarded as "undefined". Failure to initialize local variables prior to entry of a loop turned out to be a very common error and a run-time check against the use of the undefined value of local variables, although expensive, proved in many circumstances not to be a luxury. Such a run-time check is, of course, the direct implementation of the pure mathematician's answer to the question of what to do with a variable whose value is undefined, i.e. extend its range with a special value, called "UNDEFINED", and initialize upon block entry each local variable with that unique, special value. Any effort to evaluate the value of a variable having that unique, special value "UNDEFINED" can then be honoured by program abortion and an error message.

Upon closer scrutiny, however, this simple proposal leads to logical problems; for instance, it is then impossible to copy the values of any set of variables. Efforts to remedy that situation include, for instance, the possibility to inspect whether a value is defined or not. But such ability to manipulate the special value —e.g. the value "NIL" for a pointer pointing nowhere— easily leads to confusions and contradictions: one might discover a case of bigamy when meeting two bachelors married to the same "nobody".

Another way out, abolishing the variables with undefined values, has been the implicit initialization upon block entry not with a very special, but with a very common, almost "neutral" value (say "zero" for all integers and "true" for all booleans). But this, of course, is only fooling oneself; now detection of a very common programming error has been made impossible by making all sorts of nonsensical programs artificially into legal ones. (This proposal has been mitigated by the convention that initialization with the "neutral" value would only occur "by default", i.e. unless indicated otherwise, but such a default convention is clearly a patch.)

A next attack to the problem of catching the use of variables with still undefined values has been the performance of (automatic) flow analysis of the program text that could at least warn the programmer that at certain places variables would—or possibly could—be used prior to the first assignment to them. In a sense my proposal can be regarded as being inspired by that approach. I propose such a rigid discipline that:

1. the flow analysis involved is trivial;
2. at no place where a variable is referenced can there exist uncertainty as to whether this variable has been initialized.

One way of achieving this would be to make the initialization of all local variables obligatory upon block entry; together with the wish not to initialize with "meaningless" values —a wish that implies that local variables should only be introduced at a stage that their meaningful initial value is available— this, I am afraid, will lead to confusingly high depths of nesting of textual scopes. Besides that we would have to "distribute" the block entry over the various guarded commands of an alternative construct whenever the initialization should be done by one of the guarded commands of a set. These two considerations made me look for an alternative that would require less (and more unique) block boundaries. The following proposal seems to meet our requirements.

First of all we insist that upon block entry the complete nomenclature (both inherited and private) is listed. Besides the assignment statement that destroys the current value of a variable by assigning a new one to it, we have initializing statements, by syntactical means recognizable as such, that give a private variable its first value since block entry. (If we so desire we can regard the execution of its initializing statement as coinciding in time with the variable's "creation"; the earlier mentioning of its name at block entry can then be regarded as "reserving its identifier for it".)

In other words, the textual scope of a variable private (i.e. local) to a block extends from the block's opening "**begin**" until its corresponding closing "**end**" with the exception of the texts of inner blocks that do not inherit it. We propose to divide its textual scope into what we might call "the passive scope", where reference to it is not allowed and the variable is not regarded as a coordinate of the local state space, and "the active scope", where the variable can be referenced. Passive and active scopes of a variable will always be separated by an initializing statement for that variable, and initializing statements for a variable have to be placed in such a way that, independent of values of guards:

1. after block entry exactly one initializing statement for it will be executed before the corresponding block exit;
2. between block entry and the execution of the initializing statement no statement from its active scope can be executed.

The following discipline guarantees that the above requirements are met. To start with we consider the block at the syntactic grain where the enumeration of its private nomenclature is followed by a list of statements mutually separated by semicolons. Such a statement list must have the following properties:

(A) It must contain a unique statement initializing a given private variable.
(B) Statements (if any) preceding the initializing statement are in the passive scope of the variable, and if they are inner blocks they are not allowed to inherit it.
(C) Statements (if any) following the initializing statement are in the active scope of the variable, and if they are inner blocks they may inherit it.
(D) For the initializing statement itself there are three possibilities:
   (*1*) It is a primitive initializing statement.
   (*2*) It is an inner block. In this case it inherits the variable in question and the statement list following the enumeration of the inner nomenclature has again the properties (A), (B), (C), and (D).
   (*3*) It is an alternative construct. In this case the statement lists following its guards **all** have the properties (A), (B), (C), and (D).

For the BNF-addicts the following syntax (where intialization refers to one private variable) may be helpful:

⟨block⟩::= **begin** ⟨nomenclature⟩; ⟨initializing statement list⟩ **end**

⟨initializing statement list⟩::= {⟨passive statement⟩;}

   ⟨initializing statement⟩ {; ⟨active statement⟩}

⟨initializing statement⟩::= ⟨primitive initializing statement⟩|

   begin ⟨nomenclature⟩; ⟨initializing statement list⟩ **end** |

   if ⟨guard⟩ → ⟨initializing statement list⟩

   {◻ ⟨guard⟩ → ⟨initializing statement list⟩} **fi**

Note. In using ALGOL *60* the sheer size of the brackets "**begin**" and "**end**" has caused discomfort; having abolished ALGOL *60*'s compound statement, we expect to need fewer of them. (*End of note.*)

The corresponding repetitive construct is not included as a permissible form of the ⟨initializing statement⟩ because its inclusion would violate our first requirement: regardless of the sequencing initialization must occur exactly once. Such a restriction does not occur in a programming language like ALGOL *60* in which simply the (dynamically) first assignment is taken as "the initialization". The price paid for the greater freedom in an ALGOL-like language is that with programs written in such a language we cannot necessarily decide statically (i.e. for all computations) at each semicolon which variables have defined values, as is shown in the following examples in ALGOL *60*.

If *B* is a global boolean

> **begin integer** *x*, *y*; **if** *B* **then** *x*:= *1* **else** *y*:= *2*; . . . . .

and if *N* is a global integer

> **begin integer** *i*, *x*; **for** *i*:= *1* **step** *1* **until** *N* **do** *x*:= *1*; . . . . .

In the first example the value of *x* is only defined provided that *B* is true; in the second example only provided $N \geq 1$. Obviously, neither of the two constructs can be translated into our language and we have to convince ourselves that we can live with the restrictions we have imposed upon ourselves, or, even stronger, that beginning blocks as in the two examples just given are not only avoidable but, in a sense, even pointless. The intuitive argument that inside a repetitive construct we never need to execute the dynamically first assignment to a variable whose value is of relevance upon termination is as follows: such a variable must occur in either the invariant relation or the guards or both and therefore it had better be defined in the initial state of the repetitive construct as well. (In the next chapter we shall see that this position shall force us to reconsider the notion of what constitutes "a variable".)

The fact that we shall restrict ourselves to a language such that at each semicolon it is statically known which variables constitute the current state space implies that we never need to doubt —if we would write our programs in an ALGOL-like language— whether an assignment to a private variable is the dynamically first one since block entry, and as a result it is no additional restriction to require that the syntactic form of a ⟨primitive initializing statement⟩ differs from that of the true assignment statement. Upon second thought it seems only honest to use different notations, for they are very different operations: while the initializing statement is in a sense a creative one (it creates a new variable with an initial value), the true assignment statement is a destructive one in the sense that it destroys information, viz. the variable's former value.

Note. The special role of the repetitive construct should not surprise us too much, because as long as we have a language without repetition, we would never need the true assignment; we could come away with initialization only: without repetition we could program in terms of constants that are initialized once. It is only with the introduction of the repetition that we need variables in the true sense of the word, i.e. that we need that at different repetition steps the same name can evoke different values. It is the notion of the repetition that calls for the notion of variables whose value can be changed by means of an assignment statement. It is in the repetition that we *need* true assignments to variables existing outside; it is also there that we can *not* allow initialization of such variables. (*End of note.*)

A few things have still to be decided. One is where and how to indicate the type of private variables. Two possible places present themselves: either —as in ALGOL *60*— at the beginning of the block to which the variable is private and its name occurs anyhow in the enumeration of the nomenclature or at its primitive initializing statement(s).

There are two reasons, however, why I feel that we should depart from the ALGOL *60* convention and should restrict the function of the enumeration of the nomenclature at the beginning of the block purely to the definition of the textual scope of names, at least for *not* burdening this enumeration with type information. We shall develop the argument for inherited names and private names separately.

If we prescribe that each inherited name in the nomenclature should carry its type explicitly with it, what price do we pay and what have we gained? The price is not only longer texts, but also the fact that a characteristic of the outer environment, viz. the type of a global variable, diffuses all through the text. At scattered places, viz. in all nomenclatures inheriting the name, we find a copy of that type information. This is most unattractive if we would like to change the type of such a global variable to another one on which the same set of functions and operations is defined. Furthermore we had decided that the function of the explicit inheritance would be a protection of the outside world, a condensation of how the inner block can interact with its environment that we are supposed to know. Repeating the types does not tell us in condensed form anything new or anything interesting about an inner block. The only gain seems to be that the block with the global type information can to a larger extent be understood in isolation. But I am not so sure that the relevant information about the environment can be restricted to just the type of the global variables: relations which may be assumed to hold between initial values could also be essential. If we want to understand what the inner block is good for, a fuller description of the interface is required and as long as we do not intend to mechanize correctness proofs, suitable comments seem a more adequate vehicle. (Any reader who now shouts "But what about independent compilation?" is asked to realize that that remark has significance only in a very specific style of implementation and is invited to imagine himself—as I do—in an environment in which that question is utterly meaningless.)

Now we turn to the private variables. If the type is stated in the enumeration, each activation of the block will initialize the variable with that type. We have seen, however, that if the initializing statement is an alternative construct, at each activation of the block, one out of a set of primitive initializing statements will be executed. As far as I am concerned they could initialize variables of different types, something no one can object to as long as the same functions and operations are defined on them. Whether such a freedom of choice for the type of a private variable is a useful thing or not is something that seems hard to discuss at this stage; at any rate it seems unwise to choose now a notational convention that does not leave the option open. (As the attentive reader will have noticed, the option that the type of a private variable may differ between different activations of the block to which it is private gives another reason for not copying type information when describing the inheritance, viz. for its inner blocks.)

The next thing we have to decide is whether at block entry we give any indication as to the *nature* of the interference with the inherited variables. I recall that one of the reasons for enumerating at the block's beginning the variables of the surrounding context it refers to, was to restrict the amount of text that should be studied when one of these variables has been interfered with in an ill-understood manner. If such a variable acts for each activation of an inner block as "a global constant", we should like to see, right at the block's begin, that it cannot tamper with its value; more precisely, that it can inspect, but not change its value.

Let us restrict for a moment our attention to an inner block (with the context "IN"), fully within the active scope of a variable that it inherits from the immediately surrounding block (with the context "OUT").

If at the level of the context OUT, the variable is changeable, we have seen the need for two possible ways of inheritance: either it is changeable in context IN as well —i.e. the inner block may contain assignment statements, assigning new values to the variable— or the inner block inherits it as a global constant. This last fact, however, has its consequences for both contexts. For context OUT it means that when we are interested in "what can influence the value of the variable" we can skip the text of the inner block. If, however, we want to read the text of the inner block —more or less in isolation of its surroundings— and want to understand its achievement, then the fact that such a global constant is a constant and not a variable is of crucial importance. Already in the first example of the chapter "The Formal Treatment of Some Small Examples" we started with "Establish for fixed x and y the relation $R(m)$

$$(m = x \text{ or } m = y) \text{ and } m \geq x \text{ and } m \geq y"$$

The fact that x and y are to be considered fixed is an essential aspect of its task.

If, at the level of the context OUT the variable is already a constant, the inner block can only inherit it in one way: again as a constant. The inner block fully in the active scope of an inherited variable has been dealt with satisfactorily.

An inner block fully in the passive scope of a variable does not present any difficulties either: it may not inherit the variable from its surroundings.

The third case, where a block begins in the passive scope of a variable and ends in its active one deserves still some further attention: it means no more and no less than the block's obligation to initialize the variable. It has inherited what we could call "a virgin variable" for the purpose of its initialization. Both in context IN and in context OUT we can ask the question whether the variable is changeable in its active scope. In the case of the inheritance of a virgin variable, these two questions are, however, fully independent; the circumstance that at the textual level of context OUT a variable will not have its value changed after initialization does not exclude that the initialization itself (in an inner block) is a multistep affair, viz. a multistep affair when we consider the initialization not as a single, undivided act, but —at a smaller grain of interest— as a sequential process, building up the initial value.

After these explorations the time has come to be as precise as possible. We recall that we introduced the name "the textual context" of a block for the constant nomenclature (in which all names have a unique meaning) pertaining to the block's "level", i.e. its text with the exception of its inner blocks. We now consider two nested blocks, an inner one (with the context called "IN") and an outer one (with the context called "OUT"); with respect to IN we have referred to OUT as "the surrounding context".

Names of a context are of two kinds: either they are private to the block, i.e. unrelated to anything outside the block, or they are "inherited" from the surrounding context. In the case of inheritance, we must distinguish two cases: the context IN may inherit a name of a variable from the context OUT with or without the obligation for the inner block to initialize, when activated, the variable inherited. We shall distinguish these three ways by

pri ("private", i.e. unrelated to the surrounding context)
vir ("virgin", i.e. inherited from the surrounding context with the obligation to initialize)
glo ("global", i.e. inherited from the surrounding context without the obligation nor the permission to initialize).

A variable can belong to more than one textual context: to start with it belongs to the textual context of the block to which it is private and furthermore it belongs to the textual contexts of all inner blocks that inherit it from their surrounding contexts. The scope of a variable extends over the levels of all blocks to whose textual contexts the variable belongs. The scope of a variable is always subdivided into two parts, its passive scope and its active scope, and the way in which initializing statements for a variable may occur in the text has been restricted so as to guarantee with respect to each variable in time the succession:

entry to the block to which it is private;

zero or more executions of statements from its passive scope;

one initialization for it;

zero or more executions of statements from its active scope;

corresponding block exit.

Whether a variable is enumerated under the heading "**pri**" or "**vir**" makes no difference as regards the block's rights and obligations with respect to that variable; in both cases it has the obligation to initialize it. The only difference is that while the variable under the heading "**pri**" has no relation to the context OUT, the variable under the heading "**vir**" must occur in the context OUT and the inner block must start in the variable's passive scope and end in its active scope. A variable under the heading "**glo**" must occur in the context OUT and the inner block must lie entirely within its active scope.

Besides the block's external aspects as described by "**pri**", "**vir**", or "**glo**", there are internal aspects, viz. whether at the block's level in the active scope of the variable its value may be changed or not. If the variable's value may be changed, this is indicated with "**var**" (from "variable"); if it may not be changed it is indicated by "**con**" (from "constant"). Each of the three external aspects can be combined with each of the two internal aspects, giving the six possibilities "**privar**", "**pricon**", "**virvar**", "**vircon**", "**glovar**", and "**glocon**". For the six headings in the context IN we give the permissible headings in the context OUT:

IN	OUT
privar, pricon	not applicable
glovar	**privar, virvar** (only if inner block fully within active scope) or **glovar** (without restriction)
glocon	**privar, pricon, virvar, vircon** (only if inner block fully within active scope) or **glovar, glocon** (without restriction)
virvar, vircon	**privar, pricon, virvar, vircon** (only if inner block begins in passive scope)

Note 1.   As a consequence of the above, the aspect "**con**" in the context OUT excludes that after initialization inner blocks can change the value of the variable. (*End of note 1.*)

Note 2.   The aspect "**con**" in context OUT does not exclude the initialization by an inner block, at the level of which the variable may enjoy the aspect "**var**": in context OUT we may have a "**pricon** table", the initialization of which is delegated to an inner block, in whose context the "**virvar** table" will be created and built up. Once the execution of such an initializing inner block has been completed, the value of "table" will remain constant throughout the execution of the outer block (and its further inner blocks, if any). (*End of note 2.*)

The remaining decisions, although far from unimportant (they determine what our texts look like, how easily they write and read), have less far-reaching consequences; they are purely concerned with syntax. We have to decide upon notations for the ⟨nomenclature⟩ and for the ⟨primitive initializing statement⟩. I propose for the nomenclature a notation very similar to ALGOL *60*'s ⟨block head⟩, a syntax with which I have always been perfectly happy.

⟨nomenclature⟩::= ⟨nomenclature element⟩ {; ⟨nomenclature element⟩}
⟨nomenclature element⟩::= ⟨nomenclature header⟩ ⟨variable⟩
        {, ⟨variable⟩}
⟨nomenclature header⟩::= **privar** | **pricon** | **virvar** | **vircon** |
        glovar | **glocon**

Admittedly with a view to later extensions I propose to derive the initializing statements from the assignment statements by post-fixing the variable at the left-hand side by the special character "**vir**" —indicating that we deal with a virgin variable— followed by the name of its type:

⟨primitive initializing statement⟩::= ⟨variable⟩ **vir** ⟨type⟩
        := ⟨expression⟩

where, as far as types are concerned we have confined ourselves up till now to integers and booleans:

⟨type⟩::= *int* | *bool*

Note 1.   The extension to concurrent initialization and concurrent assignment and initialization is left to the ambitious reader. (*End of note 1.*)

Note 2.   The expression(s) at the right-hand side are to be regarded as still in the passive scope of the variables being initialized. (*End of note 2.*)

As an example we give the inner block that initializes the global integer variable x with the GCD(X, Y), where with regard to the inner block, X and Y are positive constants. The block uses a private variable called y.

> **begin glocon** X, Y; **virvar** x; **privar** y;
> x **vir** *int*, y **vir** *int*:= X, Y;
>   **do** $x > y \rightarrow x:= x - y$
>   ▯ $y > x \rightarrow y:= y - x$
>   **od**
> **end**

I would like to point out that my decision to indicate "**var**" or "**con**" in the nomenclature is not without arbitrariness. On the one hand someone could argue that the indication is superfluous. If he decides to abolish the convention, he is free to do so; he just reduces the headings to "**pri**" "**vir**" and "**glo**" by omitting all the **var**'s and **con**'s from my programs. If my programs were correct according to my conventions, his versions will be equally correct according to his conventions. On the other hand someone could have the wish to give more precise information than I provide the means for. He could wish to indicate, for instance,

1. that the value of a variable can only increase;
2. that the initial value of a global variable will only influence its own final value but no others;
3. that of all the ways in which the value of a global variable can be modified, only a subset will be used.

An indication like (*1*) seems too specific, for it is only applicable to types whose values have a natural ordering. An indication like (*2*) seems also too specific. What about a pair of global variables whose initial values only influence their own and each other's final value? An indication like (*3*), however, could be meaningful. Our indication "**con**" then emerges as "the subset of allowed modifiers is empty".

11 ARRAY VARIABLES

I have been trained to regard an array in the ALGOL *60* sense as a finite set of elementary, consecutively numbered variables, whose "indentifiers" could be "computed". But for two reasons this view does not satisfy me anymore.

The first reason is my abhorrence of variables with undefined values. In the previous chapter we solved this problem by introducing for each variable a passive scope and an active scope, separated by a syntactically recognizable initialization for that variable. But when we regard the array as a collection of (subscripted) variables, that solution breaks down.

The second reason is of a combinatorial nature and more fundamental. In ALGOL *60* the compound statement that causes the variables x and y to interchange their values needs an additional variable, h say,

$$h := x; \ x := y; \ y := h$$

which is cumbersome and ugly compared with the concurrent assignment

$$x, y := y, x$$

For the concurrent assignment we have insisted that all variables at the left-hand side should be different: it would be foolish to attach to "$x, x := 1, 2$" any other meaning than "error". For a long time, however, I hesitated to adopt the concurrent assignment on account of the problems it causes in cases like

$$A[i], A[j] := x, y$$

Should this be allowed when $i \neq j$, but not when $i = j$? Or is, perhaps, $i = j$ permissible if $x = y$ holds as well, as for instance in

$$A[i], A[j] := A[j], A[i] \qquad ?$$

94

If we go that route we are clearly piling one logical patch upon another. However, I have now come to the conclusion that it is not the concurrent assignment, but the notion of the subscripted variable that is to be blamed. In the axiomatic definition of the assignment statement via "substitution of a variable" one cannot afford —as in, I guess, all parts of logic— any uncertainty as to whether two variables are the same or not.

The moral of the story is that we must regard the array in its entirety as a single variable, a so-called "array variable", in contrast to the "scalar variables" discussed so far. In the following I shall restrict myself to array variables that are the analogue of one-dimensional arrays.

We can regard (the value of) a variable of type "integer" as an integer-valued function without arguments (i.e. defined on a domain consisting of a single, anonymous point), a function that does not change unless explicitly changed (usually by an assignment). It is perhaps unusual to consider functions without arguments, but we mention the viewpoint for the sake of the analogy. For, similarly, we can regard (the value of) a variable of type "integer array" as an integer-valued function of one argument with a domain in the integers, a function, again, that does not change unless explicitly changed.

But the value of a variable of type "integer array" cannot be *any* integer-valued function defined on a domain in the integers, for I shall restrict myself to such types that, given two variables of that type, we can write an algorithm establishing whether or not the two variables have the same value. If x and y are scalar variables of type "integer", then this algorithm boils down to the boolean expression $x = y$, i.e. both functions are evaluated at the only (anonymous) point of their domain and these integer values are then compared. Similarly, if ax and ay are two variables of type "integer array", their values are equal if and only if, as functions, they have the same domain and in each point of the domain their values are equal to each other. In order that all these comparisons are possible, we *must* restrict ourselves to finite domains. And what is more, besides being finite, the domains must be available in one way or another to the algorithm that is to compare the values of the array variables ax and ay.

For practical purposes I shall restrict myself to domains consisting of consecutive integers (when not empty). But even then there are at least two possibilities. In ALGOL 60 the domain is fixed by giving in the declaration —e.g. "**boolean array** $A[1:10]$, $B[1:5]$"— the lower and upper bounds for the subscript value. As a type determines the class of possible values for a variable of that type, we must come to the conclusion that the two arrays A and B in the above example are of different type: A may have *1024* different values, B only *32*. In ALGOL 60 we have as many different types "boolean array" as we can have bound pairs (and, as the bound pair may contain expressions, the type is in principle only determined upon block entry). Besides that, the necessary knowledge about the domain must be provided by other means: without further information it is impossible to write in ALGOL *60* an inner block determining whether two global boolean arrays *A* and *B* are equal!

The alternative is to introduce only one type "integer array" and only one type "boolean array" and to regard "the domain" as part (aspect) of any value of such type; we must then be able to extract that aspect from any such value. Let *ax* be an array variable; in its active scope I propose to extract the bounds of the domain from its value by means of two integer-valued functions, denoted by "*ax.lob*" and *ax.hib*" respectively, with the understanding that the domain of the function "*ax(i)*" extends over all integers *i* satisfying

$$ax.lob \leq i \leq ax.hib$$

Besides those two I propose a third (dependent) one, "*ax.dom*", equal to the number of points in the domain. The three functions satisfy

$$ax.dom = ax.hib - ax.lob + 1 \geq 0$$

(Note that even the empty domain, *dom = 0*, has a place along the number line; *lob* and *hib* remain defined and they then satisfy *hib = lob − 1*.)

We have used here a new notation, the dot as in "*ax.lob*", "*ax.hib*" and "*ax.dom*". The names following the dot are what is called "subordinate to the type of the variable whose name precedes the dot". Following the dot that follows a variable, only names subordinate to the type of that variable may occur and their meaning will be as defined with respect to that type.

Remark 1.   In other contexts, i.e. not following the dot, the same names may be used with completely different meaning. We could introduce an array variable named "*dom*" and in its active scope we could refer to "*dom.lob*", "*dom.hib*" and even "*dom.dom*"! Such perversities are not recommended and therefore I have tried to find subordinate names that, although of some mnemonic value, are unlikely candidates for introduction by the programmer himself.   (*End of remark 1.*)

Remark 2.   A further reason for using the dot notation rather than the function notation —e.g. "*dom(ax)*", etc.— is that, unless we introduce different sets of names for these functions defined on boolean arrays and integer arrays respectively (which would be awkward) we are forced to introduce functions of an argument that may be of more than one type, something I would like to avoid as long as possible.   (*End of remark 2.*)

Remark 3.   The expression "*ax(i)*" is used to denote the function value in point *i*. Only when the value of "*ax(i)*" is required does the argument *i* need to be defined and to satisfy

$$ax.lob \leq i \leq ax.hib$$

In view of the dot notation we could regard "$ax(i)$" as an abbreviation for "$ax.val(i)$", where "val" is the subordinate name indicating evaluation in the point as indicated by the value of the further argument i. For each type, such an abbreviation can be introduced just once! Note that also the type "integer" could have a subordinate name "val" that would enable us to write a little bit more explicitly

$$x := y.val$$

instead of the usual and somewhat sloppy $x := y$.   (*End of remark 3.*)

For the sake of convenience we introduce two further functions; for the array variable ax they are defined if $ax.dom > 0$. They are

$$ax.low, \text{ defined to be equal to } ax(ax.lob)$$

and

$$ax.high, \text{ defined to be equal to } ax(ax.hib)$$

They denote the function values at the lowest and the highest point of the domain respectively. They are nothing really new and are defined in terms of concepts already known; in the definition of the semantics of operations on array values we do not need to mention the effect on them explicitly.

As stated above, a scalar variable can be regarded as a function (without argument) that can be changed by assigning a new value to it: such an assignment destroys the information stored as "its old value" completely. We also need operations to change the value of an array variable (without them it would always be an array constant!) but the assignment of a new value to it that is totally unrelated to its old value will play a less central role. It is not that the assignment to an array variable presents any logical difficulties — on the contrary, I am tempted to add— but there is something wrong with its economics. With a large domain size the amount of information stored as "the value of an array variable" can be very large, and neither copying nor destroying such large amounts of information are considered as "nice" operations. On the contrary: in many programming tasks the core of the problem consists of building up an array value gradually, i.e. in a number of steps, each of which can be considered as a "nice" operation, "nice" in the sense that the new value of the array can be regarded as a "pleasant" derivation of its old value. What makes such operations "nice" or "pleasant" depends essentially on two aspects: firstly, the relation between the old and the new value should be mathematically manageable, otherwise the operations are too cumbersome for us to use; secondly, its implementation should not be too expensive for the kind of hardware that we intend to instruct with our program. The extent to which we are willing to take the latter hardware constraints into account is not a scientific question, but a political one, and as a consequence I don't feel obliged to give an elaborate justification of my choices. For the sake of convenience I shall be somewhat more liberal than many programmers would be, particularly those that are working daily with machinery, the conceptual design of which is ten or more years old; on the other hand I hope to be sufficiently aware of the possible technical consequences of my choices that they remain, if not realistic, at least not totally unrealistic.

Our first modification of the value of an array variable, *ax* say, does not change the domain size, nor the set of function values, nor their order; it only shifts the domain over a number of places, *k* say, upwards along the number line. (If $k < 0$ it is a shift over $-k$ places in the other direction; if $k = 0$ it is the identity transformation, semantically equivalent to "*skip*".) We denote it by

$$ax:shift(k)$$

Here we have introduced the colon ":". Its lowest dot indicates in the usual manner that the following name is subordinate to the type of the variable mentioned to its left; the upper dot is just an embellishment (inspired by the assignment operator ":="), indicating that the value of the variable mentioned to its left is subject to redefinition.

Immediately we are confronted with the question whether we can give an axiomatic definition of the predicate transformer wp("*ax:shift(E)*", *R*). Well, it must be a predicate transformer similar to the one of the axiom of assignment to a scalar variable, but more complicated —and this will be true as well for all the other modifiers of array values— because the value of a scalar value is fully defined by one (elementary) value, while the value of an array variable involves the domain itself and a function value for all points of the domain. Because the value of the array variable *ax* is fully determined by

the value of *ax.lob*,
the value of *ax.dom* and
the value of *ax(i)* for $ax.lob \leq i < ax.lob + ax.dom$

we can, in principle at least, restrict ourselves to post-conditions *R* referring to the array value only in terms of "*ax.lob*", "*ax.dom*" and "*ax(arg)*" where "*arg*" may be any integer-valued expression. For such a post-condition *R* the corresponding weakest pre-condition

$$wp("ax:shift(E)", R)$$

is derived from *R* by simultaneously replacing

1. all occurrences of *ax.lob* by (*ax.lob* + (*E*)) and
2. all occurrences of (sub)expressions of the form *ax(arg)* by *ax*((*arg*) − (*E*))
   Note. If *E* itself depends on the value of *ax*, the safest way is to evaluate first for the given *R* with a completely new name, *K* say, wp("*ax:shift(K)*", *R*), in which then the actual expression *E* is substituted for *K*. We have

already encountered the same complication when applying the axiom of assignment to statements such as $x := x + f(x)$.   (*End of note.*)

We give a few examples. Let R be $ax.lob = 10$, then

$$\text{wp}(\text{“}ax\text{:}shift(ax.lob)\text{”}, R) = (ax.lob + ax.lob = 10)$$
$$= (ax.lob = 5)$$

Let R be (**A** i: $0 \leq i < ax.dom$: $ax(ax.lob + i) = i$); then

$$\text{wp}(\text{“}ax\text{:}shift(7)\text{”}, R) = (\mathbf{A}\ i\text{:}\ 0 \leq i < ax.dom\text{:}\ ax(ax.lob + 7 + i - 7) = i)$$
$$= R$$

An alternative way of formulating the weakest pre-condition is

$$\text{wp}(\text{“}ax\text{:}shift(E)\text{”}, R) = R_{ax' \to ax}$$

(i.e. a copy of R, in which every occurrence of ax is replaced by ax'), where

$ax'.lob = ax.lob + E$

$ax'.dom = ax.dom$

$ax'(arg) = ax(arg - E)$ for any value of arg.

From these three definitions it follows that

$$ax'.hib = ax.hib + E$$
$$ax'.low = ax.low$$
$$ax'.high = ax.high$$

Note.   Such equalities are meant to imply that if the right-hand side is undefined, the left-hand side is undefined as well.   (*End of note.*)

For the definition of our further operators we shall follow the latter technique: it describes more clearly how the final value ax' depends on the initial value ax.

The next operators extend the domain at either the high or the low end with one point. The function value in the new point is given as parameter which must be of the so-called "base type" of the array, i.e. boolean for a boolean array, etc. The operators are of the form

$$ax\text{:}hiext(x) \quad \text{or} \quad ax\text{:}loext(x)$$

The semantic definition of *hiext* is given by

$$\text{wp}(\text{“}ax\text{:}hiext(x)\text{”}, R) = R_{ax' \to ax}$$

where

$ax'.lob = ax.lob$

$ax'.hib = ax.hib + 1$

$ax'.dom = ax.dom + 1$

$$ax'(arg) = x \qquad \text{for } arg = ax.hib + 1$$
$$\quad = ax(arg) \qquad \text{for } arg \neq ax.hib + 1$$

The semantic definition of *loext* is given by

$$\text{wp}(\text{``}ax:loext(x)\text{''}, R) = R_{ax' \to ax}$$

where

$$ax'.lob = ax.lob - 1$$
$$ax'.hib = ax.hib$$
$$ax'.dom = ax.dom + 1$$
$$ax'(arg) = x \qquad \text{for } arg = ax.lob - 1$$
$$\quad = ax(arg) \qquad \text{for } arg \neq ax.lob \overset{*}{-} 1$$

Note. Our earlier remark that also the empty domain would have its place along the number line was to ensure that the extension operators *hiext* and *loext* are also defined when applied to an array variable with $dom = 0$. (*End of note.*)

The next two operators remove a point from the domain at either the high or the low end. They are only defined when initially $dom > 0$ holds for the array to which they are applied; when applied to an array with $dom = 0$, they lead to abortion. They destroy information in the sense that one of the function values gets lost.

The semantic definition of *hirem* is given by

$$\text{wp}(\text{``}ax:hirem\text{''}, R) = (ax.dom > 0 \text{ and } R_{ax' \to ax})$$

where

$$ax'.lob = ax.lob$$
$$ax'.hib = ax.hib - 1$$
$$ax'.dom = ax.dom - 1$$
$$ax'(arg) = \text{undefined} \qquad \text{for } arg = ax.hib$$
$$\quad = ax(arg) \qquad \text{for } arg \neq ax.hib$$

The semantic definition of *lorem* is given by

$$\text{wp}(\text{``}ax:lorem\text{''}, R) = (ax.dom > 0 \text{ and } R_{ax' \to ax})$$

where

$$ax'.lob = ax.lob + 1$$
$$ax'.hib = ax.hib$$
$$ax'.dom = ax.dom - 1$$
$$ax'(arg) = \text{undefined} \qquad \text{for } arg = ax.lob$$
$$\quad = ax(arg) \qquad \text{for } arg \neq ax.lob$$

For the sake of convenience we introduce two further operations, the semantics of which can be expressed in terms of the functions and operations already introduced; they are

x, ax:$hipop$, semantically equivalent to "x:= $ax.high$; ax:$hirem$"

and

x, ax:$lopop$, semantically equivalent to "x:= $ax.low$; ax:$lorem$"

They are given in a notation which is reminiscent of the one for the concurrent assignment; the name following the ":" must be subordinate to the type of the variable immediately before the ":". Obviously, the other variable x must be of the base type of the array variable ax.

The above modifiers all change the domain of the function, either only its place along the number line or also its size. Two further modifiers will be introduced, modifiers that leave the domain as it stands but only affect one or two function values.

A very important modifier does not introduce new function values, but only rearranges them. It is of the form

$$ax\!:\!swap(i, j)$$

It leads to abortion when invoked without both i and j lying in the domain. Its semantics are given by

$$\mathrm{wp}("ax\!:\!swap(i, j)", R) = (ax.lob \leq i \leq ax.hib \textbf{ and}$$
$$ax.lob \leq j \leq ax.hib \textbf{ and}$$
$$R_{ax' \to ax})$$

where

$$ax'.lob = ax.lob$$
$$ax'.hib = ax.hib$$
$$ax'.dom = ax.dom$$
$$ax'(arg) = ax(j) \qquad \text{for } arg = i$$
$$= ax(i) \qquad \text{for } arg = j$$
$$= ax(arg) \qquad \text{for } arg \neq i \textbf{ and } arg \neq j$$

Note. Initially $i \neq j$ is not required: if initially $i = j$ holds, the value of the array variable remains unaffected. (*End of note.*)

Our last modifier redefines a single function value; it is of the form

$$ax\!:\!alt(i, x)$$

It leads to abortion when invoked without i lying in the domain; the second parameter x must be of the array variable's base type. Its semantics are given by

$$\text{wp}(\text{``}ax:alt(i, x)\text{''}, R) = (ax.lob \leq i \leq ax.hib \textbf{ and}$$
$$R_{ax' \to ax})$$

where

$ax'.lob = ax.lob$

$ax'.hib = ax.hib$

$ax'.dom = ax.dom$

$ax'(arg) = x$ for $arg = i$

      $= ax(arg)$ for $arg \neq i$

The operation denoted above as "$ax:alt(i, x)$" is semantically equivalent to what FORTRAN or ALGOL 60 programmers know as "the assignment to a subscripted variable". (They would write "$AX(I) = X$" and "$ax[i] := x$" respectively.) I have introduced this operation in the form "$ax:alt(i, x)$" in order to stress that such an operation affects the array ax as a whole: two functions with the same domain are different functions if they differ in at least one point of the domain. The "official" —or, if you prefer, "puritan"— notation "$ax:alt(i, x)$" is, however, even to my taste too cumbersome and too unfamiliar and I therefore propose (I too have my weaker moments!) to use instead

$$ax:(i) = x$$

a notation which is somewhat shorter, reminiscent of the so much more familiar assignment statement, and still reflects by its opening "$ax:$" that we must view it as affecting the array variable ax. (The decision to write "$ax:(i) = x$" is not much different from the decision to write "$ax(i)$" instead of the more pompous "$ax.val(i)$".)

None of the previous operators can be used for initialization. They can only change the value of an array under the assumption that it has already a value; they can only occur in the active scope of the array variable. We have not yet introduced the assignment

$$ax := bx$$

a construct that would do the job. I am, however, very hesitant to do so, because in its full generality "assignment of a value" usually implies "copying a value" and if the domain of the function bx is large, this is not to be regarded as a "nice" operation in present technology. Not that I am absolutely unwilling to introduce "unpleasant" operations, but if I do so, I would not like them to appear on paper as innocent ones. A programming language in which "$x := y$" should be regarded as "nice" but "$ax := bx$" should have to be regarded as "unpleasant" would be misleading; it would at least mislead me. A way out of this dilemma is to admit as the right-hand side of the assignment to an array variable only enumerated constants, e.g. of the form

$$(\langle integer \rangle \{, \langle value\ of\ the\ base\ type \rangle \})$$

such that

$$bx := (5,\ true,\ true,\ false,\ true)$$

would establish

$bx.lob = 5$	$bx(5) = true$
$bx.hib = 8$	$bx(6) = true$
$bx.dom = 4$	$bx(7) = false$
	$bx(8) = true$

The consequence of such a restriction is that assignment of or initialization with a value with a large domain size cannot be written down unnoticed. My expectation is that most initializations will be with values with $dom = 0$.

A few concluding remarks are in order.

There is, to start with, the question of economics. My basic assumption is that all operations mentioned in this chapter can be performed at roughly the same price. Some assumption of this nature has to be made, for without it the programming task does not make sense. For instance, instead of writing

$$ax:(5) = 7$$

we could have written the inner block

```
begin glovar ax; privar bx;
  if ax.lob ≤ 5 and 5 ≤ ax.hib →
  bx vir int array := (0);
  do ax.hib ≠ 5 → bx:hiext(ax.high); ax:hirem od;
  ax:hirem; ax:hiext(7);
  do bx.dom ≠ 0 → ax:hiext(bx.high); bx:hirem od
  fi
end
```

but I would like to reject that inner block as a worthy substitute, not so much on account of the length of the text, but on account of its inefficiency. I will not even regard "$ax:(5) = 7$" as an abbreviation of the above inner block.

With the possible exception of the assignment of an enumerated value, I assume in particular the price of all operations independent of the values of the arguments supplied to it: the price of executing $ax:shift(k)$ will be independent of the value of k, the price of executing $ax:swap(i, j)$ will be independent of the values of i and j, etc. With present-day technology these assumptions are not unrealistic.

It is in such considerations that the justification is to be found for my willingness to introduce otherwise superfluous names; we could have restrict-

ed ourselves to *ax.lob* and *ax.dom*, for whenever we would need *ax.hib*, we
could write

$$ax.lob + ax.dom - 1$$

instead, but that would make the effective use of *ax.hib* "twice as expensive"
as the effective use of *ax.lob* and our consciousness of this fact could easily
twist our thinking (worse, it is guaranteed to do so).

I said that the prices are of the same order of magnitude. What I also
mean is "of the same order of magnitude as other things that we consider
as primitive". If the array operations were orders of magnitude more expensive than other operations, we would, for instance, find ourselves invited to
replace

$$ax:swap(i, j)$$

by

$$\textbf{if } i \neq j \longrightarrow ax:swap(i, j) \,\rlap{[}\,]\, i = j \longrightarrow skip \textbf{ fi}$$

and very quickly we should need to know both the exact price ratios and a
very good estimate for the probability of hitting the case "$i = j$" in order to
be able to decide whether our replacement of $ax: swap(i, j)$ by the alternative
construct is actually an improvement or not. I know of mathematicians who
revel in such optimization problems, sometimes thinking that they constitute
the central problems of computer programming. I leave these problems
gladly to them if they are happy with them; the operations that we prefer
to consider as primitive should not confront us with such conflicts. I like to
believe that we have more important problems to worry about.

A final remark about implementation. It is conceivable that upon initialization of the array variable *ax* some limits are given: a lower limit for *ax.lob*,
or an upper limit for *ax.hib*, or both, or perhaps only an upper limit for
ax.dom. If such "hints to the compiler" are included, a wealth of traditional
storage management techniques becomes exploitable. I prefer, however, to
regard such "hints to the compiler" not as part of the program. They only
make (on some equipment!) a cheaper implementation possible; they represent for the implementation the permission (but not the obligation!) to abort
a program execution in which such a stated limit is exceeded.

12 THE LINEAR SEARCH THEOREM

Let B be a boolean function defined on the integers and consider the following beginning of a block:

> **begin privar** i;
> i **vir** $int := 0$;
> **do** $B(i) \rightarrow i := i + 1$ **od**;
> $\ldots$

For this repetitive construct we can formulate the invariant relation

$P(i)$: $\qquad\qquad (\mathbf{A}\, j: 0 \leq j < i: B(j))$

Proof. As $P(0)$ is true, $P(i)$ is established upon initialization. Furthermore

$$(P(i) \text{ and } B(i)) = P(i + 1)$$
$$= wp(\text{``}i := i + 1\text{''}, P(i)) \qquad\qquad \text{Q.E.D.}$$

Without further knowledge about the boolean function B we cannot prove that the repetitive construct will terminate. If, however,

$$(\mathbf{E}\, j: j \geq 0: \text{non } B(j))$$

the assumption of nontermination leads to the usual contradiction: the existence of at least one value $j \geq 0$ such that

$$\text{non } B(j)$$

holds is sufficient to guarantee termination. Upon termination, however, we know

$$P(i) \text{ and non } B(i) =$$
$$(\mathbf{A}\, j: 0 \leq j < i: B(j)) \text{ and non } B(i)$$

i.e. i is the *minimum* value ≥ 0, such that **non** $B(i)$ holds. In other words, when we look for the *minimum* value (at least equal to some lower bound) that satisfies some criterion, our program investigates values (starting at that lower bound) in *increasing* order. Searching in increasing order translates the *first* satisfactory value encountered into the *smallest* satisfactory value existing. Similarly, when looking for a maximum value, we shall search in decreasing order.

Very often, the two statements have the form

$$x := xnought;$$

$$\textbf{do } B(x) \longrightarrow x := F(x) \textbf{ od}$$

This program searches in the sequence of values given by

$$x_0 = xnought$$

for $i > 0$: $x_i = F(x_{i-1})$

the value x_i with the minimum value of i (≥ 0), such that **non** $B(x_i)$ holds. (More formal proofs of the above are left as an exercise to the industrious reader, if so inclined.)

The insights described in this chapter are referred to as the "Linear Search Theorem". In the next chapter we shall use it as part of our reasoning for actually finding a solution; simple as it is, the Linear Search Theorem has often proved to be of significant heuristic value.

13 THE PROBLEM OF THE NEXT PERMUTATION

We are requested to write an inner block operating on a global integer array variable, named c, with

$$c.lob = 1 \quad \text{and} \quad c.hib = n$$

for some constant value of n (> 1). Furthermore it is given that the ordered sequence of values $c(1)$, $c(2)$, ..., $c(n)$ is some permutation of the values from 1 through n, but **not** the alphabetically last one: n, $n - 1$, ..., 1. The inner block has to transform the sequence $c(1)$, $c(2)$, ..., $c(n)$ into its immediate alphabetic successor. (For the notion of "alphabetic order", see the last example of the chapter "The Formal Treatment of Some Small Examples".) For instance, with $n = 9$, the sequence

$$1\ 4\ 6\ 2\ 9\ 5\ 8\ 7\ 3$$

should be transformed into

$$1\ 4\ 6\ 2\ 9\ 7\ 3\ 5\ 8$$

As the above example shows, we may have at the low end a number of function values that remain unaffected. The transformation to be performed is restricted to permuting the values at the high end and our first duty seems to be to find that split, i.e. to determine the value of i, such that

$$c(k) \text{ remains unaffected for } 1 \leq k < i$$

$$c(k) \text{ is changed for } k = i$$

That value of i is characterized as the maximum value of i ($< n$) such that

$$c(i) < c(i + 1)$$

(It could not be larger, for then we would be restricted to permuting an initially monotonically decreasing sequence, an operation that cannot give rise to a sequence that is higher in the alphabetic order; it should not be smaller either, because then we would never generate the immediate alphabetic successor.)

   Note. The fact that the initial sequence is not the alphabetically last one guarantees the existence of an i $(0 < i < n)$ such that $c(i) < c(i + 1)$. (*End of note.*)

   Having found i, we must find from "the tail", i.e. among the values $c(j)$ with $i + 1 \leq j \leq n$, the new value $c(i)$. Because we are looking for the immediate successor, we must find that value of j in the range $i + 1 \leq j \leq n$, such that $c(j)$ is the smallest value satisfying

$$c(j) > c(i)$$

   Having found j, we can see to it that $c(i)$ gets adjusted to its final value by "$c{:}swap(i,j)$". This operation has the additional advantage that the total sequence remains a permutation of the numbers from 1 through n; the final operation is to rearrange the values in the tail in monotonically increasing order. The overall structure of the program we are considering is now

> determine i;
>
> determine j;
>
> $c{:}swap(i,j)$;
>
> sort the tail

(In our example $i = 6$, $j = 8$ and the final result would be reached via the intermediate sequence *1 4 6 2 9 7 8 5 3*.)

   When determining i, we look for a maximum value of i; the Linear Search Theorem tells us that we should investigate the potential values for i in decreasing order.

   When determining j, we look for a minimum value $c(j)$; the Linear Search Theorem tells us that we must investigate $c(j)$ values in increasing order. Because the tail is a monotonically decreasing function (on account of the way in which i was determined), this obligation boils down to inspecting $c(j)$ values in decreasing order of j.

   The operation "$c{:}swap(i,j)$" does not destroy the monotonicity of the function values in the tail (prove this!) and "sort the tail" reduces to inverting the order. (In doing so, our program "borrows" the variables i and j that have done their job. Note that the way in which the tail is reflected works equally well with an even number as with an odd number of values in the tail.)

```
begin glovar c; privar i, j;
    i vir int:= c.hib − 1; do c(i) ≥ c(i + 1) → i:= i − 1 od;
    j vir int:= c.hib; do c(j) ≤ c(i) → j:= j − 1 od;
    c:swap(i, j);
    i:= i + 1; j:= c.hib;
    do i < j → c:swap(i, j); i, j := i + 1, j − 1 od
end
```

Remark 1.   Nowhere have we used the fact that the values $c(1)$, $c(2)$, ... , $c(n)$ were all different from each other. As a result one would expect that this program would correctly transform the initial sequence into its immediate alphabetic successor also if some values occurred more than once in the sequence. It does indeed, thanks to the fact that, while determining i and j, we have formed our guards by "mechanically" negating the required condition $c(i) < c(i + 1)$ and $c(j) > c(i)$ respectively. I once showed this program, when visiting a university, to an audience that absolutely refused to accept my guards with equality included. They insisted on writing, when you knew that all values were different

$$\textbf{do } c(i) > c(i + 1) \rightarrow \ldots$$

and

$$\textbf{do } c(j) < c(i) \rightarrow \ldots$$

Their unshakable argument was "that it was much more expensive to test for equality as well". I gave up, wondering by what kind of equipment on the campus they had been brainwashed.   (*End of remark 1.*)

Remark 2.   Programmers unaware of the Linear Search Theorem often code "determine j" erroneously in the following form:

$$j \textbf{ vir } int:= i + 1; \textbf{do } c(j + 1) > c(i) \rightarrow j:= j + 1 \textbf{ od}$$

They argue that this program will only assign to j the value $j + 1$ after it has been established that this new value is acceptable in view of the goal $c(j) > c(i)$. Analyze why their version of "determine j" may fail to work properly.   (*End of remark 2.*)

Remark 3.   One time I had the unpleasant obligation to examine a student whose inventive powers I knew to be strictly limited. Because he had studied the above program I asked him to write a program transforming the initial permutation, known not to be the alphabetically first, into its immediate alphabetic predecessor. I hope that this exercise takes you considerably less than the hour he needed.   (*End of remark 3.*)

Remark 4.   This program is a particular friend of mine, because I remember having tackled this problem in my student days, in the Stone Age of machine code programming (even without index registers: in the good old von Neumann tradition, programs had to modify their own instructions in store!). And I also remember that, after a vain struggle of more than two hours, I gave up! And that at a moment when I was already an experienced programmer! A few years ago, needing an example for lecturing purposes, I suddenly remembered that old problem and solved it without hesitation (and could even explain it the next morning to a fairly inexperienced audience within twenty minutes). That now one can explain within twenty minutes to an inexperienced audience what twenty years before an experienced programmer could not find shows the dramatic improvement of the state of the art (to the extent that it is now even hard to believe that then I could not solve this problem!).   (*End of remark 4.*)

Remark 5.   Equivalent to our criterion for i ("the maximum value of i ($< n$), such that $c(i) < c(i + 1)$") is "the maximum value of i ($< n$) such that $(\mathbf{E}\, j : i < j \leq n : c(i) < c(j))$". The latter criterion is, however, less easily usable and whoever starts with the latter one had better discover the other one (in one way or another).   (*End of remark 5.*)

14 THE PROBLEM OF THE DUTCH NATIONAL FLAG

There is a row of buckets numbered from *1* through *N*. It is given that

    P1: each bucket contains one pebble

    P2: each pebble is either red, white, or blue.

A mini-computer is placed in front of this row of buckets and has to be programmed in such a way that it will rearrange (if necessary) the pebbles in the order of the Dutch national flag, i.e. in order from low to high bucket number first the red, then the white, and finally the blue pebbles. In order to be able to do so, the mini-computer has been equipped with one output command that enables it to interfere with pebble positions, viz.

"buck:swap(i,j)" for $1 \leq i \leq N$ and $1 \leq j \leq N$:

    for $i = j$: the pebbles are left as they are

    for $i \neq j$: two computer-controlled hands pick up the pebbles from buckets *nrs. i* and *j* respectively and then drop them in each other's bucket respectively. (This operation leaves relations *P1* and *P2* invariantly true.)

and one input command that can inspect the colour of a pebble, viz.

"buck(i)"   for $1 \leq i \leq N$:

when the computer program prescribes the evaluation of this function of type "colour", a movable "eye" is directed upon bucket *nr. i*, and delivers to the mini-computer as the value of the function the colour (i.e. red, white, or blue) of the pebble currently lying in the bucket, the contents of which is inspected by the "eye".

The constant N is a global constant from the context in which our program is to be embedded as an inner block. Our program, however, has to meet three special requirements:

1. It must be able to cope with all possible forms of "degeneration" as presented by missing colours: the buckets may have been filled with pebbles of two colours only, of one colour only, or of no colour at all (if $N = 0$).
2. The mini-computer has a very small store compared with the values of N it should be able to cope with, and therefore we are not allowed to introduce arrays of any sort, only a fixed number of variables of the types "integer" and/or variables of type "colour". (With variables of type integer we mean here variables that cannot take on much more than N different values.)
3. The program may direct the "eye" at most once upon each pebble (it is assumed that the input operation is so time-consuming that looking twice at the same pebble would lead to an inacceptable loss of time).

Furthermore, regarding programs of the same degree of complication, the one that needs (on the average) the fewer swaps is to be preferred.

Although our pebbles are of only three different colours, the fact that our eye can only inspect pebbles one at a time, together with requirement (3), implies that halfway through the rearrangement process, we have to distinguish between pebbles of four different categories, viz. "established red" (ER), "established white" (EW), "established blue" (EB), and "as yet uninspected" (X). Requirement (2) excludes that pebbles of these different categories lie arbitrarily mixed: inside the mini-computer we then cannot store "who is what". Our only way out is to divide the row of buckets into a fixed number of (possibly empty) zones of consecutively numbered buckets, each zone being reserved for pebbles of a specific category. Because four different zones is the minimum, the introduction of just four zones seems the first thing to try. But in what order? I found that many programmers tend to decide without much thinking upon the order "ER", "EW", "EB", "X", but this is a rash decision. As soon as anyone is of the opinion that it is attractive to place the zone "ER" at the low end, considerations of symmetry should suggest that the zone "EB" at the high end is equally attractive. Still sticking to our earlier decision of only four different zones, we come to the conclusion that the zones "EW" and "X" should be in the middle in some order (convince yourself that it is now immaterial in which order!), for instance:

$$\text{"ER", "X", "EW", "EB"}$$

Once we have chosen the above "general situation", our problem is essentially solved, for here we have a general situation of which both the initial state (all buckets in zone "X") and the final state (zone "X" empty) are special cases! We can establish it, and then a repetitive construct has to decrease the size of zone "X" while maintaining this general situation. In our mini-computer we need three integer variables for keeping track of the place of the zone boundaries, e.g. "r", "w", and "b" with the meanings

$1 \leq k < r$: the kth bucket is in zone "ER"
(number of buckets $r - 1 \geq 0$)

$r \leq k \leq w$: the kth bucket is in zone "X"
(number of buckets $w - r + 1 \geq 0$)

$w < k \leq b$: the kth bucket is in zone "EW"
(number of buckets $b - w \geq 0$)

$b < k \leq N$: the kth bucket is in zone "EB"
(number of buckets $N - b \geq 0$)

Establishing the relation P to be kept invariant means initializing these three variables in accordance with "all buckets in zone "X"", and the overall structure of our program could be:

```
begin glovar buck; glocon N; privar r, w, b;
    r vir int, w vir int, b vir int := 1, N, N; {P has been established}
    do w ≥ r → "decrease number of buckets in zone "X"
                under invariance of P"
    od
end
```

Immediately we are faced with the question: by which amount shall the guarded statement decrease the number of buckets in zone "X"? There are three arguments —and as the reader will notice, they are of a fairly general nature— in favour of trying first whether we can come away with "decrease the number of buckets in zone "X" by 1". The arguments are:

1. Decreasing by 1 is sufficient.
2. As we have chosen our guard "$w \geq r$", we can guarantee the presence of at most one bucket in zone "X"; for two, we would have needed the guard "$w > r$".
3. The one pebble inspected will face us with three different cases, inspecting two confronts us already with nine different cases; this multiplicative building up of cases to be considered should be interpreted, in principle, as a heavy price to pay for whatever we can gain by it.

The next question to be settled is: which one of the uninspected pebbles will be looked at? This question is not necessarily irrelevant, because in the meantime in the ordering "ER","X", "EW","EB" an asymmetric situation has been created. No experienced programmer will suggest an arbitrary one, the ones at the low and the high end respectively are the most likely candidates. With equal probabilities for the three colours, an inspection of the pebble in the rth bucket will give rise to $(0 + 1 + 2)/3 = 1$ swap; inspection of the pebble in the wth bucket, however, will give rise only to $(1 + 0 + 1)/3 = 2/3$ swap, and this settles the choice. Thus we arrive at the following program:

```
begin glovar buck; glocon N; privar r, w, b;
   r vir int, w vir int, b vir int := 1, N, N;
   do w ≥ r →
   begin glovar buck, r, w, b; pricon col;
      col vir colour := buck(w);
      if col = red → buck:swap(r, w); r:= r + 1
      ▯ col = white → w:= w − 1
      ▯ col = blue → buck:swap(w, b); w, b := w − 1, b − 1
      fi
   end
   od
end
```

Note. The program is robust in the sense that it will lead to abortion when fed with erroneous data such as one of the pebbles being green. (*End of note.*)

In the case that all pebbles are red and no swaps are necessary, our program will prescribe N swaps and as conscious programmers we should investigate how complicated a possibly more refined solution becomes: perhaps we have acted too cowardly in rejecting it. (As a general strategy I would recommend not to try the more refined solution before having constructed the more straightforward one; that strategy gives us, besides a working program, an inexpensive indication of what the considered refinement as such has to compete with.) I have always thought the above solution perfectly satisfactory, and up till now I have never considered a more complicated one. So, here we go!

Inspecting just one can be extended to "inspecting one or two" or "inspecting as many as we can conveniently place". In view of the case "all pebbles red" something along the latter line seems indicated. Before inspecting the uninspected pebble at the high end we could try to move the boundary indicated by r to the high end as much as we possibly can without swapping, because it seems a pity to replace a red pebble in a perfectly OK-position by another red pebble. The outer repetition could then begin with

```
do w ≥ r →
begin glovar buck, r, w, b; privar colr;
    colr vir colour := buck(r);
    do colr = red and r < w → r:= r + 1; colr:= buck(r) od;
```

The inner repetition stops, either because all pebbles have been inspected ($r = w$) or because we have hit a nonred pebble. The case $r = w$, where *colr* may have one of three different values, reduces to the alternative clause of the earlier program but for the fact that the "*buck:swap(r, w)*" —r and w being equal to each other— can be omitted. The case $r < w$ implies *colr* $\neq$ *red*; now we *must* be willing to inspect another pebble, for otherwise our solution reduces to the one which always inspects the pebble at the low end of the zone "X" and of that solution we know that on the average it generates more swaps than our first effort. Because $r < w$, there is indeed another uninspected pebble and the one in the wth bucket is the obvious candidate.

Again, with *colr* = *white*, it seems a pity to swap the pebble in the rth bucket with a white one in the wth bucket and in case of $r < w$ it seems indicated to enter a new inner block

```
begin glovar buck, r, w, b; glocon colr; privar colw;
    colw vir colour := buck(w);
    do colw = white and w > r + 1 → w:= w − 1; colw:= buck(w) od;
```

We have now for *colr* the two possibilities *white* or *blue*, for *colw* the three possibilities *red*, *white*, or *blue*, and the set of uninspected pebbles may be empty or not. For a moment I feared that I might have to distinguish between about *12* cases! But after looking at it for a long time (and after one false start), I discovered that the way to proceed now is first to place the pebble now in the wth bucket and to see to it that in all three cases the pebble originally in the rth bucket is left in the (new) wth bucket. Then the three alternatives can merge and a single text deals uniformly with the second pebble, the colour of which is still given by *colr*.

```
if colw = red → buck:swap(r, w); r:= r + 1
▯ colw = white → w:= w − 1
▯ colw = blue → buck:swap(w, b); w, b := w − 1, b − 1;
                buck:swap(r, w)
fi;
if colr = white → w:= w − 1
▯ colr = blue → buck:swap(w, b); w, b := w − 1, b − 1
fi
```

Note 1. It is nice that we could achieve that the concatenation of two alternative constructs caters to the $2*3$ colour-combinations! (*End of note 1.*)

Note 2. Convince yourself that the case *colw* = *white* has been correctly dealt with, because in this case $w = r + 1$ initially. (*End of note 2.*)

Remark. For pedagogical reasons I slightly regret that the final treatment of "two inspected pebbles in wrong buckets" did not turn out to be worse; perhaps I should have resisted the temptation to do even this messy job as decently as I could. (*End of remark.*)

I leave the final composition of our second program to the reader, if he still so desires (I hope he does not!); I think the point has been made. I have carried the case-analysis up to this stage in order to drive home the message that such a case-analysis, also known under the name "combinatorial explosion", should nearly always be avoided like the plague. It lengthens the program texts, and that may easily impair the efficiency! It always impairs the program's reliability, for it imposes upon the poor programmer's shoulders a burden under which he usually succumbs (not in the last place because the work becomes so boring). The reader may interpret the above exercise as a hint to software managers not to grade their programmers by the number of lines of code produced per month; I would rather let them pay the punched cards they use out of their own pocket.

I have solved this problem often with students, either arriving at zones in the order "ER", "X", "EW", "EB" or in the order "ER", "EW", "X", "EB". When asked which pebble to inspect, their first suggestion had always been "the leftmost one". I had the idea that this preference could be traced to our habit of reading from left to right. Later I encountered students that suggested first the rightmost one: one was an Israeli computing scientist, the other one was of Syrian origin. It is somewhat frightening to discover the devious ways in which our habits influence our thinking!

And this concludes my treatment of the problem of the Dutch national flag, a problem that I owe to W.H.J. Feijen.

15 UPDATING A SEQUENTIAL FILE

When the guarded commands had emerged and the word got around, a graduate student that was occupying himself mainly with business-oriented computer applications expressed his doubts as to whether our approaches were of any value outside (what he called) the scientific/technical applications area. To support his doubt he confronted us with what he regarded as a typical business application, viz. the updating of a sequential file. (For a more precise statement of his problem, see below.) He could show the flow-chart of a program that was supposed to solve the problem, but that had arrows going from one box to another in such a wild manner that that solution (if it was one, for we could never find out!) was considered a kludge by both of us. With some pride he showed us a decision table —his decision table— that, according to him, would solve the problem; but the size of that transition table terrified us. As the gauntlet was thrown to us, the only thing left for us to do was to pick it up. Our first two efforts, although cleaner than anything we had seen, did not yet satisfy W.H.J. Feijen, whose solution I shall describe in this chapter. It turned out that our first efforts had been relatively unsuccessful because by the way in which the problem had been presented to us, we had erroneously been led to believe that this special nut was particularly hard to crack. Quod non. I include the treatment of the file updating problem in this monograph for three reasons. Firstly, because it gives us the opportunity to publish Feijen's neat solution to a common type of problem for which, apparently, very messy solutions are hanging around. Secondly, because it can be found by exactly the same argument that led to the elegant solution of the problem of the Dutch national flag. Finally, it gives us the opportunity to cast some doubts on the opinion that business programs are of a special nature. (If there is something special, it might be the nature of business programmers . . . .)

There is given a file, i.e. ordered sequence, of records or, more precisely, of values of type "*record*". If x is (the value of) a variable of type *record*, a boolean function $x.norm$ and an integer function $x.key$ are defined, such that for some constant *inf*

$$x.norm \Rightarrow (x.key < inf)$$
$$(\textbf{non } x.norm) \Rightarrow (x.key = inf)$$

The given file of records is called "*oldfile*" and successive records in the sequence have monotonically increasing values of their "*key*"; only for the last record of oldfile "*x.norm*" is *false*.

Furthermore there is given a file, called "*transfile*", which is an ordered sequence of transactions or, more precisely, of values of type "*transaction*". If y is (the value of) a variable of type *transaction*, the boolean $y.norm$ and the integer $y.key$ are defined, such that for the same constant *inf* as above

$$y.\,norm \Rightarrow (y.key < inf)$$
$$(\textbf{non } y.norm) \Rightarrow (y.key = inf)$$

Successive transactions of "transfile" have monotonically nondecreasing values of their "key", only the last transaction is abnormal and has "$y.key = inf$". If $y.norm$ is *true*, three further booleans are defined, viz. "*y.upd*", "*y.del*" and "*y.ins*", such that always exactly one of them is *true*.

Furthermore, with x of type *record* and y of type *transaction*, such that $y.norm$ is *true*, three operations modifying x are defined:

$x:update(y)$ only defined if $x.norm$ **and** $y.upd$ **and** $(x.key = y.key)$; upon completion $x.norm$ **and** $(x.key = y.key)$ still holds

$x:delete(y)$ only defined if $x.norm$ **and** $y.del$ **and** $(x.key = y.key)$; upon completion $x.norm = false$

$x:insert(y)$ only defined if **non** $x.norm$ **and** $y.ins$; upon completion $x.norm$ **and** $(x.key = y.key)$ holds

With x of type *record*, we have furthermore the operation "$x:setabnorm$" which leaves $x.norm = false$.

The program has to generate a record file, called "*newfile*", whose final value depends on the initial value of the input files "*oldfile*" and "*transfile*" in the following way. We can merge the records of *oldfile* and the transactions of *transfile* in the order of nondecreasing key with the rule that if a given key-value occurs (once!) in *oldfile* and also (once or more) in *transfile*, the record with that key-value precedes the transaction(s) with that key-value in the merged sequence. The internal order of the transactions with the same key-value is not to be destroyed by this merging process. As long as there is still a transaction in the merged sequence, the merged sequence is subjected to the transformation to be described below; the remaining sequence, consisting of records only, is the desired final value of "*newfile*". The transformation is described as follows.

Let y be the first transaction in the merged sequence, let x be the immediately preceding record (if any):

if *y.upd* and there is a preceding record x with *x.key* = *y.key*, the latter is modified by *x:update(y)* and y is removed from the sequence;

if *y.del* and there is a preceding record x with *x.key* = *y.key*, both x and y are removed from the sequence;

if *y.ins* and there is *not* a preceding record x with *x.key* = *y.key*, y is replaced by a record as results from the insert-operation;

if **non** *norm.y*, transaction y is removed;

if the first transaction satisfies none of these four criteria, it is removed from the sequence under execution of the operation "*error message*", which, for the purpose of this discussion, needs no further description.

We shall model this as an inner block operating on three global arrays:

record **array** *oldfile* , only referred to by "*lopop*" and eventually empty (i.e. *oldfile.dom* = 0)

transaction **array** *transfile* , only referred to by "*lopop*" and eventually empty (i.e. *transfile.dom* = 0)

record **array** *newfile* , only referred to by "*hiext*" and initially empty (i.e. *newfile.dom* = 0)

We see some of the complications of this problem when we realize that the merged sequence might contain a sequence of transactions, all with the same key-value, and, for instance, successively characterized by the truth of

$$ins, ins, upd, del, del, upd, ins, upd, del$$

where the second "*ins*", the second "*del*" and the second "*upd*" will all give rise to "*error message*" and the whole sequence contributes nothing at all to the final value of *newfile*; such a sequence may occur with or without a normal record following it.

As lengths of the files are unknown, our program will consist of a prelude, one or more repetitive constructs, and possibly a (nonrepetitive) code closing the *newfile* with an abnormal record. In general a new record for *newfile* can only be generated provided that the record with the next higher key from *oldfile* and also the transaction with the next higher key from *transfile* have already been "seen". (Think about a new record derived from the transaction file only.) For this reason, we introduce a variable x of type "*record*" and a variable y of type "*transaction*", in which the record and the transaction with these next higher keys will be stored; upon creation of a record of *newfile*, "*x*, followed by the remaining records of *oldfile*" will represent the still unprocessed records, "*y*, followed by the remaining transactions of *transfile*" will represent the still unprocessed transactions. This applies when a new normal record has been added to *newfile*; the final abnormal record will be attached by the coda. Because an unknown number of new records can still be generated as long as one of the two input files is not yet exhausted, the overall structure suggested for our program is now

> **begin glovar** *oldfile, transfile, newfile*; **privar** *x, y*;
>   *x* **vir** *record, oldfile:lopop*;
>   *y* **vir** *transaction, transfile:lopop*;
>   **do** *x.norm* **or** *y.norm* $\longrightarrow$
>   "process at least one record or transaction such as to
>   ensure progress"
>   **od**;
>   "extend newfile with abnormal record"
> **end**

In designing repetitive constructs the crucial decision is how to synchronize the progress of the computation with the cycling, the decision regarding how much shall be done by each guarded statement list when selected for execution. In this example we get into trouble when we synchronize with *oldfile* or *transfile*, because either of them may already be exhausted; we get into similar trouble when we try to synchronize with the generation of records for *newfile*, because, though none of the input files is exhausted, we may have generated the last normal record for newfile. The answer to the question of synchronization is given in exactly the same manner as with the problem of the Dutch national flag, when the number of pebbles to be inspected had to be decided: the guarded statement will do exactly as much work —no more and no less— as needs to be done and can be done, when its guard is true.

If our guard *x.norm* **or** *y.norm* is true, the *only* conclusion we can draw is that the unprocessed parts of the input files contain for at least one key-value such that *key* < *inf* a record and/or transactions: the guarded statement list will therefore process all records and/or transactions with that key-value!

In the first statement —an alternative construct— that key-value is determined and recorded in the local constant "*ckey*" (short for "current key"). Also the variable "*xx*" of type *record* is initialized; it is in this variable that the new record that may result is being built up. If the current key is derived from *oldfile*, the only record with that key is processed, otherwise *oldfile* will be left untouched.

In the second statement —a repetitive construct— all transactions with that key-value are processed; as the processing of transactions is fully restricted to this repetitive construct, the distinction between the various kinds of transactions is well concentrated.

In the third statement —an alternative construct— a new record may be added to *newfile*.

```
begin glovar oldfile, transfile, newfile; privar x, y;
    x vir record, oldfile:lopop;
    y vir transaction, transfile:lopop;
    do x.norm or y.norm →
        begin glovar oldfile, transfile, newfile, x, y;
            pricon ckey; privar xx;
            if x.key ≤ y.key → ckey vir int:= x.key; xx vir record:= x;
                                x, oldfile:lopop
            ▯ x.key > y.key → ckey vir int:= y.key; xx vir record:setabnorm
            fi {ckey < inf and ckey < x.key and ckey ≤ y.key};
            do y.key = ckey → {y.key < inf, i.e. y.norm}
                if y.upd and xx.norm → xx:update(y)
                ▯ y.del and xx.norm → xx:delete(y)
                ▯ y.ins and non xx.norm → xx:insert(y)
                ▯ y.ins = xx.norm → error message
                fi; y, transfile:lopop
            od {ckey < x.key and ckey < y.key};
            if xx.norm → newfile:hiext(xx) ▯ non xx.norm → skip fi
        end
    od; newfile:hiext(x) {newfile closed with abnormal record}
end
```

Remark 1. In the way in which we have presented this problem, one of the possible values of a variable x of type *record* was the abnormal value with $x.norm = false$; in the problem statement this value was used to mark the end of *oldfile*. Thanks to that convention it was possible to restrict references to *oldfile* to the operation "*lopop*"; if, however, "*oldfile.dom*" would also have been available, such an abnormal value as end marker of the file would not have been necessary and the whole problem could have been stated in terms of a type "*normal record*". For the purpose of this program we would then need linguistic means for introducing the type "*record*" as used in our solution. Programming languages without such means force its users to meet such a need for instance by introducing a pair of variables, say a variable "*xx*" of type "*normal record*" and a boolean variable "*xxnorm*", and then to write a program explicitly manipulating the variables of this pair; *xxnorm* has then to indicate whether the value of *xx* is significant. Such "conditional significance" is incompatible with our idea of explicit initialization with meaningful values. In the case $x.key \leq y.key$ both xx and $xxnorm$ can be given meaningful initial values; in the case $x.key > y.key$, however, only

$$xxnorm \ \textbf{vir} \ bool := false$$

would be really meaningful: our conventions would oblige us to initialize xx then with some dummy value. We have circumvented this problem by assuming the type *record* to include the abnormal value as well, thus postponing a discussion of the linguistic means that would be needed for the introduction of new types.   (*End of remark 1.*)

16 MERGING PROBLEMS REVISITED

In the two preceding chapters we have followed a pattern of reasoning that was rather different from our earlier formal treatments, where we derived the guards once the invariant relation and the variant function (for the repetitive construct) or the post-condition (for the alternative construct) and the statement (list) to be guarded had been decided. In dealing with the problem of the Dutch national flag and the file updating problem, however, we started our reasoning about the repetitive construct with the guard and from there argued what the guarded statement could be like, a more classical approach. Particularly with respect to the file updating program I can imagine that earlier chapters have made some of my readers so suspicious that they wonder why I dare to believe that last chapter's program is correct; against all rules, I have not even mentioned an invariant relation! The current chapter is included, among other reasons, to supply the omitted material; simultaneously it will give us an opportunity to deal with a somewhat wider class of problems in a more abstract manner.

Let x, y, and z be sets (and we can restrict ourselves without loss of generality to sets of integers —there are enough of them!). We recall that, by definition of the notion "set", all its elements are different from each other; in this respect a "set of integers" differs from "a collection of numbers that may contain duplicates". Two sets are equal ($x = y$), if and only if every element of one set occurs in the other as well and vice versa.

We denote the union of two sets by a "$+$", i.e. if $z = x + y$, then z contains an element if and only if that element occurs in either x, or y, or both.

We denote the intersection of two sets by a "$*$", i.e. if $z = x * y$, then z contains an element if and only if that element occurs in both x and y.

123

We denote the empty set by "$\varnothing$", i.e. $z = \varnothing$ if and only if z contains no element at all.

We now consider the task of computing for fixed sets X and Y the value Z, given by

$$Z = X + Y$$

(In the course of this discussion X and Y, and therefore Z, are regarded as constants: Z is the desired final value of a variable to be introduced later.) Our program is requested to do so by manipulating —i.e. inspecting, changing, etc.— sets element by element.

Before proceeding to think in more detail about the algorithm, we realize that halfway through the computational process, some of the elements of Z will have been found and some not, that is, there exists for the set Z a partitioning

$$Z = z1 \mp z2$$

Here the symbol "$\mp$" is a shorthand for

$$Z = z1 + z2 \quad \textbf{and} \quad z1 * z2 = \varnothing$$

(We may think of $z1$ as the set of elements whose membership of Z has been definitely established, and of $z2$ as the set of Z's remaining elements.)

Similarly, halfway through the computational process, the sets X and Y can be partitioned

$$X = x1 \mp x2 \quad \text{and} \quad Y = y1 \mp y2$$

(Here we may think of the sets $x1$ and $y1$ as those elements of X and Y respectively which do not need to be taken into account anymore, as they have been successfully processed.)

These interpretations of the partitionings of Z, X, and Y are, however, of later concern. We shall first prove, quite independent of what might be happening during the execution of our program, a theorem about such partitionings.

THEOREM.

If $Z = X + Y$ (1)

$X = x1 \mp x2$ (2)

$Y = y1 \mp y2$ (3)

$z1 = x1 + y1$ (4)

$z2 = x2 + y2,$ (5)

then $Z = z1 \mp z2 \Leftrightarrow (x1 * y2 = \varnothing \quad \textbf{and} \quad y1 * x2 = \varnothing)$ (6)

Proof. To show that the left-hand side of (6) implies its right-hand side, we argue as follows:

$$Z = z1 \mp z2 \Rightarrow z1 * z2 = \varnothing$$

substituting (4) and (5), we find

$$(x1 + y1)*(x2 + y2) =$$
$$(x1 * x2)+(x1 * y2)+(y1 * x2)+(y1 * y2) = \varnothing$$

which implies the right-hand side of (6). To show that the right-hand side of (6) implies its left-hand side, we have to show that it implies

$$z1 * z2 = \varnothing \quad \textbf{and} \quad Z = z1 + z2$$
$$z1 * z2 = (x1 + y1)*(x2 + y2)$$
$$= (x1 * x2)+(x1 * y2)+(y1 * x2)+(y1 * y2)$$
$$= \varnothing + \varnothing + \varnothing + \varnothing = \varnothing$$
$$z1 + z2 = (x1 + y1)+(x2 + y2)$$
$$= x1 + x2 + y1 + y2$$
$$= X + Y = Z \qquad\qquad (End\ of\ proof.)$$

If relations (1) through (5) hold, the right-hand side of (6), and, therefore,

$$Z = z1 \mathrel{\mp} z2$$

is also implied by

$$z1 * x2 = \varnothing \quad \textbf{and} \quad z1 * y2 = \varnothing \qquad\qquad (7)$$

and from (1) through (5) and (7) it follows that if the partitioning of Z has been chosen, the other two partitionings are uniquely defined.

Armed with the above knowledge, we return to our original problem, in which our program should establish

R: $\qquad\qquad\qquad\qquad z = Z$

Not unlike our treatment of earlier problems, we introduce two variables x and y and could try the invariant relation

P: $\qquad\qquad\qquad\qquad z + (x + y) = Z$

which has the pleasant property that it is trivially satisfied by

$P0$: $\qquad\qquad z = \varnothing \quad \textbf{and} \quad x = X \quad \textbf{and} \quad y = Y$

while, together with $(x + y) = \varnothing$, it implies R.

Our theorem now suggests to identify x with $x2$, y with $y2$, and z with $z1$ (the asymmetry reflecting that X and Y are known sets, while Z has to be computed). After this identification, (2) through (5) define all sets in terms of x and y. If we now synchronize the shrinking of x and y in such a way as to keep the right-hand side of (6) or

$$z * x = \varnothing \quad \textbf{and} \quad z * y = \varnothing \qquad\qquad (7')$$

invariant as well, then we know that

$$Z = X + Y = z1 \mathrel{\mp} z2$$

Extending z ($= z1$) with an element e implies, because $z1 \between z2$ is a partitioning of the constant set Z, taking away that element e from $x + y$ ($= z2$). In order that such an element exists, the union should not be empty, i.e. $(x + y) \neq \varnothing$ or, equivalently, "$x \neq \varnothing$ **or** $y \neq \varnothing$"; the element e should either be a member of x but not of y, or a member of y but not of x, or a member of both x and y, and it should be taken away either from x or from y or from both respectively. The program structure we are considering is:

$x, y, z := X, Y, \varnothing$;
do $x \neq \varnothing$ **or** $y \neq \varnothing \longrightarrow$ "transfer an element from $(x + y)$ to z" **od**

We now assume (the elements of) the set x to be represented by the values $ax(i)$ with $ax.lob \leq i < ax.hib$ and (the elements of) the set y by the values $ay(i)$ with $ay.lob \leq i < ay.hib$, where ax and ay are monotonically increasing integer functions with $ax.high = ay.high = inf$. The advantage of that additional value inf is that, even if x or y is empty, $ax.low$ and $ay.low$ are still defined. The advantage of the monotonically increasing order is that for a nonempty set x, $ax.low$ equals its minimum element, and similarly for y. As a result, if not both sets are empty, there is one element from the union, for which it is very easy to determine whether it belongs to x, to y, or to both, viz.

$$min(ax.low, ay.low)$$

If, for instance $ax.low < ay.low$, the element equals $ax.low$ and occurs in x but cannot occur in y because all y's elements are larger than it; its removal from x is then duly represented by $ax: lorem$, leaving x's remaining elements still represented by a monotonically increasing function.

If (the elements of) the set z must be represented according to the same convention, we choose to represent it by all values $az(i)$ with $az.lob \leq i \leq az.hib$; the last value inf can then be added only at the end of the computation. The resulting function az will be monotonically increasing if its value is only changed by $az: hiext(K)$, such that initially either $az.dom = 0$ or $az.dom > 0$ **and** $az.high < K$. Our program will satisfy those constraints.

Assuming the array variables ax and ay properly initialized (i.e. with $ax.high = ay.high = inf$) and az with $az.dom = 0$, the following two statements would perform the desired transformation:

do $ax.low \neq inf$ **or** $ay.low \neq inf \longrightarrow \{min(ax.low, ay.low) < inf\}$
    if $ax.low < ay.low \longrightarrow az: hiext(ax.low); ax: lorem$
    [] $ax.low > ay.low \longrightarrow az: hiext(ay.low); ay: lorem$
    [] $ax.low = ay.low \longrightarrow az: hiext(ax.low); ax: lorem; ay: lorem$
    fi $\{az.high < min(ax.low, ay.low)\}$
od $\{az.dom = 0 \textbf{ cor } (az.dom > 0 \textbf{ and } az.high < inf)\}$;
$az: hiext(inf)$

EXERCISES

1. Modify this program such that it will establish $u = U$ as well, where U is given by $U = X * Y$.

2. Make a similar program, such that it will establish $z = Z$, where Z is given by $Z = W + X + Y$.

3. Make a similar program, such that it will establish $z = Z$, where Z is given by $Z = W + (X * Y)$.

4. Make a program establishing $z = X + Y$, but without assuming (nor introducing!) the value "*inf*" marking the high ends of the domains; empty sets may be detected by *ax.dom* $= 0$ and *ay.dom* $= 0$ respectively. (*End of exercises.*)

At the expense of still some more formal machinery we could have played our formal game in extenso.

Let, for any predicate $P(z)$, the semantics of "$z := x \mathbin{\overline{\mp}} y$" be given by

$$\mathrm{wp}(\text{``}z := x \mathbin{\overline{\mp}} y\text{''}, P(z)) = (x * y = \varnothing \ \textbf{and} \ P(x + y))$$

here the first term expresses that the intersection of x and y should be empty for $x \mathbin{\overline{\mp}} y$ to be defined.

Let, for any predicate $P(z)$, the semantics of $z := x \simeq y$ be given by

$$\mathrm{wp}(\text{``}z := x \simeq y\text{''}, P(z)) = (x * y = y \ \textbf{cand} \ P(x \simeq y))$$

where the first term expresses that y should be fully contained in x for $x \simeq y$ to be defined and $x \simeq y$ then represents the unique solution of $(x \simeq y) \mathbin{\overline{\mp}} y = x$.

Eliminating $x1$, $x2$, $y1$, $y2$, $z1$, and $z2$, we find that we have to maintain in terms of x, y, and z the relations:

P1: $\qquad\qquad\qquad x * X = x$

P2: $\qquad\qquad\qquad y * Y = y$

P3: $\qquad\qquad\qquad z = (X \simeq x) + (Y \simeq y)$

P4: $\qquad\qquad\qquad x * (Y \simeq y) = \varnothing$

P5: $\qquad\qquad\qquad y * (X \simeq x) = \varnothing$

and we can ask ourselves under what initial circumstances the execution of

S: $\qquad\qquad\qquad z, x := z \mathbin{\overline{\mp}} \{e\}, x \simeq \{e\}$

will leave these relations invariant for some element e. We begin by investigating when this concurrent assignment is defined, i.e.

$$\mathrm{wp}(S, T) = (z * \{e\} = \varnothing \ \textbf{and} \ x * \{e\} = \{e\})$$

Because

$$(P1 \text{ and } x *\{e\} = \{e\}) \Rightarrow (X \simeq x)*\{e\} = \varnothing$$
$$(P2 \text{ and } P4 \text{ and } x *\{e\} = \{e\}) \Rightarrow (Y \simeq y)*\{e\} = \varnothing$$

$Q \Rightarrow \text{wp}(S, T)$ with

$$Q = (P1 \text{ and } P2 \text{ and } P3 \text{ and } P4 \text{ and } x *\{e\} = \{e\})$$

It is now not too difficult to establish

$$Q \Rightarrow \text{wp}(S, P1 \text{ and } P2 \text{ and } P3 \text{ and } P4)$$

However:

$$
\begin{aligned}
\text{wp}(S, P5) &= (\text{wp}(S, T) \text{ and } y *(X \simeq (x \simeq \{e\})) = \varnothing) \\
&= (\text{wp}(S, T) \text{ and } y *((X \simeq x) \mp \{e\}) = \varnothing) \\
&= (\text{wp}(S, T) \text{ and } P5 \text{ and } y *\{e\} = \varnothing)
\end{aligned}
$$

and consequently, the guard for S such that $P1$ through $P5$ remain invariant is

$$x *\{e\} = \{e\} \text{ and } y *\{e\} = \varnothing$$

i.e. e should be an element of x, but not of y, et cetera.

The above concludes my revisiting of merging problems. In the last two chapters I have given treatments of different degrees of formality and which one of them my reader will prefer will depend as much on his needs as on his mood. But it seems instructive to go through the motions at least once! (As the result in all probability shows, the writing of this chapter created considerably more difficulties than anticipated. It is at least the fifth version; that, in itself, already justifies its inclusion.)

17 AN EXERCISE ATTRIBUTED TO R.W. HAMMING

The way the problem reached me was: "To generate in increasing order the sequence *1, 2, 3, 4, 5, 6, 8, 9, 10, 12,* . . . of all numbers divisible by no primes other than *2, 3,* or *5*." Another way of stating which values are in the sequence is by means of three axioms:

Axiom *1*. The value *1* is in the sequence.
Axiom *2*. If *x* is in the sequence, so are *2 ∗ x, 3 ∗ x*, and *5 ∗ x*.
Axiom *3*. The sequence contains no other values than those that belong to it on account of Axioms *1* and *2*.

(We leave to the number theorists the task of establishing the equivalence of the two above definitions.)

We include this exercise because its structure is quite typical for a large class of problems. Being interested only in terminating programs, we shall make a program generating only the, say, first *1000* values of the sequence. Let

P0(n, q) mean: the value of "*q*" represents the ordered set of the first "*n*" values of the sequence.

Then Axiom *1* tells us that *1* is in the sequence and, as *2 ∗ x, 3 ∗ x*, and *5 ∗ x* are functions whose value is $> x$ for $x > 0$, Axiom *2* tells us that *1* is the minimum value whose membership of the sequence can be established on account of the first two axioms. Axiom *3* then tells us that *1* is the minimum value occurring in the sequence and therefore *P0(n, q)* is easily established for *n = 1*: "*q*" then contains the value *1* only. The obvious program structure is:

"establish $P0(n, q)$ for $n = 1$";
do $n \neq 1000 \rightarrow$
    "increase n by 1 under invariance of $P0(n, q)$"
od

Under the assumption that we can extend a sequence with a value "$xnext$", provided that the value "$xnext$" is known, the main problem of "increase n by 1 under invariance of $P0(n, q)$" is how to determine the value "$xnext$". Because the value 1 is already in q, $xnext > 1$, and $xnext$'s membership of the sequence must therefore rely on Axiom 2. Calling the maximum value occurring in q "$q.high$", $xnext$ is the minimum value $> q.high$, that is, of the form $2 * x$ or $3 * x$ or $5 * x$ such that x occurs in the sequence. But because $2 * x$, $3 * x$, and $5 * x$ are all functions whose value is $> x$ for $x > 0$, that value of x must satisfy $x < xnext$; furthermore, x cannot satisfy $x > q.high$, for then we would have

$$q.high < x < xnext$$

which would contradict that $xnext$ is the minimum value $> q.high$. Therefore we have $x \leq q.high$, i.e. x must already occur in q, and we can sharpen our definition of $xnext$: $xnext$ is the minimum value $> q.high$, that is of the form $2 * x$ or $3 * x$ or $5 * x$, such that x occurs in q. (It is for the sake of the above analysis that we have initialized $P0(n, q)$ for $n = 1$; initialization for $n = 0$ would have been just as easy, but then $q.high$ would not be defined.)

A straightforward implementation of the above analysis would lead to the introduction of the set qq, where qq consists of all values $xx > q.high$, such that xx can be written as

$$xx = 2 * x, \quad \text{with } x \text{ in } q,$$

or as

$$xx = 3 * x, \quad \text{with } x \text{ in } q,$$

or as

$$xx = 5 * x, \quad \text{with } x \text{ in } q$$

The set qq is nonempty and $xnext$ would be the minimum value occurring in it. But upon closer inspection, this is not too attractive, because the adjustment of qq would imply (in the notation of the previous chapter)

$$qq := (qq \simeq \{xnext\}) + \{2 * xnext, 3 * xnext, 5 * xnext\}$$

where the "$+$" means "forming the union of two sets". Because we have to determine the minimum value occurring in qq, it would be nice to have the elements of q ordered; forming the union in the above adjustment would then require an amount of reshuffling, which we would like to avoid.

A few moments of reflection, however, will suffice for the discovery that we do not need to keep track of the whole set qq, but can select $xnext$ as the minimum value occurring in the much smaller set

$$qqq = \{x2\} + \{x3\} + \{x5\},$$

where

$x2$ is the minimum value $> q.high$, such that $x2 = 2 * x$
and x occurs in q,
$x3$ is the minimum value $> q.high$, such that $x3 = 3 * x$
and x occurs in q and
$x5$ is the minimum value $> q.high$, such that $x5 = 5 * x$
and x occurs in q.

The above relation between q, $x2$, $x3$, and $x5$ is denoted by $P1(q, x2, x3, x5)$.

A next sketch for our program is therefore:

"establish $P0(n, q)$ for $n = 1$";
do $n \neq 1000 \rightarrow$
    "establish $P1(q, x2, x3, x5)$ for the current value of q";
    "increase n by 1 under invariance of $P0(n, q)$, i.e.
        extend q with $min(x2, x3, x5)$"
od

A program along the above lines would be correct, but now "establish $P1(q, x2, x3, x5)$ for the current value of q" would be the nasty operation, even if —what we assume— the elements of the ordered set q are as accessible as we desire. The answer to this is a standard one: instead of computing $x2$, $x3$, and $x5$ as a function of q afresh when we need them, we realize that the value of q only changes "slowly" and try to "adjust" the values, which are a function of q, whenever q changes. This is such a standard technique that it is good to have a name for it; let us call it "taking the relation outside (the repetitive construct)". Its application is reflected in the program of the following structure:

"establish $P0(n, q)$ for $n = 1$";
"establish $P1(q, x2, x3, x5)$ for the current value of q";
do $n \neq 1000 \rightarrow$
    "increase n by 1 under invariance of $P0(n, q)$, i.e.
        extend q with $min(x2, x3, x5)$";
    "re-establish $P1(q, x2, x3, x5)$ for the new value of q"
od

The re-establishment of $P1(q, x2, x3, x5)$ has to take place after extension of q, i.e. after increase of $q.high$; as a result, the adjustment of $x2$, $x3$, and $x5$ is either the empty operation, or an increase, viz. a replacement by the corresponding multiple of a higher x from q. Representing the ordered set q by means of an array *aq*, i.e. as the values *aq(1)* through *aq(n)* in monotonically increasing order, we introduce three indices *i2*, *i3*, and *i5*, and extend *P1* with

... **and** $x2 = 2 * aq(i2)$ **and** $x3 = 3 * aq(i3)$ **and** $x5 = 5 * aq(i5)$

Our inner block, initializing the global array variable *aq* with the desired final value could be:

> **begin virvar** *aq*; **privar** *i2, i3, i5, x2, x3, x5*;
>   *aq* **vir** *int* **array**:= $(1, 1)$; {*P0* established}
>   *i2* **vir** *int*, *i3* **vir** *int*, *i5* **vir** *int*:= *1, 1, 1*;
>   *x2* **vir** *int*, *x3* **vir** *int*, *x5* **vir** *int*:= *2, 3, 5*; {*P1* established}
>   **do** *aq.dom* $\neq$ *1000* $\rightarrow$
>   **if** $x3 \geq x2 \leq x5 \rightarrow$ *aq:hiext(x2)*
>   ⫿ $x2 \geq x3 \leq x5 \rightarrow$ *aq:hiext(x3)*
>   ⫿ $x2 \geq x5 \leq x3 \rightarrow$ *aq:hiext(x5)*
>   **fi** {*aq.dom* has been increased by *1* under invariance of *P0*};
>   **do** $x2 \leq aq.high \rightarrow i2:= i2 + 1$; $x2:= 2 * aq(i2)$ **od**;
>   **do** $x3 \leq aq.high \rightarrow i3:= i3 + 1$; $x3:= 3 * aq(i3)$ **od**;
>   **do** $x5 \leq aq.high \rightarrow i5:= i5 + 1$; $x5:= 5 * aq(i5)$ **od**
>   {*P1* has been re-established}
>   **od**
> **end**

In the above version it is clearly expressed that after re-establishing *P1* we have $x2 > aq.high$ **and** $x3 > aq.high$ **and** $x5 > aq.high$. Apart from that we could have used "... $= aq.high$" instead of "... $\leq aq.high$" as well.

Note 1.   In the last three inner repetitive constructs each guarded statement list is selected for execution at most once. Therefore, we could have coded them

> **if** $x2 = aq.high \rightarrow i2:= i2 + 1$; $x2:= 2 * aq(i2)$
> ⫿ $x2 > aq.high \rightarrow$ *skip*
> **fi**;   etc.

When I start to think about this choice, I come out with a marked preference for the repetitive constructs, for what is so particular about the fact that a repetition terminates after zero or one execution as to justify expression by syntactic means? Very little, I am afraid. Any hesitation to recognize "zero or one times" as a special instance of "at most *k* times" is probably due to our linguistic inheritance, as all Western languages distinguish between singular and plural forms. (If we had been classical Greeks (i.e. used to thinking in terms of a dual form as well) we might have felt obliged to introduce in addition special syntactical gear for expressing termination after at most two executions!) To end in "Updating a sequential file" with

do *xx.norm* $\longrightarrow$ *newfile:hiext(xx)*; *xx:setabnorm* **od**

instead of with

if *xx.norm* $\longrightarrow$ *newfile:hiext(xx)* ▯ **non** *xx.norm* $\longrightarrow$ *skip* **fi**

would, in a sense, have been more "honest", for the output obligation as expressed by *xx.norm* has been met.   (*End of note 1.*)
Note 2.   The last three inner repetitive constructs could have been combined into a single one:

> **do** $x2 \leq aq.high \longrightarrow i2:= i2 + 1; x2:= 2 * aq(i2)$
> ▯ $x3 \leq aq.high \longrightarrow i3:= i3 + 1; x3:= 3 * aq(i3)$
> ▯ $x5 \leq aq.high \longrightarrow i5:= i5 + 1; x5:= 5 * aq(i5)$
> **od**

I prefer, however, not to do so, and not to combine the guarded commands into a single set when the execution of one guarded statement list cannot influence the truth of other guards from the set. The fact that the three repetitive constructs, separated by semicolons, now appear in an arbitrary order does not worry me: it is the usual form of over-specification that we always encounter in sequential programs prescribing things in succession that could take place concurrently.   (*End of note 2.*)

The exercise solved in this chapter is a specific instance of a more general problem, viz. to generate the first N values of the sequence given axiomatically by

Axiom *1*.   The value *1* is in the sequence.
Axiom *2*.   If x is in the sequence, so are $f(x)$, $g(x)$, and $h(x)$, where f, g, and h are monotonically increasing functions with the property $f(x) > x$, $g(x) > x$, and $h(x) > x$.
Axiom *3*.   The sequence contains no other values than those that belong to it on account of Axioms *1* and *2*.

Note that if nothing about the functions f, g, and h were given, the problem could not be solved!

EXERCISES

1.   Solve the problem if Axiom *2* is replaced by:
Axiom *2*.   If x is in the sequence, so are $f(x)$ and $g(x)$, where f and g have the property $f(x) > x$ and $g(x) > x$.

2. Solve the problem if Axiom 2 is replaced by:

Axiom 2.   If x and y are in the sequence, so is $f(x, y)$, where f has the properties

1. $f(x, y) > x$
2. $(y1 > y2) \Rightarrow (f(x, y1) > f(x, y2))$

(*End of exercises.*)

The inventive reader who has done the above exercises successfully can think of further variations himself.

18 THE PATTERN MATCHING PROBLEM

The problem that is solved in this chapter is a very famous one and has been tackled independently by many programmers. Yet we hope that our treatment gives some pleasure to even those of my readers who considered themselves thoroughly familiar with the problem and its various solutions.

We consider as given two sequences of values

$$p(0), p(1), \ldots, p(N-1) \qquad \text{with } N \geq 1$$

and

$$x(0), x(1), \ldots, x(M-1) \qquad \text{with } M \geq 0$$

(usually M is regarded as being many times larger than N). The question to be answered is: how many times does the "pattern", as given by the first sequence, occur in the second sequence?

Using

$$(\mathbf{N}i: 0 \leq i < m: B(i))$$

to denote "the number of different values of i in the range $0 \leq i < m$ for which $B(i)$ holds", a more precise description of the final relation R that is to be established is

R: $\qquad count = (\mathbf{N}i: 0 \leq i \leq M - N: match(i))$

where the function $match(i)$ is given by

for $0 \leq i \leq M - N$: $match(i) = (\mathbf{A}j: 0 \leq j < N: p(j) = x(i+j))$
for $i < 0$ or $i > M - N$: $match(i) = false$

(To define $match(i) = false$ for those further values of i, thus making it a total function, is a matter of convenience.)

If we take as invariant relation

$P1$: $\qquad count = (\mathbf{N}i: 0 \leq i < r: match(i))$ and $r \geq 0$

135

we have one which is trivially established by "*count, r*:= *0, 0*" and, further-more, is such that

$$(P1 \text{ and } r > M - N) \Rightarrow R$$

(The "matter of convenience" referred to above is that now the above inequal-ity will do the job.) This gives a sketch for the program:

> *count, r*:= *0, 0*;
> **do** $r \leq M - N \rightarrow$ "increase r under invariance of *P1*" **od**

and the reader is invited to work out for himself the refinement in which r is always increased by *1*; in the worst case, the time taken by the execution of that program will be proportional to $M * N$.

Depending on the pattern, however, much larger increases of r seem sometimes possible: if, for instance, the pattern is (*1, 2, 3, 4, 5*) and *match(r)* has been found to hold, "*count, r*:= *count + 1, r + 5*" would leave *P1* invari-ant! Considering the invariant relation

P2: $(\mathbf{A}j: 0 \leq j < k: p(j) = x(r + j))$ **and** $0 \leq k \leq N$

(which can be expected to play a role in the repetitive construct computing *match(r)*), we can investigate what we can gain by taking that relation outside the repetitive construct, i.e. we consider:

> *count, r, k*:= *0, 0, 0*;
> **do** $r \leq M - N \rightarrow$ "increase r under invariance of *P1* **and** *P2*" **od**

(relation *P2* being vacuously satisfied by $k = 0$).

In view of the validity of relation *P2* and the formula for *match(r)*, the most natural thing to start the repeatable statement with is to try to determine *match(r)*; as the truth of *match(r)* can be concluded from *P2* **and** $k = N$, we prescribe that k be increased as long as is necessary and possible:

> **do** $k \neq N$ **cand** $p(k) = x(r + k) \rightarrow k:= k + 1$ **od**   (*1*)

upon termination of which —and termination is guaranteed— we have

$$P2 \text{ and } (k = N \text{ cor } p(k) \neq x(r + k))$$

from which we can conclude that *match(r)* = ($k = N$). Thus it is known whether increasing r by *1* should be accompanied by "*count*:= *count + 1*" or not. We would like to know by how much r can be increased without further increase of *count* and without taking any further x-values into account. (The taking into account of x-values is done in statement (*1*); to do so is its specific purpose! Here we are willing to exploit only properties of the — constant— pattern.)

If $k = 0$, we conclude (because $N > 0$) that *match(r)* = *false*; the relation *P1* then justifies an increase of r by *1* (leaving *P1* invariant by leaving *count* unchanged) but *P2* does not justify any higher increase of r, and $k = 0$ (making *P2* vacuously true) is maintained.

For general k, however, there is the following argument. Define for $0 < i \leq k \leq N$ the boolean function

$$dif(i, k) = (\mathbf{E}j: 0 \leq j < k - i: p(j) \neq p(i + j))$$

From this it follows that $dif(k, k) = false$. If, however, $dif(i, k) = true$, we conclude —because $0 \leq i + j < k$— on account of the truth of $P2$

$$(\mathbf{E}j: 0 \leq j < k - i: p(j) \neq x(r + i + j))$$

that is, $dif(i, k) \Rightarrow \mathbf{non}\ match(r + i)$. Therefore, the variable "$count$" needs no further adjustments (besides the one on account of the value of $match(r)$) when r is increased by $d(k)$, where $d(k)$ is the $minimum$ solution for i with $0 < i \leq k$ of the equation $dif(i, k) = false$, or

$$(\mathbf{A}j: 0 \leq j < k - i: p(j) = p(i + j)) \qquad (2)$$

The fact that $d(k)$ is a solution of (2) implies

$$(\mathbf{A}j: 0 \leq j < k - d(k): p(j) = p(d(k) + j))$$

which, with $P2$, amounts to

$$(\mathbf{A}j: 0 \leq j < k - d(k): p(j) = x(r + d(k) + j))$$

and as a result (besides the adjustment of "$count$" as implied by the value of $match(r)$) both $P1$ and $P2$ are kept invariant by "$r, k := r + d(k), k - d(k)$".

Because the minimum solution of (2) depends on k and p only, we find:

```
begin glocon p, N, x, M; virvar count; privar r, k; pricon d;
    "initialize d";
    count vir int, r vir int, k vir int := 0, 0, 0;
    do r ≤ M − N →
        do k ≠ N cand p(k) = x(r + k) → k := k + 1 od;
        if k = N → count := count + 1; r, k := r + d(k), k − d(k)
        ▯ 0 < k < N → r, k := r + d(k), k − d(k)
        ▯ k = 0 → r := r + 1
        fi
    od
end
```

The only job left is the initialization of the array variable d, i.e. to establish for each k satisfying $1 \leq k \leq N$ the minimum solution for i of (2). The Linear Search Theorem tells us that we should try i-values in increasing order. It pays, however, to realize that this minimum value for i has to be determined for a whole sequence of k-values. Let $k1 > k2$ and let $d(k1)$ be the minimum solution for i of (2) with $k = k1$. From

$$(\mathbf{A}j: 0 \leq j < k1 - d(k1): p(j) = p(d(k1) + j))\ \mathbf{and}\ k1 > k2$$

follows:

$$(\mathbf{A}j: 0 \leq j < k2 - d(k1): p(j) = p(d(k1) + j))$$

i.e. for $k = k2$, $d(k1)$ is also a solution for i of (2), but not necessarily the smallest! From that we conclude that $d(k)$ is a monotonically nondecreasing function of k. And the algorithm therefore investigates increasing values of i, each time deciding whether for one or more k-values $i = d(k)$ can be concluded (should be established). More precisely, let $j(i)$ for given value of i be the maximum value $\leq N - i$, such that

$$(Aj: 0 \leq j < j(i): p(j) = p(i + j))$$

then $d(k) = i$ for all k such that $k - i \leq j(i)$ (or $k \leq j(i) + i$), for which no solution $d(k) < i$ exists. As the values of i will be tried in increasing order and, upon identification as minimal solution, will be recorded in the monotonically nondecreasing function d, the condition is

$$d.hib < k \leq j(i) + i$$

and we get the following program:

```
"initialize d":
begin glocon p, N; virvar d; privar i;
    d vir int array, i vir int:= (1), 0;
    do d.hib ≠ N →
        begin glocon p, N; glovar d, i; privar j;
            j vir int:= 0; i:= i + 1;
            do j < N − i cand p(j) = p(i + j) → j:= j + 1 od;
            do d.hib < j + i → d:hiext(i) od
        end
    od
end
```

EXERCISES

1.   Give a formal correctness proof for the above initialization.
2.   With "$r, k:= r + d(k), r - d(k)$" for $0 < k$, our algorithm adjusts r and k without changing $r + k$. Investigate the slight gain that is possible for $0 < k < N$ if it is known that the x-values are two-valued. (*End of exercises.*)

Remark.   Our final algorithm is one whose execution time I consider to grow proportional to $M + N$. Once one has set his goal to find, if possible, an algorithm with such a performance, its actual development does not seem to require much more than the usual care; the crucial point seems the refusal to be satisfied (without further investigation) with the obvious $M * N$-algorithm, the development of which I have left as an exercise to the reader. A slight reformulation of the problem, however, enables us to recognize also here a general design principle, which might be called the Search for the

Small Superset. Suppose that we had not been asked to count the number of matches, but to generate the sequence of r-values for which $match(r)$ holds.

When a program has to generate the members of a set A, there are (roughly) only two situations. Either we have a simple, straightforward "successor function" by means of which a next member of A can be generated —and then the whole set can be trivially generated by means of repeated application of that successor function— or we do not have a function like that. In the latter case, the usual technique is to generate the members of a set B instead, where:

1. Each member of A is a member of B as well.
2. There exists a generator for successive members of B.
3. There exists a test whether a member of B belongs to A as well.
The algorithm then generates and inspects all members of B in turn.

If this technique is to lead to a satisfactory performance, three conditions should be satisfied:

1. The members of set B should be reasonably efficient to generate.
2. The test whether an element of B belongs to A as well should be reasonably efficient (particularly in the case that it does *not*, for, usually, B is an order of magnitude larger than A).
3. Set B should not be unnecessarily large.

The trained problem solver, aware of the above, will consciously look for a smaller set B than the obvious one. In this example, the set of *all* r-values satisfying $0 \leq r \leq M - N$ is the obvious one. Note that in the previous chapter "An Exercise Attributed to R. W. Hamming" the replacement of the set "qq" by the much smaller set "qqq" was another application of the principle of the Search for the Small Superset. And besides "taking a relation outside the repetitive construct" this illustrates the second strategical similarity between the solutions presented in the current and in the previous chapter.

(End of remark.)

19 WRITING A NUMBER AS THE SUM OF TWO SQUARES

Suppose we are requested to design a program that will generate for any given $r \geq 0$ all the essentially different ways in which r can be written as the sum of two squares, more precisely, it has to generate all pairs (x, y), such that

$$x^2 + y^2 = r \text{ and } x \geq y \geq 0 \qquad (1)$$

The answer will be delivered in two array variables xv and yv, such that for i from $xv.lob(= yv.lob)$ through $xv.hib(= yv.hib)$ the pairs $(xv(i), yv(i))$ will enumerate all solutions of (1). The standard way of ensuring that our sequential algorithm will find *all* solutions to (1) is to order the solutions of (1) in some way, and I propose to order the solutions of (1) in the order of increasing value of x (no two different solutions having the same x-value, this ordering is unique). We propose to keep the following relation invariant

P1: $xv(i)$ will be a monotonically increasing function with the same domain as the monotonically decreasing function $yv(i)$, such that the pairs $(xv(i), yv(i))$ are all solutions of (1) with $xv(i) < x$

P1 is easily established by initializing both xv and yv with an empty domain and choosing x not too large. If the pair $(xv(i), yv(i))$ is a solution of (1), we shall always have $2 * xv(i)^2 \geq xv(i)^2 + yv(i)^2 = r$, and, therefore, because $xv(i) < x$, the *smallest* value $x \geq 0$, such that $2 * x^2 \geq r$ is not too large. This smallest value for x can be established by using the Linear Search Theorem. However, because each $xv(i)$ will satisfy $xv(i)^2 \leq r$, we know that *P1* and $x^2 > r$ implies that all solutions have been recorded.

Our first sketch can therefore be:

```
begin glocon r; virvar xv, yv; privar x;
    x vir int:= 0; do 2 * x² < r → x:= x + 1 od;
    xv vir int array, yv vir int array:= (1), (1);
    do x² ≤ r → "increase x under invariance of P1" od
end
```

From this program we conclude that the invariant relation is really the stronger relation

$P1'$: $$P1 \text{ and } 2 * x^2 \geq r$$

It is too much to hope to determine for each value of x the value y, such that $x^2 + y^2 = r$, for such a value need not exist. What we can do is establish

$$x^2 + y^2 \leq r \text{ and } x^2 + (y + 1)^2 > r$$

From that relation we can conclude not only that if $x^2 + y^2 = r$, a solution of (1) has been found, but also that if $x^2 + y^2 < r$, for that value of x no value y exists that would complete the pair. Taking the relation

$P2$: $$x^2 + (y + 1)^2 > r$$

as invariant relation for an inner repetitive construct, we can program

```
"increase x under invariance of P1'":
begin glocon r; glovar xv, yv, x; privar y;
    y vir int:= x; {on account of P1', P2 has been established}
    do x² + y² > r → y:= y − 1 od; {x² + y² ≤ r and P2}
    if x² + y² = r → xv:hiext(x); yv:hiext(y); x:= x + 1
    ▯ x² + y² < r → x:= x + 1
    fi
end
```

Observing, however, that the last alternative construct will not destroy the validity of P2, we can improve the efficiency of this program considerably by taking the relation P2 outside the outer repetitive construct:

```
begin glocon r; virvar xv, yv; privar x, y;
    x vir int, y vir int:= 0, 0;
    do x² + y² < r → x, y:= x + 1, y + 1 od;
    xv vir int array, yv vir int array:= (1), (1);
    do x² ≤ r → do x² + y² > r → y:= y − 1 od;
                if x² + y² = r → xv:hiext(x); yv:hiext(y); x:= x + 1
                ▯ x² + y² < r → x:= x + 1
                fi
    od
end
```

The latter improvement is the outcome of a Search for a Small Superset, viz. for y; it has been implemented by taking a relation outside a repetitive construct, viz. relation *P2*.

Note.   Obvious improvements, such as testing whether r **mod** $4 = 3$, and exploiting the recurrence relation $(x + 1)^2 = x^2 + (2 * x + 1)$ are left as exercises.   (*End of note.*)

Remark.   The above program, which is due to W. H. J. Feijen, is distinctly superior to the program as we wrote it a few years ago, when, for instance, the demonstration that no solutions had been missed always required a drawing.   (*End of remark.*)

20 THE PROBLEM OF THE SMALLEST PRIME FACTOR OF A LARGE NUMBER

In this chapter we shall tackle the problem of finding the smallest prime factor of a large number $N > 1$ (by "large" I mean here a number of the order of magnitude of, say, 10^{16}), under the assumption that the program is intended for a small machine whose additive operations and comparisons are assumed to be very fast compared with arbitrary multiplications and divisions. (Nowadays, these assumptions are realistic for most so-called "minicomputers"; the algorithm to be described was developed years ago for what, in spite of its physical size, would now be called "a micro-computer".)

A straightforward application of the Linear Search Theorem tells us that, when looking for the smallest prime factor of N, we should investigate prime numbers as possible factors in increasing order of magnitude. Because a divisible number has at least one prime factor not exceeding its square root, the investigation need not go beyond the square root; if then still no factor has been found, the number N must be prime. An algorithm of the following structure would do the job:

```
begin glocon N; virvar p; privar f;
    f vir int:= 2;
    do N mod f ≠ 0 and f² < N →
        "increase f to the next prime number"
    od;
    if N mod f ≠ 0 → p vir int:= N
    ▯ N mod f = 0 → p vir int:= f
    fi
end
```

This algorithm, however, is "begging the question", for how do we intend to increase f to the next prime number? We have assumed a small machine and that is supposed to exclude storing a table of successive primes up to 10^8. (In a straightforward technique, that would require $5 * 10^7$ bits and that is not what is called —not even today!— "a small memory".) Instead of determining the next prime number by looking it up in a stored table, it could be computed; but the usual way to do that is, in principle, to investigate the sequence

$$f + 1, f + 2, f + 3, \ldots$$

until the first prime is found. But the investigation of whether a number is a prime is usually reduced to the question of whether it equals its smallest prime factor!

There is an absolutely unsophisticated way out of this dilemma. For $N > 1$, the smallest prime factor of N is also the smallest natural number ≥ 2, dividing N. This property gives us a method for finding the smallest prime factor of N without referring to the concept "prime number" any more

```
begin glocon N; virvar p; privar f;
    f vir int:= 2;
    do N mod f ≠ 0 and (f + 1)² ≤ N → f:= f + 1 od;
    if N mod f ≠ 0 → p vir int:= N
    ▯ N mod f = 0 → p vir int:= f
    fi
end
```

The main trouble with this algorithm is that we have only assumed that additive operations and comparisons would be fast, but have allowed the computations of $N \bmod f$ and of $(f + 1)^2$ to be so slow as to be avoided in the inner cycle, if possible.

The only way out seems to find some way of applying the technique of "taking a relation outside the repetitive construct", i.e. seeking to store and maintain such information that after the computation of $r = N \bmod f$, the computation of the next value of r (for $f + 1$) can profit from it. What can we store?

We can start with the observation that $r = N \bmod f$ is the solution of the equation

$$N = f * q + r \text{ and } 0 \leq r < f,$$

and we could store q as well. Then we know that

$$N = (f + 1) * q + (r - q)$$

and, in general, we can expect to have "gained" in the sense that $(r - q)$ will be closer to zero than the original N and, therefore, "easier" to reduce modulo $(f + 1)$. But, particularly for smaller values of f (and r) and —therefore— larger values of q, we cannot expect to have gained very much.

As far as that new value of r is concerned, viz. $(r - q) \bmod (f + 1)$, we are, however, not interested in q itself at all! Any smaller value, congruent q modulo $(f + 1)$, would be equally welcome and decreasing r by it would have disturbed it less. In other words: we would prefer to decrease r not by q but, say, by $q \bmod (f + 1)$. So why not store that? Repeating the argument, we are led to write down the equations:

$$N = f * q_0 + r_0 \qquad \text{with} \quad 0 \leq r_i < f + i$$
$$q_0 = (f + 1) * q_1 + r_1 \qquad \text{for} \quad 0 \leq i \leq n$$
$$q_1 = (f + 2) * q_2 + r_2$$
$$\vdots$$
$$q_{n-1} = (f + n) * q_n + r_n$$
$$q_n = 0.$$

Eliminating the q's we get:

$$N = r_0 +$$
$$f * r_1 +$$
$$f * (f + 1) * r_2 +$$
$$f * (f + 1) * (f + 2) * r_3 +$$
$$\vdots$$
$$f * (f + 1) * (f + 2) * \ldots * (f + n - 1) * r_n \qquad (1)$$

which clearly shows how N is fully determined by f and the finite sequence of r's.

Replacing f by $f + 1$ and compensating the increase in each line by a decrease of the term immediately above it, we get for N the alternative representation:

$$N = (r_0 - r_1) +$$
$$(f + 1) * (r_1 - 2 * r_2) +$$
$$(f + 1) * (f + 2) * (r_2 - 3 * r_3) +$$
$$(f + 1) * (f + 2) * (f + 3) * (r_3 - 4 * r_4) +$$
$$\vdots$$
$$(f + 1) * (f + 2) * (f + 3) * \ldots * (f + n) * r_n.$$

The above transformation is effected by the program

```
f:= f + 1; i:= 0;
do i < n → r_i := r_i − (i + 1)*r_{i+1}; i:= i + 1 od
```

but for the fact that it would not do the job as far as the inequalities

$$0 \leq r_i < f + i$$

are concerned: r's could become negative. But this is easily remedied, because
(1) shows that an increase $r_0 := r_0 + f$ can be compensated by a decrease
$r_1 := r_1 - 1$. In general: $r_i := r_i + (f + i)$ is compensated by $r_{i+1} := r_{i+1} - 1$.
As a result, the complete transformation is correctly described by

$$f := f + 1; i := 0;$$
$$\textbf{do } i < n \rightarrow$$
$$\qquad r_i := r_i - (i + 1) * r_{i+1};$$
$$\qquad \textbf{do } r_i < 0 \rightarrow$$
$$\qquad\qquad r_i := r_i + (f + i); r_{i+1} := r_{i+1} - 1$$
$$\qquad \textbf{od};$$
$$\qquad i := i + 1$$
$$\textbf{od};$$
$$\textbf{do } r_n = 0 \rightarrow n := n - 1 \textbf{ od}$$

Under the assumption that multiplication by small integers presents no
serious problems —that could be done by repeated addition— the computation of successive values of N **mod** f has been reduced to the repertoire of
admissible operations. Furthermore, the test ($f^2 < N$ in our earliest version,
$(f + 1)^2 \leq N$ in our next version) whether it is still worthwhile to proceed or
that the square root has been reached, can be replaced by $n > 1$, for $(n \leq 1)$
$\Rightarrow (N < (f + 1)^2)$.

With $ar(k) = r_k$ for $0 \leq k \leq ar.hib$, we arrive at the following program:

```
begin glocon N; virvar p; privar f, ar;
    begin glocon N; virvar ar; privar x, y;
        ar vir int array:= (0); x vir int, y vir int:= N, 2;
        do x ≠ 0 → ar:hiext(x mod y); x, y:= x div y, y + 1 od
    end {ar has been initialized};
    f vir int:= 2 {relation (1) has been established};
    do ar(0) ≠ 0 and ar.hib > 1 →
        begin glovar f, ar; privar i;
            f:= f + 1; i vir int:= 0;
            do i ≠ ar.hib →
                begin glocon f; glovar ar, i; pricon j;
                    j vir int:= i + 1; ar:(i) = ar(i) − j * ar(j);
                    do ar(i) < 0 → ar:(i) = ar(i) + f + i;
                                    ar:(j) = ar(j) − 1
                    od;
                    i:= j
                end
```

```
        od
     end;
       do ar.high = 0 ⟶ ar:hirem od
   od;
   if ar(0) = 0 ⟶ p vir int:= f
   ▯ ar(0) ≠ 0 ⟶ p vir int:= N
   fi
end
```

Remark 1.   One might think that the algorithm could be speeded up by a factor *2* by separately dealing with even values of *N* and with odd values of *N*. For the latter we then could restrict the sequence of *f*-values to *3, 5, 7, 9, 11, 13, 15,* . . . ; the analogy of

$$r_i := r_i - (i + 1)*r_{i+1}$$

then becomes

$$r_i := r_i - 2*(i + 1)* r_{i+1}$$

and this more violent disturbance will cause the next loop, which has to bring r_i within range again, to be repeated on the average about twice as many times. The change is hardly an improvement and has mainly the effect of messing up the formulae.   (*End of remark 1.*)

Remark 2.   A well-known technique for discovering where to invest one's energy optimizing code is executing a program by an implementation that, upon completion of the computation, will print the complete histogram, indicating how many times each statement has been executed: it tells where one should optimize. If that technique is applied to this program, it will indicate that the innermost loop, bringing $ar(i)$ again within range, absorbs most of the computation time, particularly when the operations on and functions of the array variable are relatively time-consuming. In this example, this information is not only trivial, but also misleading in the sense that one should **not** decide to start optimizing that inner loop! (Optimizing it, reducing the number of "subscriptions", is easily done by introducing two scalar variables, *ari* and *arj*, equal to $ar(i)$ and $ar(j)$ respectively, but again it makes the text longer and more messy.) The point is that the computation is only time-consuming if *N* is prime or its smallest prime factor is near its square root. In that case we shall have for the major part of the computation time *ar.hib* = 2 (i.e. as soon as *f* has passed the cube root of *N*). The technique is to replace in the outer loop the guard by

$$ar(0) \neq 0 \text{ and } ar.hib > 2$$

and to deal in the final stage with three scalar variables *r0*, *r1*, and *r2*. In the coding of that final stage one can then invest all one's ingenuity.

(*End of remark 2.*)

Remark 3.   If the outcome of this computation is $p = N$, that result is very hard to check. Even in the face of a computer which is not ultra-reliable, this algorithm gives us the opportunity to increase the confidence level of the result considerably: upon completion, the relation $N = f * r_1 + r_0$ should hold! If somewhere in the arithmetic something has gone wrong, it is highly improbable that, in spite of that, the last equality eventually holds. From the point of view of reliability this algorithm, all the time computing the new r's as a function of all the old ones, is far superior to the one that selects the next prime number as trial factor from a table: the table may be corrupted and, besides that, each divisibility test is a completely isolated computation. It seems worth noticing that this tremendous gain in safety has been made possible by "taking a relation outside the repetitive construct" and by nothing else. The algorithm described in this chapter has not only been used to produce highly reliable factorizations (of the type $p = N$), it has also been used to check the reliability of a machine's arithmetic unit.

(*End of remark 3.*)

Consolation.   Those of my readers who found this a difficult chapter will be pleased to hear that it took even my closest collaborators more than an hour to digest it: programs can be very compact.   (*End of consolation.*)

21

THE PROBLEM OF THE MOST ISOLATED VILLAGES

We consider n villages $(n > 1)$, numbered from 0 through $n - 1$; for $0 \leq i < n$ and $0 \leq j < n$, a computable function $f(i, j)$ is given, satisfying for some given positive constant M:

$$\text{for } i \neq j : 0 < f(i, j) < M$$

$$\text{for } i = j : f(i, j) = M$$

For the ith village, its isolation degree "id(i)" is given by

$$\text{id}(i) = \underset{j \neq i}{\text{minimum}} f(i, j) = \underset{j}{\text{minimum}} f(i, j)$$

(Here $f(i, j)$ can be interpreted as the distance from i to j; the rule $f(i, i) = M$ has been added for the purpose of the above simplification.)

We are requested to determine the set of maximally isolated villages, i.e. the set of all values of k such that

$$(\text{A } h: 0 \leq h < n: \text{id}(h) \leq \text{id}(k)).$$

The program is expected to deliver this set of values as

$$miv(miv.lob), \ldots, miv(miv.hib)$$

Note that eventually all values $1 \leq miv.dom \leq n$ are possible.

A very simple and straightforward program computes the n isolation degrees in succession and keeps track of their maximum value found thus far. On account of the bounds for $f(i, j)$ we can take as the minimum of an empty set the value M and as the maximum of an empty set 0.

149

begin glocon n, M; **virvar** miv; **privar** max, i;
miv **vir** int **array** $:= (0)$; max **vir** int, i **vir** $int := 0, 0$;
do $i \neq n \longrightarrow$
begin glocon n, M; **glovar** miv, max, i; **privar** min, j;
min **vir** int, j **vir** $int := M, 0$;
do $j \neq n \longrightarrow$
  do $f(i, j) < min \longrightarrow min := f(i, j)$ **od**;
  $j := j + 1$
od $\{min = \text{id}(i)\}$;
if $max > min \longrightarrow skip$
  〚 $max = min \longrightarrow miv:hiext(i)$
  〚 $max < min \longrightarrow miv := (0, i)$; $max := min$
fi;
$i := i + 1$
end
od
end

The above is a very unsophisticated program: in the innermost loop the value of *min* is monotonically nonincreasing in time, and the following alternative construct will react equivalently to *any* value of *min* satisfying $min < max$. Combining these two observations, we conclude that there is only a point in continuing the innermost repetition as long as $min \geq max$. We can replace the line "**do** $j \neq n \longrightarrow$" therefore by

"**do** $j \neq n$ **and** $min \geq max \longrightarrow$"

and the assertion after the corresponding **od** by

$\{\text{id}(i) \leq min < max \text{ **or** } \text{id}(i) = min \geq max\}$.

Let us call the above modification "Optimization 1".
   A very different optimization is possible if it is given that

$$f(i, j) = f(j, i)$$

and, because the computation of f is assumed to be time-consuming, it is requested never to compute $f(i, j)$ for such values of the argument that $f(j, i)$ has already been computed. Starting from our original program we can achieve that for each unordered argument pair the corresponding f-value will only be computed once by initializing j each time with $i + 1$ instead of with 0 —only scanning the upper triangle of the symmetric distance matrix, so to speak. The program is then only guaranteed to compute *min* correctly provided that we initialize *min* instead of with M with

$$\underset{0 \leq h < i}{\text{minimum}} f(i, h)$$

This can be catered for by introducing an array, b say, such that for k satisfying $i \leq k < n$:

$$\text{for } i = 0 : b(k) = M$$
$$\text{for } i > 0 : b(k) = \underset{0 \leq h < i}{\text{minimum}} f(k, h)$$

(In words: $b(k)$ is the minimum distance connecting village k that has been computed thus far.)

The result of Optimization 2 is also fairly straightforward.

```
begin glocon n, M; virvar miv; privar max, i, b;
  miv vir int array := (0); max vir int, i vir int := 0, 0;
  b vir int array := (0); do b.dom ≠ n → b:hiext(M) od;
  do i ≠ n →
  begin glocon n; glovar miv, max, i, b; privar min, j;
    min vir int, b:lopop; j vir int := i + 1;
    do j ≠ n →
    begin glocon i; glovar min, j, b; privar ff;
      ff vir int := f(i, j);
      do ff < min → min:= ff od;
      do ff < b(j) → b:(j)= ff od;
      j:= j + 1
    end
    od {min = id(i)};
    if max > min → skip
    ▯ max = min → miv:hiext(i)
    ▯ max < min → miv:= (0, i); max:= min
    fi;
    i:= i + 1
  end
  od
end
```

To try to combine these two optimizations presents a problem. In Optimization 1 the scanning of a row of the distance matrix is aborted if min has become small enough; in Optimization 2, however, the scanning of the row is also the scanning of a column and that is done to keep the values of $b(k)$ up to date. Let us apply Optimization 1 and replace the line "do $j \neq n \rightarrow$" by

$$\text{"do } j \neq n \text{ and } min \geq max \rightarrow \text{"}$$

The innermost loop can now terminate with $j < n$; the values $b(k)$ with $j \leq k < n$ for which updating is still of possible interest are now the ones with $b(k) \geq max$, the other ones are already small enough. The following insertion will do the job:

```
do j ≠ n →
    if b(j) < max → j:= j + 1
    ▯ b(j) ≥ max →
        begin glocon i; glovar j, b; privar ff;
            ff vir int := f(i, j);
            do ff < b(j) → b:(j)= ff od;
            j:= j + 1
        end
    fi
od
```

The best place for this insertion is immediately preceding "$i:= i + 1$", but after the adjustment of max; the higher max, the larger the probability that a $b(k)$ does not need any more adjustments.

The two optimizations that we have combined are of a vastly different nature. Optimization 2 is just "avoiding redoing work known to have been done", and its effectiveness is known a priori. Optimization 1, however, is a strategy whose effectiveness depends on the unknown values of f: it is just one of the many possible strategies in the same vein.

We are looking for those rows of the distance matrix whose minimum element value S exceeds the minimum elements of the remaining rows and the idea of Optimization 1 is that for that purpose we do not need to compute for the remaining rows the actual minimum if we can find for each row an upper bound B_i for its minimum, such that $B_i < S$. In an intermediate stage of the computation, for some row(s) the minimum S is known because all its/their elements have been computed; for other rows we only know an upper bound B_i. And now the strategic freedom is quite clear: do we first compute the smallest number of additional matrix elements still needed to determine a new minimum, in the hope that it will be larger than the minimum we had and, therefore, may exceed a few more B's? Or do we first compute unknown elements in rows with a high B in the hope of cheaply decreasing that upper bound? Or any mixture?

My original version combining the two strategies postponed the "updating of the remaining $b(k)$" somewhat longer, in the hope that in the meantime max would have grown still further, but whether it was a more efficient program than the one published in this chapter is subject to doubt. It was certainly more complicated, needing yet another array for storing a sequence of village numbers. The published version was only discovered when writing this chapter.

In retrospect I consider my ingenuity spent on my original program as wasted: if it was "more efficient" it could only be so "on the average". But on what average? Such an average is only defined provided that we postulate —quite arbitrarily!— a probability distribution for the distance matrix $f(i, j)$. On the other hand it was not my intention to tailor the algorithm to a specific subclass of distance matrices!

The moral of the story is that, in making a general program, we should hesitate to yield to the temptation to incorporate the smart strategy that would improve the performance in cases that might never occur, if such incorporation complicates the program notably: simplicity of the program is a less ambiguous target. (The problem is that we are often so proud of our smart strategies that it hurts to abandon them.)

Remark. Our final program combines two ideas and we have found it by first considering —as "stepping stones", so to speak— two programs, each incorporating one of them, but not the other. In many instances I found such stepping stones most helpful. (*End of remark.*)

22

THE PROBLEM OF THE SHORTEST SUBSPANNING TREE

Two points can be connected by one point-to-point connection; three points can be interconnected by two point-to-point connections; in general, N points can be fully interconnected by $N - 1$ point-to-point connections. Such a set of interconnections is called a "tree" or, if we wish to stress that it connects the N points to each other, a "subspanning tree" and the connections are called "its branches". Cayley has been the first to prove that the number of different possible trees between N given points equals N^{N-2}. (Verify this for $N = 4$, but not for $N = 5$.)

We now assume that the length of each of the $N*(N - 1)/2$ possible branches has been given. Defining the length of a tree as the sum of the lengths of its branches, we can ask ourselves how to determine the shortest tree between those N points. (For the time being, we assume that the given lengths are such that the shortest tree is unique.)

Note. The points are not necessarily in a Euclidean plane; the given lengths need not have any relation to a Euclidean distance. (*End of note.*)

An apparently straightforward solution would generate all trees between the N points, would determine their lengths, and select the shortest one. But Cayley's theorem tells us that, as N increases, this rapidly becomes very expensive, even prohibitively so. We would like to find a more efficient algorithm.

When faced with such a problem (we have already done so quite explicitly when solving the problem of the Dutch national flag), it is often very instructive, keeping in mind that we try to design a sequential algorithm, to consider what intermediate states of the computation to expect. As our final answer consists of $N - 1$ branches whose membership of the shortest tree will —

hopefully— be established in turn, we are led to investigate what we can say when a number of branches of the shortest tree are known.

Immediately we are faced with the choice whether we shall consider the general case in which an arbitrary subset of these branches is known, or whether we confine our attention to certain types of subsets only, in the hope that these will turn out to be the only subsets that will occur in our computation and, also, that this restriction will simplify our analysis. This is at least a choice that presents itself if we can think of a natural type of subset. In this example, the natural type of subset that suggests itself is that the known branches, instead of being randomly distributed over the points, themselves already form a tree. As this special case indeed seems simpler than the general one, we rephrase our question. Is there anything helpful that we can say when a subtree of the shortest subspanning tree is known?

For the sake of this discussion we colour red the branches of the known subtree and the points connected by it and colour all remaining points blue. Can we then think of a branch that must belong to the shortest tree as well? Because the final tree connects all points with each other, the final tree must contain at least one branch connecting a red point to a blue one. Let us call the branches between a red point and a blue one "the violet branches". The obvious conjecture is that the shortest violet branch belongs to the shortest tree as well.

The correctness of this conjecture is easily proved. Consider a tree T between the N points that contains all the red branches but not the shortest violet one. Add the shortest violet branch to it. This closes a a cycle with at least one red and at least one blue point, a cycle which, therefore, contains at least one other (and longer) violet branch. Remove such a longer violet branch from the cycle. The resulting graph is again a tree. In tree T we have replaced a longer violet branch by a shorter one, and, therefore, tree T cannot have been the shortest one. (A tree between N points is a graph with the following three properties:

1. It interconnects the N points.
2. It has $N - 1$ branches.
3. It has no cycles.

Any two of these properties imply that the graph is a tree and, therefore, also enjoys the third property.)

But now we have the framework for an algorithm, provided that we can find an initial subtree to colour red. Once we have that, we can select the shortest violet branch, colour it and its blue endpoint red, etc., letting the red tree grow until there are no more blue points. To start the process, it suffices to colour an arbitrary point red:

```
colour an arbitrary point red and
the remaining points blue;
do number of red points ≠ N →
    select the shortest now violet branch;
    colour it and its blue endpoint red
od
```

As it stands, the main task will be: "select the shortest now violet branch", because the number of violet branches may be quite large, viz. $k*(N-k)$, where k = number of red points. If "select the shortest now violet branch" were executed as an isolated operation, it would require on the average a number of comparisons proportional to N^2 and the amount of work to be done by the algorithm as a whole would grow as N^3. Observing, however, that the operation "select the shortest now violet branch" does not occur in isolation, but as component of a repetitive construct, we should ask ourselves whether we can apply the technique of "taking a relation outside the repetitive construct", i.e. whether we can arrange matters in such a way that subsequent executions of "select the shortest now violet branch" may profit from the preceding one. There is considerable hope that this may be possible, because one set of violet branches is closely related to the next: the set of violet branches is defined by the way in which the points have been partitioned in red ones and blue ones, and this partitioning is each time only changed by painting one blue point red.

Hoping for a drastic reduction in searching time when selecting the shortest branch from a set means hoping to reduce the size of that set; in other words, what we are looking for is a *subset* of the violet branches —call it the "ultraviolet" ones— that will contain the shortest one and can be used to transmit helpful information from one selection to the next. We are envisaging a program of the structure:

```
colour an arbitrary point red
and the remaining ones blue;
determine the set of ultraviolet branches;
do number of red points ≠ N →
    select the shortest now ultraviolet branch;
    colour it and its blue endpoint red;
    adjust the set of ultraviolet branches
od
```

where the notion "ultraviolet" should be chosen in such a way that:

1. It is guaranteed that the shortest violet branch is among the ultraviolet ones.

2. The set of ultraviolet branches is, on the average, much smaller than the set of violet ones.

3. The operation "adjust the set of ultraviolet branches" is relatively cheap.

(We require the first property because then our new algorithm is correct as well; we require the second and the third properties because we would like our new algorithm to be more efficient than the old one.)

Can we find such a definition of the notion "ultraviolet"? Well, for lack of further knowledge, I can only suggest that we try. Considering that the set of violet branches leading from k red points to $N - k$ blue points, has $k*(N - k)$ members, and observing our first criterion, two obvious possible subsets immediately present themselves:

1. Make for each red point the shortest violet branch ending in it ultraviolet; the set of ultraviolet branches has then k members.

2. Make for each blue point the shortest violet branch ending in it ultraviolet; the set of ultraviolet branches has then $N - k$ members.

Our aim is to keep the ultraviolet subset small, but we won't get a clue from their sizes: for the first choice the size will run from 1 through $N - 1$, for the second choice it will be the other way round. So, if there is any chance of deciding, we must find it in the price of the operation "adjust the set of ultraviolet branches".

Without trying different adjustments, however, there is one observation that suggests a strong preference for the second choice. In the first choice, different ultraviolet branches may lead to the same blue point and then we know a priori that at most one of them will be coloured red; with the second choice each blue point is connected in only one way to the red tree, i.e. red and ultraviolet branches form all the time a subspanning tree between the N points. Let us therefore explore the consequences of the second definition for our notion "ultraviolet".

Consider the stage in which we had a red subtree R and in which from the set of corresponding ultraviolet branches (according to the second definition; I shall no longer repeat that qualification) the shortest one and its originally blue endpoint P have been coloured red. The number of ultraviolet branches has been decreased by 1 as it should be. But, are the remaining ones the correct ones? They represent for each blue point the shortest possible connection to the originally red tree R, they should represent the shortest possible connection to the new red tree $R + P$. But this question is settled by means of one simple comparison for each blue point B: if the branch BP is shorter than the ultraviolet branch connecting B to R, the latter is to be replaced by BP, otherwise it is maintained as, apparently, the growth of the red tree did not result in a shorter way of connecting B with it. As a result, both selection of the shortest ultraviolet branch and adjustment of the set of ultraviolet ones have become operations in price proportional to N, the price of the total algorithm grows with N^2 and the introduction of this concept "ultraviolet" has, indeed, accomplished the savings we were hoping for.

EXERCISE

Convince yourself that the rejected alternative for the concept "ultraviolet" is not so helpful. (*End of exercise.*)

Because "adjust the set of ultraviolet branches" implies checking for each ultraviolet branch whether it has to be kept or has to be replaced, it is tempting to combine this process with the selection of the shortest one of the adjusted set into one single loop. Instead of transmitting the adjusted set of ultraviolet branches to the next repetition, we shall transmit the unadjusted set together with the "*lcr*", the ordinal number of the point lastly coloured red. The initialization problem can be solved nicely if we know that all branches have a length $< inf$; we shall assume the knowledge of this constant available and shall initialize the ultraviolet branches of the unadjusted set all with length inf (and connect the blue points to a hypothetical point with ordinal number 0).

We assume the N given points numbered from 1 through N, and we assume the length of the branch between points p and q given by the symmetric function "$dist(p, q)$". The answer required is a tree of $N - 1$ branches, each branch being identified by the ordinal numbers of its endpoints; the answer is an (unordered) set of (unordered) pairs. We shall represent them by two arrays, "*from*" and "*to*" respectively, such that for $1 \leq h \leq N - 1$ "*from(h)*" and "*to(h)*" are the (ordinal numbers of the) two endpoints of the hth branch. In our final answer the branches will be ordered (by h); the only order that makes sense is the order in which they have been coloured red. This suggests to use, during our computation, the arrays "*from*" and "*to*" for representing the ultraviolet branches as well, with the aid of the convention that

for $1 \leq h < k$: the hth branch is red
for $k \leq h < N$: the hth branch is ultraviolet.

A local array uvl ("ultraviolet length") is introduced in order to avoid recomputation of lengths of ultraviolet branches, i.e. we shall maintain

for $k \leq h < N$: $uvl(h) = $ length of the hth branch.

Furthermore, because there is a one-to-one correspondence between ultraviolet branches and blue points, we can represent which points are blue by means of the convention that the hth ultraviolet branch connects the red point "*from(h)*" with the blue point "*to(h)*".

In the following program, point N is chosen as the arbitrary point that is initially coloured red.

Note. With respect to the array "*from*" and the scalar variable "*suv*" one could argue that we have not been able to avoid meaningless initializations; they refer, however, to a virtual point 0 at a distance "*inf*" from all the others and to an equally virtual 0th ultraviolet branch. (*End of note.*)

```
begin glocon N, inf; virvar from, to; privar uvl, k, lcr;
    from vir int array := (I); to vir int array := (I);
    uvl vir int array := (I);
    do from.dom ≠ N − 1 →
        from:hiext(0); to:hiext(from.dom); uvl:hiext(inf)
    od;
    k vir int, lcr vir int := 1, N;
    do k ≠ N →
    begin glocon N, inf; glovar from, to, uvl, k, lcr; privar suv, min, h;
        suv vir int, min vir int, h vir int := 0, inf, k;
        do h ≠ N →
        begin glocon to, lcr; glovar from, uvl, suv, min, h; privar len;
        len vir int:= dist(lcr, to(h));
        if len ≤ uvl(h) → uvl:(h)= len; from:(h)= lcr
        ▯ len ≥ uvl(h) → len:= uvl(h)
        fi {len = uvl(h)};
        do len < min → min:= len; suv:= h od {min = uvl(suv)};
        h:= h + 1
        end
    od {the suv-th branch is the shortest ultraviolet one};
    from:swap(k, suv); to:swap(k, suv); uvl:swap(k, suv);
    lcr:= to(k); k:= k + 1; uvl:lorem
    end
    od
end
```

In spite of the simplicity of the final program —it is not much more than a loop inside a loop— the algorithm it embodies is generally not regarded as a trivial one. It is, as a matter of fact, well-known for being highly efficient, both with respect to its storage utilization and with respect to the number of comparisons of branch lengths that are performed. It may, therefore, be rewarding to review the major steps that led to its ultimate discovery.

The first crucial choice has been to try to restrict ourselves to such intermediate states that the red branches, i.e. the ones known to belong to the final answer, always form a tree by themselves. The clerical gain is that then the number of red points exceeds the number of red branches by exactly one and that we are allowed to conclude that a branch leading from one red point to another is *never* a candidate for being coloured red: it would erroneously close a cycle. (And now we see an alternative algorithm: sort all branches in the order of increasing length and process them in that order, where processing means if the branch, together with the red branches, forms a cycle, reject it, otherwise colour it red. Obviously, this algorithm establishes the membership of the final answer for the red branches in the order of increasing length. The algorithm is less attractive because, firstly, we have to sort all the branches and, secondly, the determination of whether a new branch will close a cycle is not too attractive either. That problem will be the subject of a next chapter.) The moral of the story is that the effort to reach the final goal via "simple" intermediate states is usually worth trying!

A second crucial step was the formulation of the conjecture that the shortest violet branch could be painted red as well. Again, that conjecture has not been pulled out of a magic hat; if we wish to "grow" a red tree, a violet branch is what we should be looking for, and the fact that then the shortest one is a likely candidate is hardly surprising.

The decision not to be content with an N^3-algorithm —a decision which led to the notion "ultraviolet"— is sometimes felt to be the most unexpected one. People argue: "But suppose that it had not entered my head to investigate whether I could find a better algorithm?" Well, that decision came at a moment that we *had* an algorithm, and the mathematical analysis of the original problem essentially had been done. It was only an optimization for which, for instance, no further knowledge of graph theory was anymore required! Besides that, it was an optimization that followed a well-known pattern: taking a relation outside the loop. The moral of the story is that once one has an algorithm, one should not be content with it too soon, but investigate whether it can still be massaged. When one has made such reconsiderations a habit, it is unlikely that the notion of "ultraviolet" would in this example have escaped one's attention.

Note. It follows from the algorithm that the shortest subspanning tree is unique if no two different branches have equal lengths. Verify that if there is more than one shortest subspanning tree, our algorithm may construct any of them. (*End of note.*)

A very different algorithm places the branches in arbitrary order, but, whenever after placement of a branch, a cycle is formed, the (or a) longest branch of that cycle is removed before the next branch is placed.

23

REM'S ALGORITHM
FOR THE RECORDING
OF EQUIVALENCE CLASSES

In a general graph (which need not be a tree) the points are usually called "vertices" and the connections are usually called "edges" rather than branches. A graph is called "connected" if and only if it contains only one vertex or its edges provide at least one path between any two different vertices from it. Because many of the possible edges of a graph with N vertices may be missing, a graph need not be connected. But each graph, connected or not, can always be partitioned uniquely into connected subgraphs, i.e. the vertices of the graph can be partitioned in subsets, such that any pair from the same subset is connected, while the edges provide no path between any two vertices taken from two different subsets. (For the mathematicians: "being connected" is a reflexive, symmetric, and transitive relation, which, therefore, generates equivalence classes.)

We consider N vertices, numbered from 0 through $N - 1$, where N is supposed to be large ($10,000$, say), and a sequence of graphs $G_0, G_1, G_2, \ldots$ which result from connecting these vertices via the edges of the sets E_0, $E_1, E_2, \ldots$, where E_0 is empty and $E_{i+1} = E_i + \{e_i\}$ and $e_0, e_1, e_2, \ldots$ is a given sequence of edges. The edges $e_0, e_1, e_2, \ldots$ have to be processed in that order and when n of them have been processed (i.e. the last edge processed, if any, is e_{n-1}) we must be able to determine for any pair of vertices whether they are connected in G_n or not. The main problem to be solved in this chapter is: "How do we store the relevant information as derived from the edge sequence $e_0, e_1, \ldots, e_{n-1}$?"

We could, of course, store the edge sequence "$e_0, e_1, \ldots, e_{n-1}$" itself, but that is not a very practical solution. For, firstly, it stores a lot of irrelevant information; e.g. if the edges $\{7, 8\}$ and $\{12, 7\}$ have been processed, a new edge $\{12, 8\}$ does not tell us anything new! And, secondly, the answer to the

161

question "Are vertices p and q connected?" —our goal!— is deeply hidden.

At the other extreme we could store the complete connectivity matrix, i.e. N^2 bits (or, if we exploit its symmetry, $N*(N+1)/2$ bits), such that the question whether p and q are connected is the stored boolean value $\text{conn}_{p,q}$. (The fact that we talk about a matrix, while the array variable more resembles a vector, need not bother us; we could use an array variable, "*acon*" say, and maintain

$$\text{conn}_{p,q} = acon(N*p+q) \qquad \text{for } 0 \leq p < N \text{ and } 0 \leq q < N.)$$

I called this "the other extreme" because it stores indeed the readymade answer to any possible question of the form "Are vertices p and q connected?"; but it stores too much, because many of these answers are in general not independent of each other. The decision to store the information in such a redundant form should not be taken lightly, because the more redundant information we store, the more may have to be updated when a new edge has to be processed.

A more compact way to represent which vertices are connected to each other is to name (for instance, to number) the subsets of the current partitioning. Then the question whether vertex p is connected to vertex q boils down to the question of whether they belong to the same subset, i.e. to the value of the boolean expression

$$subset(p) = subset(q)$$

Because there are at most N different subsets, this does not require more than $N*{}_2\log(N)$ bits (compared to the N^2 of the complete connectivity matrix).

To answer the question whether p and q are connected, an array variable storing the function "*subset*" would be extremely helpful, but . . . its updating can be very painful! For, suppose that $subset(p) = P$ and $subset(q) = Q$ with $P \neq Q$ and suppose that the next edge to be processed is $\{p, q\}$. As a result, the two subsets have to be combined into a single one and, if the subsets are already large, that requires a lot of updating. Besides that, if the array variable "*subset*" is the only thing we have, how do we find, for instance, all values of k such that $subset(k) = Q$ (assuming that P will be the name of the new subset formed by the combination) otherwise than by scanning the function "*subset*" over its complete domain?

The way out of this dilemma is not to store the function "*subset*", but a different function, "*f*" say, with the properties that

1. For given value of p, the knowledge of the function f allows, at least on the average, an easy computation of the value $subset(p)$.
2. The processing of a new edge $\{p, q\}$ allows, at least on the average, an easy updating of the function f.

Can we invent such a function?

Because the primary information given by a new edge to be processed is that from now on the one vertex belongs to the same subset as the other one, it is suggested to store a function f, with $f(k)$ meaning

"vertex $nr.$ k belongs to the same subset as vertex $nr.$ $f(k)$"

i.e. the argument of f and the function value of f are both interpreted as vertex numbers.

Because, at the beginning, E_0 is empty, each vertex is then the only member of the subset it belongs to, and this function, therefore, must be initialized:

$$f(k) = k \qquad \text{for } 0 \leq k < N$$

and the most natural nomenclature for the N different subsets is then the number of the only vertex it contains. The obvious generalization to subsets of more vertices is that each subset will be identified by the vertex number of one of the vertices it contains —which one need not be considered now; with this convention, we can now consider a function f such that

if $f(k) = k$, vertex $nr.$ k belongs to subset $nr.$ k, and
if $f(k) \neq k$, vertex $nr.$ k belongs to the same subset as vertex
$\quad nr.$ $f(k)$.

Repeated computation of the function f will lead us from one vertex of the subset to another vertex of the same subset. If we can see to it that this will not lead us into a cycle before we have been led to the "identifying vertex of the subset", i.e. the one whose number has been inherited by the subset as a whole, the knowledge of the function f will indeed enable us to compute $subset(p)$ for any value of p.

More precisely, with the notational convention

$$f^0(p) = p,$$

and for $i > 0$

$$f^i(p) = f(f^{i-1}(p))$$

there exists for a vertex p belonging to subset ps a value j such that

for $i < j$: $\qquad\qquad\qquad f^i(p) \neq ps$
for $i \geq j$: $\qquad\qquad\qquad f^i(p) = ps$

From this it follows that for $0 \leq j1 < j2 \leq j: f^{j1}(p) \neq f^{j2}(p)$ and

"ps **vir** $int := p$; **do** $ps \neq f(ps) \rightarrow ps := f(ps)$ **od**"

will terminate with $ps = subset(p)$.

The fact that the function f leads —possibly after repeated application— for all points of subset $nr.$ qs to the same identifying vertex $nr.$ qs, merging that subset with subset $nr.$ ps and identifying the result with $nr.$ ps only requires a minute change in the function f; instead of $f(qs) = qs$, eventually

$f(qs) = ps$ should hold. Processing the edge $\{p, q\}$ can therefore be done by the following inner block:

> **begin glocon** p,q; **glovar** f; **privar** ps, qs;
> ps **vir** $int := p$; **do** $ps \neq f(ps) \longrightarrow ps := f(ps)$ **od**; $\{ps = subset(p)\}$
> qs **vir** $int := q$; **do** $qs \neq f(qs) \longrightarrow qs := f(qs)$ **od**; $\{qs = subset(q)\}$
> $f:(qs) = ps$
> **end**

Although correct, the above processing of a new edge is not too attractive, as its worst case performance can become very bad: the cycles may have to be repeated very many times. It seems advisable to "clean up the tree"; for both vertex p and vertex q we now know the current identifying vertex and it seems a pity to trace those paths possibly over and over again. To remedy this situation, we offer the following inner block (we have also incorporated an effort to reduce the number of f-evaluations)

> **begin glocon** p, q; **glovar** f; **pricon** ps;
> **begin glocon** p, f; **virvar** ps; **privar** $ps0$;
> $ps0$ **vir** int, ps **vir** $int := p, f(p)$;
> **do** $ps0 \neq ps \longrightarrow ps0, ps := ps, f(ps)$ **od**
> **end** $\{ps = subset(p)\}$;
> **begin glocon** p, ps; **glovar** f; **privar** $ps0, ps1$;
> $ps0$ **vir** int, $ps1$ **vir** $int := p, f(p)$;
> **do** $ps0 \neq ps1 \longrightarrow f:(ps0) = ps$; $ps0, ps1 := ps1, f(ps1)$ **od**
> **end** {vertices encountered from *nr. p* "cleaned up"};
> **begin glocon** q, ps; **glovar** f; **privar** $qs0, qs1$;
> $qs0$ **vir** int, $qs1$ **vir** $int := q, f(q)$;
> **do** $qs0 \neq qs1 \longrightarrow f:(qs0) = ps$; $qs0, qs1 := qs1, f(qs1)$ **od**;
> $f:(qs0) = ps$
> **end** {vertices encountered from *nr. q* "cleaned up" and the
> whole subset combined with *nr. ps*}
> **end**

EXERCISES

1. Give a more formal proof of the correctness of the above algorithm.

2. We have quite arbitrarily decided that *subset*(p) would remain unchanged and that *subset*(q) would be redefined. Can you exploit this freedom to advantage?

(End of exercises.)

The above algorithm has not been included for its beauty. As a matter of fact, I would not be amazed if it left the majority of my readers dissatisfied. It is, for instance, annoying that it is not a trivial task to estimate how much we have gained by going from the first to the second version. It has been included for two other reasons.

Firstly, it gave me in a nicely compact setting the opportunity to discuss alternative ways for representing information and to illustrate the various economic considerations. Secondly, it is worthwhile to point out that we allow as intermediate state a nonunique representation of the (unique) current partitioning and allow the further destruction of irrelevant information to be postponed until a more convenient moment arrives. I have encountered such use of nonunique representations as the basis for a few, otherwise very surprising, inventions.

When M. Rem read the above text, he became very pensive —my solution, indeed, left him very dissatisfied— and shortly afterwards he showed me another solution. Rem's algorithm is in a few respects such a beauty that I could not resist the temptation to include it as well. (The following reasoning about it is the result of a joint effort, in which W.H.J. Feijen participated as well.)

In the previous solution it is not good form that, starting at p, the path to the root of that tree is traced twice, once to determine ps, and then, with the knowledge of ps, a second time in order to clean it up. Furthermore it destroys the symmetry between p and q.

The two scans of the path from p were necessary because we wanted to perform a complete cleaning up of it. Without knowing the number of the identifying vertex we could, however, at least do a partial cleaning up in a single scan, if we knew a *direction* towards "a cleaner tree". It is therefore suggested to exploit the ordering relation between the vertex numbers and to choose for each subset as identifying vertex number, say, the *minimum* value; then, the smaller the f-values, the cleaner the tree. Because initially $f(k) = k$ for all k and our target has now become to decrease f-values, we should restrict ourselves to representations of the partitioning satisfying

$$f(k) \leq k \qquad \text{for } 0 \leq k < N.$$

This restriction has the further advantage that it is now obvious that the only cycles present are the stationary points for which $f(k) = k$ (i.e. the identifying vertices).

For the purpose of a more precise treatment we introduce the following notation: a function "*part*" and a binary operator "$".

$part(f)$ denotes the partitioning represented by f
$part(f)\$(p, q)$ denotes the partitioning resulting when in $part(f)$ the subset containing p and the subset containing q are combined into a single one. If and only if in $part(f)$ the vertices p and q are already in the same subset, we have

$$part(f) = part(f)\$(p, q)$$

Denoting the initial value of f by f_{init}, the processing of an edge (p, q) can be described as establishing the relation

R: $$part(f) = part(f_{init})\$(p, q)$$

This is done (in the usual fashion!) by introducing two local variables, $p0$ and $q0$ say, (or, if you prefer, a local edge) satisfying the relation

P: $$part(f)\$(p0, q0) = part(f_{init})\$(p, q)$$

which is trivially established by the initialization

$$p0 \text{ vir } int, q0 \text{ vir } int := p, q$$

After the establishment of P the algorithm should massage f, $p0$, and $q0$ under invariance of P until we can conclude that

Q: $$part(f) = part(f)\$(p0, q0)$$

holds, as $(Q \text{ and } P) \Rightarrow R$.

Relation R has in general many solutions for f, but the cleaner the one we can get, the better; it is therefore proposed to look for a massaging process such that each step decreases at least one f-value. Then termination is ensured (as monotonically decreasing variant function we can take the sum of the N f-values) and we must try to find enough steps such that BB, the disjunction of the guards, is weak enough so that $(\text{non } BB) \Rightarrow Q$.

We can change the value of the function f in point $p0$, say, by

$$f: (p0) = \text{something}$$

but in order to ensure an effective decrease of the variant function, that "something" must be smaller than the original value of $f(p0)$, i.e. smaller than $p1$ if we introduce

$P1$: $$p1 = f(p0) \quad \text{and} \quad q1 = f(q0)$$

(The second term has been introduced for reasons of symmetry.)

Because $part(f)\$(p0, q0)$ has to remain constant, obvious candidates for the "something" are $q0$ and $q1$; but because $q1 \leq q0$, the choice $q1$ will in general be more effective, and we are led to consider

$$q1 < p1 \rightarrow f: (p0) = q1$$

where the guard is fully caused by the requirement of effective decrease of the variant function. The next question is whether after this change of f we can readjust $(p0, q0)$ so as to restore the possibly destroyed relation P. The connection (from $p0$) to $p1$ being removed, a safe readjustment has to reestablish the (possibly) destroyed connection with $p1$. After the change of f caused by $f: (p0) = q1$, we know that

$$part(f)\$(p1, x) = part(f_{init})\$(p, q)$$

for x equal to $p0$, $q0$, or $q1$. The relation P is most readily re-established (because for x, $q0$ may be chosen) by "$p0 := p1$", which, in view of $P1$ is coded as

$$p0, p1 := p1, f(p1)$$

Thus we are led to the following program, the second guarded command being justified by symmetry considerations,

```
begin glocon p, q; glovar f; privar p0, p1, q0, q1;
   p0 vir int, q0 vir int := p, q {P has been established};
   p1 vir int, q1 vir int := f(p0), f(q0) {P1 has been established};
   do q1 < p1 → f:(p0)= q1; p0, p1 := p1, f(p1)
    ▯ p1 < q1 → f:(q0)= p1; q0, q1 := q1, f(q1)
   od
end
```

The repetitive construct has been constructed in such a way that termination is ensured: upon completion we can conclude $p1 = q1$, which on account of $P1$ implies $f(p0) = f(q0)$, from which Q follows! Q.E.D.

Note. For the controlled derivation of this program —even for an a posteriori correctness proof— the introduction of "*part*" and "$", or a similarly powerful notation, seems fairly essential. Those readers who doubt this assertion are invited to try for themselves a proof in terms of the N values of $f(k)$, rather than in terms of a nicely captured property of the function f as a whole, as we have done.   (*End of note.*)

Advice. Those readers who have not fully grasped the compelling beauty of Rem's algorithm should reread this chapter very carefully. (*End of advice.*)

24

THE PROBLEM
OF THE CONVEX HULL
IN THREE DIMENSIONS

In order to forestall the criticism that I only show examples that admit a nice, convincing solution, and, in a sense, do not lead to a difficult program, we shall now tackle a problem which I am pretty sure will turn out to be much harder. (For my reader's information: while starting to write this chapter, I have never seen a program solving the problem we are going to deal with.)

Given a number of different points on a straight line —by their coordinates, say— we can ask to select those points P, such that all other points lie at the same side of P. This problem is simple: scanning the coordinates once we determine their minimum and their maximum value.

Given, by means of their x-y-coordinates, a number of different points in a plane such that no three points lie on the same straight line, we can ask to select those points P through which a straight line can be drawn such that all other points lie at the same side of that line. These points P are the vertices of what is called "the convex hull of the given points". The convex hull itself is a cyclic ordering of these points with the property that the straight line connecting two successive ones has all remaining points at one of its sides. The convex hull is the shortest closed line such that each point lies either on it or inside it.

In this chapter we shall tackle the analogous problem for three dimensions. Given, by their x-y-z-coordinates, N different points (N large) such that no four different points lie in the same plane, select all those points P through which a plane can be "drawn", such that all other points lie at the same side of that plane. These points are the vertices of the convex hull around those N points, i.e. the minimal closed surface such that each point lies either on it or inside it. (The restriction that no four points lie in the

168

same plane has been introduced to simplify the problem; as a result all the faces of the convex hull will be triangles.)

For the time being we leave the question open as to whether the convex hull should be produced as the collection triangles forming its faces, or as the graph of its vertices and edges —where the edges are the lines through two different vertices such that a plane through that line can be "drawn" with all other points at the same side of it.

The reason why we postpone this decision is exactly the reason why the problem of the three-dimensional convex hull is such a hairy one. In the two-dimensional case, the convex hull is one-dimensional and its "processing" (scanning, building up, etc.) is quite naturally done by a sequential algorithm with a linear store. In the three-dimensional case, however, neither the representation of the "two-dimensional" answer with the aid of a linear store nor the "sequencing" in manipulating it are obvious.

All algorithms that I know for the solution to the two-dimensional problem can be viewed as specific instances of the abstract program:

> construct the convex hull for two or three points;
> **do** there exists a point outside the current hull →
>   select a point outside the current hull;
>   adjust the current hull so as to include
>   the selected point as well
>
> **od**

The known algorithms differ in various respects. A subclass of these algorithms select in the action "select a point outside the current hull" only points that are a vertex of the final answer. These fall into two subsubclasses: in the one subsubclass not only the new vertex but also one of the new edges will belong to the final answer; in the other subsubclass the new vertex of the final answer is selected with the aim of reducing the number of points still outside the hull as much as possible. The worst case and best case effectiveness of such a strategy is, however, dependent on the positions of the given points and its "average effectiveness" is only defined with respect to a population of sets of points from which our input can be regarded as a random sample. (In general, an algorithm with widely different worst and best case performance is *not* an attractive tool; the trouble is that often these two bounds can only be brought more closely together by making *all* performances equally bad.)

The second aspect in which the various known algorithms for the two-dimensional case differ is the way in which it is discovered which points lie within the current hull (and, therefore, can be discarded). To determine whether an arbitrary point lies within the current hull, we can scan the edges (in sequence, say): if it lies at the inner side of all of them, it lies inside the current hull. Instead of scanning all vertices, we can also exploit that a point lies only inside the convex hull if it lies inside a triangle between three of its vertices and we can try to find such a triple of vertices according to some strategy aiming at "quickest inclusion". Some of these strategies can, on "an" average, be speeded up quite considerably by some additional book-keeping, by trading storage space versus computation time.

From the above we can only expect that for the three-dimensional case, the collection of algorithms worthy of the predicate "reasonable" will be of a dazzling variety. It would be vain to try anything approaching an exhaustive exploration of that class, and I promise that I will be more than happy if I can find one, perhaps two "reasonable" algorithms that do not seem to be unduly complicated.

Personally I find such a global exploration of the potential difficulty, as given above, very helpful, as it indicates how humbly I should approach the problem. In this case I interpret the indications as pointing towards a very humble approach and it seems wise to refrain from as much complicat-ing sophistication as we possibly can, before we have discovered —if ever! — that, after all, the problem is not as bad as it seemed at first sight. The most drastic simplification I can think of is confining our attention to the topo-logy, and refraining from all strategic considerations based upon expecta-tion values for the numbers of points inside given volumes.

It seems that the most sensible thing to do is to look at the various ways of solving the two-dimensional problem and to investigate their generaliza-tion to three dimensions.

A simple solution of the two-dimensional problem deals with the points in arbitrary order, and it maintains the convex hull for the first n points, initializing with $n = 3$. Whenever a next point is taken into consideration two problems have to be solved:

1. It has to be decided whether the new point lies inside or outside the current hull.
2. If it is found to lie outside the current hull, the current hull should be adjusted.

One way of doing this is to search for the set of k consecutive (!) edges such that the new point lies at their wrong side. Those k edges (and $k - 1$ points) have to be removed during the adjustment; they will be replaced by 1 point and 2 edges. If the search fails to find such a set, the new point lies inside.

Assuming the current vertices cyclically arranged, such that for each vertex we can find its predecessor as well as its successor, the least sophisti-cated program investigates these edges in order. In the three-dimensional problem the equivalents of the edges are the triangular faces, the equivalent of a set of consecutive edges is a set of connected triangles which are topologically equivalent to a circle. Let us call this "a cap".

The convex hull for the two-dimensional problem has to be divided into two "sections", the set of edges to be maintained or to be rejected respectively, where the two sections are separated by two points; in the three-dimensional problem the convex hull has to be divided into two caps separated by a cyclic arrangement of points and edges.

We could start confronting the new point with an arbitrary face and take this as the starting face of one of the two caps; that cap can be extended one face at a time, and the process will terminate either because the cap comprises all faces (and the other cap is empty; the new point lies inside the current hull) or because it is fully surrounded by faces belonging to the other cap.

The key problem seems to be to maintain a floating population of faces in such a way that given a cap we can find a face with which we can extend it such that the new set of faces again forms a cap. We can do so by maintaining (in cyclic order) the points (and the edges) of the cap boundary. A new face to be added must have an edge, and therefore two points in common with the cap boundary: if the third point occurs in the cap boundary as well, it must in the old boundary be adjacent to one of the other two.

I would not like the effort to find a face with which the cap can be extended to imply a search through the remaining faces, i.e. given an edge of the boundary, I would prefer quick access to the necessary data defining the other face to which this edge belongs. A desire to tabulate —we would like to use arrays— suggests that we should maintain a population of numbered edges as well.

The fact that an edge defines two points as well as two faces, and that a face is defined equally well by its three points as by its three edges, suggests that we should try to carry out as much of the administration as we can in terms of edges. We seem to get the most symmetrical arrangement if we number each undirected edge twice, i.e. regard it as a superposition of two numbered, directed edges.

Let i be the number of a directed edge of the convex hull; then we can define

$inv(i) =$ the number of the directed edge that connects the same points as the directed edge $nr.\ i$, but in the inverse direction.

Furthermore, when we associate with each face the three directed edges of its clockwise boundary, each directed edge is a clockwise edge of exactly one face, and we can give the complete topology by one further function

$suc(i) =$ the number of the directed edge that is the next clockwise edge of the face of which $nr.\ i$ is a clockwise edge; with "next" is meant that the edge "$suc(i)$" begins where the edge "i" ends.

As a result "i", "$suc(i)$" and "$suc(suc(i))$" are the numbers of the edges forming in that order a clockwise boundary of a face. Because all faces are triangles, we shall have

$$suc(suc(suc(i))) = i$$

The functions "inv" and "suc" give the complete topological description of the convex hull in terms of directed edge names. If we want to go from there to point numbers, we can introduce a third function

$end(i) =$ the number of the point in which the directed edge $nr.$ i ends.

We then have $end(inv(i)) = end(suc(suc(i)))$, because both expressions denote the number of the point in which the directed edge $nr.$ i begins; the left-hand expression is to be preferred, not so much because it is simpler, but because it is independent of the assumption that all faces are triangles.

To find for a given point, say $nr.$ k, the set of edges ending in it is very awkward, and therefore must be avoided. Rather than storing "k", we must store "ek" such that $end(ek) = k$. Then, for instance,

$$ek := inv(suc(ek))$$

will switch ek to the next edge ending in k; by repeated application of that transformation we shall be able to rotate ek along all edges ending in point $nr.$ k (and thus we have access to all faces with point $nr.$ k on their boundary).

Note. As $inv(inv(i)) = i$ and I expect to be rather free in assigning numbers to edges, we can probably assign numbers $\neq 0$ and introduce the convention $inv(i) = -i$; in that case we do not need to store the function inv at all. (*End of note.*)

Our task is to try to separate with respect to the new point the current hull into two caps. I take the position that establishing at which side of a face the new point lies will be the time-consuming operation and would like to confront the new point at most once with each face (and possibly with some faces not at all).

To use a metaphor, we can regard the new point as a lamp that illuminates all faces on which its rays fall from outside. Let us call them the "light" faces and all the other ones the "dark" faces. The light faces have to be removed; only if the point lies inside the current hull, does it leave all faces dark.

After the colouring of the first face I only expect to colour new faces adjoining a coloured one. The two main questions that I find myself pondering now are:

1. Do we insist that, as long as only faces of the same colour have been found, the next face to investigate should form a cap with the already coloured ones, or do we admit "holes"? The reason is that the test whether a new face, when added, will give rise to a hole does not seem too attractive.

2. As soon as two colours have been used, we know that the new point lies outside the current hull and we also know an edge between two differently coloured faces. Should we change strategy and from then on try to trace the boundary between dark and light faces, rather than colour all faces of our initial colour?

It took me a very long time to find a suitable answer to these questions. Because we have taken the position that we shall confront each face at most once with a new point, we have in general three kinds of faces: "dark", "light", and "undecided yet". And a certain amount of this information has to be recorded in order to avoid reconfrontation of the same face with the new point. But faces have no names! A face is only known as "the face along edge i", i.e. with edge i on its clockwise boundary, and for each face there are three such edges. So it seems more advantageous to carry out the administration not so much in terms of faces, but in terms of edges, the more so because in the first phase we are searching for an *edge* between a light and a dark face.

For a new point to be confronted with the faces we introduce for the purpose of this discussion two constants, called "right" and "wrong": "right" is the colour (dark or light respectively) of the (arbitrarily chosen) first face that has been confronted with the new point, "wrong" (light or dark respectively) is the other colour.

Let K be the set of edges i such that

1. the face along edge i is right (and this has been established);
2. the face along edge $-i$ has not been inspected yet.

The initialization of K consists then of the three edges of the clockwise boundary of the first face confronted. As long as the set K is not empty, we select an arbitrary edge from it, say edge x, and the face along edge $-x$ is confronted (for the first time, because edge x satisfied criterion (2)) with the new point. If the new face is wrong, the first edge between two differently coloured faces has been found and we enter the second phase, the discussion of which is postponed. If the new face, however, is also right we consider the edges y for $y = -x$, $y = suc(-x)$ and $y = suc(suc(-x))$, i.e. the edges of the clockwise boundary of the new right face, and for each of the three values we perform

> **if** edge $-y$ is in $K \longrightarrow$ remove edge $-y$ from K
> ▯ edge $-y$ is not in $K \longrightarrow$ add edge y to K
> **fi**

For, in the first case the edge $-y$ no longer satisfies criterion (2), and in the second case edge y (which cannot be in K already because it did not satisfy criterion (1)) now satisfies criterion (1) and also criterion (2) (for if the face along $-y$ had been inspected earlier, edge $-y$ would still have been in K).

In the meantime we have, at least tentatively, made up our mind about questions *1* and *2*: we do not insist that the established right faces always form a cap and we do intend to change strategy as soon as the first edge of the boundary between the caps has been found. (These decisions were made during a period that I did not write; it included an evening walk through the village. My first remark to myself was that tracing the boundary between the two caps as soon as one of its edges has been found reduces a two-dimensional search to a one-dimensional one and is, therefore, not to be discarded lightly. Then I realized that as soon as it has been decided to adopt that strategy, there does not seem to be much of a point anymore in sticking during the first phase to established right faces always forming a cap. Then for some time I tried to figure out how to carry out the first phase in terms of faces being right or uninspected, until I remembered what I had temporarily forgotten, viz. that I had already decided to express the structure in terms of edges. Confident that now it could be worked out I returned to my desk and wrote the above.)

Now we must tackle the second phase. Let x be an edge of the clockwise boundary of the right cap. How do we find, for instance, the next edge of that clockwise boundary? We have seen how to scan the faces having a point in common; the only question is whether the knowledge of set K is sufficient to stick to our principle that no face should be confronted with the new point more than once.

Well, that seems more than we can hope for, because in the meantime we have found a wrong face, and on the one hand we cannot expect to deal definitely with it, i.e. with all its adjoining faces, and on the other hand we would not like to confront the wrong face more than once with the new point either. The simplest suggestion seems to maintain a similar administration for edges with respect to wrong faces, viz. let H be the set of edges i such that

1. the face along edge i has been established wrong;
2. the face along edge $-i$ has not been inspected yet.

Can we come away with that? We observe that the intersection of K and H is empty, because no edge i can be a member of both K and H.

Can we maintain both sets K and H if the new face is right, and also if the new face is wrong? Let x be an edge of set K and let us consider again the three edges y for $y = -x$, $y = suc(-x)$, and $y = suc(suc(-x))$. In the following, B is the set of discovered edges of the clockwise boundary of the right cap.

If the new face is right, its three edges y have each to be processed by:

if edge $-y$ is in $K \rightarrow$ remove edge $-y$ from K
  ⫿ edge $-y$ is in $H \rightarrow$ remove edge $-y$ from H and
                add edge y to B
  ⫿ edge $-y$ is not in $(H + K) \rightarrow$ add edge y to K
fi

If the new face is wrong, its three edges y have each to be processed by:

  if edge $-y$ is in $K \rightarrow$ remove edge $-y$ from K and
                add edge $-y$ to B
  ⫿ edge $-y$ is in $H \rightarrow$ remove edge $-y$ from H
  ⫿ edge $-y$ is not in $(H + K) \rightarrow$ add edge y to H
fi

Looking at the above, I have one of the many surprises of my life! When H is still empty and the new face is right, the adjustment reduces —and that is not very surprising— to the adjustment of the first phase. But nowhere have we used that x was a member of K: if x would have been a member of H, the algorithm would have worked equally well. We only insist that x should be a member of the union $H + K$ in order to avoid reconfrontation and thus to ensure termination! As far as logical considerations are concerned, we can initialize K with the edges of the clockwise boundary of the first face and initialize H and B empty. Then we can select as long as possible an *arbitrary* edge x from the union $H + K$ and subject the clockwise edges y of the face along the edge $-x$ to the above treatment. This process ends when $H + K$ is empty; the new point is already inside the current hull if and only if finally B is still empty!

Before proceeding, a few retrospective remarks seem in order. I have introduced the restriction to confront each face only once with the new point for reasons of efficiency, after having made the logically irrelevant assumption that that would be the time-consuming operation. I should not have worried about efficiency so early in the game; I should have focussed my attention more on the logical requirement of guaranteed termination. If I had done so, I would never have worried about "caps" —a herring that is becoming redder and redder— and I would not have considered the two phases as logically different! (My long hesitation as to how to answer questions (*1*) and (*2*) should have made me more suspicious!) For what remains? It boils down to the observation that as soon as the edges in a nonempty B form a cycle, we can stop, even if $H + K$ is not empty yet and knowing that, we can try to exploit our freedom in choosing x from $H + K$ so as to find all edges of that cycle as quickly as possible. In our effort to keep things as simple as possible we feel now entitled to postpone the conscious tracing of the boundary between the two caps as an optimization that can be expected to be easily plugged in at a later stage.

The introduction of the concepts right/wrong also seems to have been a mistake, seeing how we can select an edge x from the union $H + K$. (It was not only a mistake, it was a stupid mistake. I hesitated very long before I did so and then I had unusual difficulties in finding suitable names for them and in phrasing their definitions, but I ignored this warning, fooling myself in believing that I had done something "smart".) We shall drop these concepts and carry our administration out in the original concepts light/dark. With this, we must be able to accomplish three simplifications:

1. We do not need to treat the first face inspected separately; its three edges y can be treated as those of any other face.
2. The two alternative constructs for dealing with the three edges of a newly inspected face (for a right face and for a wrong face respectively) as given above can be mapped on a single alternative construct.
3. We don't need to invert the edges of B if it was the clockwise boundary of the dark cap.

The further details will be postponed until we have explored the next operation: adjusting the convex hull so as to include the new point as well.

Having found a nonempty boundary we must remove the inner edges of the light cap, if any, and add the edges connecting the new point to the points on the cap boundary. As the number of edges to be removed is totally unrelated to the number of edges to be added, we propose to deal with these two tasks separately. In the unrefined search for the boundary, in the course of which all faces have been inspected, simultaneous removal of all inner edges of the light cap could easily have been incorporated. Because I would like to keep the option for optimization of the search for the boundary open, we have to solve the problem of finding the set of inner edges of the white cap when its nonempty clockwise boundary B is given, regardless of how that boundary has been found.

Because the problem of finding the set of inner edges of the light cap is a (not so special) instance of a more general problem —of which the exercise attributed to R.W. Hamming and the traversal of a binary tree are more special instances— we shall tackle the general problem (which is really the problem of finding the transitive closure) first.

Given a (finite) set of elements. For each element x zero or more other elements are given as "the consequences of x". For any set B, a set $S(B)$ is given by the following three axioms:

    Axiom 1.   Each element of B belongs to $S(B)$.
    Axiom 2.   If x belongs to $S(B)$, then the consequences of x, if any, belong to $S(B)$ as well.

Axiom 3.   The set $S(B)$ contains only those elements that belong to it on account of Axioms *1* and *2*.

For given B it is required to establish the relation

R: $$V = S(B)$$

The idea of the algorithm is quite simple: initialize with $V := B$, and as long as V contains an element x whose consequences do not all belong to V, extend V with those consequences and stop when no such element can be found anymore. A refinement of this algorithm can be found by observing that once for a given element y it has been established that all its consequences are in V as well, that relation will continue to hold, because the only modification V is subjected to is the extension with new elements. The refinement consists of keeping track of the subset of such elements y, because their consequences need not to be taken into consideration anymore. The set V is therefore split into two parts, which we may call C and $V \simeq C$. Here $V \simeq C$ contains all elements of which it has been established that their consequences are already all in V, while C (possible "causes") contains all remaining elements which may have a consequence outside V. The algorithm deals with one element of C at a time. Let c be an element of C; it is removed from C (and, therefore, added to $V \simeq C$) and all its consequences outside V are added to V and C. The algorithm stops when C is empty. Termination is guaranteed for finite $S(B)$ because, although the number of elements of C may increase, the number of elements of $V \simeq C$ increases by one at each step, and this number is bounded from above by $S(B)$. (The number of steps is independent of the choice of the element c from C!)

The above informal description of the intended computational process may satisfy some of my readers —it satisfied me for more than fifteen years. I hope that in the meantime it will dissatisfy some of them as well. For without stating the invariance relation and without stating clearly the nature of the inductive argument, the best we can reach is: "Well, I don't see how the above computational process could fail to accomplish the desired result."

The argument should express clearly what is meant by the intuitive remark that there is no point in investigating the consequences of a given element more than once. For this purpose we introduce the functions $S_C(B)$ which are defined by the same axioms as $S(B)$ but for another set of consequences, viz.

if x belongs to C, x has no consequences,
if x does not belong to C, x has the consequences as originally given.

Because $S_\phi(B) = S(B)$, it is suggested to choose as invariant relations

$P1$: $V = S_C(B)$ and $P2$: C is a subset of V,

relations which are easily established by the assignment $V, C := B, B$.

The crucial properties of the function $S_C(B)$ are the following:

1. $S_C(B)$ is a monotonic function of C; that is, if $C2$ is a subset of $C1$, then $S_{C1}(B)$ is a subset of $S_{C2}(B)$.
2. $S_C(B)$ is not changed if C is extended with elements not belonging to $S_C(B)$.

Let c be an arbitrary element of C; extension of C with the consequences of c that do not belong to V leaves the relation $P1$ undisturbed on account of the second property. Subsequent removal of c from C means that, on account of the first property, all elements already in V remain in V, which (maintaining $P1$ and restoring $P2$) is adjusted by

$$V := V + \{\text{the set of consequences of } c\}$$

(where "$+$" is used to denote set union). The forming of the set union boils down to extension of V with the consequences of c not belonging to V, i.e. the elements that just have been added to C; but as these new elements "have no consequences", this completes the adjustment.

Remark. The algorithm for the transitive closure is of general interest, not in the last place because it shows how the usual recursive solution for traversing a binary tree is a special case of this one. The role of C is then taken over by the stack and the test whether a consequence of c does already belong to V can be omitted because absence of loops in the tree guarantees that each node will be encountered only once. This observation casts some doubts upon opinions held high by some members of the Artificial Intelligentsia. The one is that recursive solutions, thought of as in some sense "more basic", come more natural than repetitive ones, an opinion which has given rise to the development of (semi-)automatic program rewriting systems that translate recursive solutions into —presumably more efficient— repetitive ones. The other opinion is that in the case of searching through a finite portion of a potentially infinite set the linguistic tool of recursive co-routines is needed. The point is that from a nonempty C *any* element may be chosen to act as "c" and any operating system designer knows that a last-in–first-out strategy engenders the danger of individual starvation; any operating system designer also knows how to exorcize this danger. It is not excluded that later generations will pronounce as their judgment that in the last fifteen years, recursive solutions have been placed upon too high a pedestal. If this judgment is correct, the phenomenon itself will be explained by the fact that up to some years ago we had no adequate mathematical tool for dealing with repetition and assignment to variables. *(End of remark.)*

In our example we can take for B (as used in the above general treatment) the B as used in our treatment of the convex hull, i.e. the edges of the clockwise boundary of the light cap. As "consequences of edge i" we can take

1. none, if $suc(i)$ belongs to B;

2. $suc(i)$ and $-suc(i)$ if $suc(i)$ does not belong to B.

The final value of V is then $B +$ {the set of inner edges of the white cap}.

Removing the inner edges of the white cap presents us with a minor clerical problem. Because we want to tabulate the functions $suc(i)$ and $end(i)$, we would like to number the edges of the convex hull —zero excluded— with consecutive numbers ranging from $-n$ through $+n$; and of course we can begin to do so (extending the arrays at both ends as n grows), but as soon as edges are removed, we get "holes" in our numbering system. Two ways out present themselves: either we renumber the remaining edges of the convex hull so as to use again consecutive numbers, or we keep track of the "holes" and use them —if present— as names for edges to be added. Renumbering the remaining edges is, in general, not a very attractive solution, because it means the updating of all references to the edge being renumbered. Although in this case the updating of the administration seems quite feasible, I prefer to use the more general technique of keeping track of the "holes", i.e. the unused names in the range from $-n$ through $+n$.

The standard technique is to use holes in last-in–first-out fashion, and to exploit one of the function values, e.g. suc, for keeping track of the stack of holes. More precisely:

$i = 0$ is permanently the oldest hole

if i ($\neq 0$) is a hole, then $suc(i)$ is the next older hole.

Finally we introduce one integer variable, yh say (short for "youngest hole"). Removal of edge i, i.e. making a hole of it, is performed by

$$suc: (i) = yh;\ yh := i;$$

if there are no holes, except zero, we have $yh = 0$; otherwise we have $yh \neq 0$ and assigning to i the value of the youngest hole is then done by

$$i := yh;\ yh := suc(i)$$

In order not to duplicate the administration we shall associate with the *single* hole i the edge *pair* $\{+i, -i\}$.

We seem to approach the moment of coding, and of fixing the ways in which the argument is given and the answer is to be delivered. Given is a cloud of $N \geq 4$ points, by means of three array constants x, y, and z, such that

$$x.lob = y.lob = z.lob = 1$$

$$x.hib = y.hib = z.hib = N$$

and $x(i)$, $y(i)$, and $z(i)$ are for $1 \leq i \leq N$ the x-, y- and z-coordinates respectively of point *nr. i*.

We propose to deliver the convex hull by means of two arrays, *"suc"* and *"end"* and a single integer *"start"* such that

$$suc.lob = end.lob = -suc.hib = -end.hib$$

and

(a) *start* is the number of a directed edge of the convex hull.
(b) If i is the number of a directed edge of the convex hull:
    (b1) $-i$ is the number of the directed edge in the opposite direction;
    (b2) *end*(i) is the number of the point towards which the directed edge i points;
    (b3) *suc*(i) is the number of the "next" directed edge of the clockwise boundary of the face "along" edge i (for the definitions of "next" and "along" in this context, see far above).

The admission of holes implies that there may be (even *will* be) values of i such that finally $0 \leq abs(i) \leq suc.hib$, while i is not the number of an edge of the final answer; the introduction of the variable *"start"* allows us not to make any commitments regarding the value of *suc*(i) and *end*(i) for such a value of i. Symbolically, we can now describe the function of the inner block to be designed by

$$\text{"}(suc, end, start) \textbf{ vir } hull := \text{convex hull of } (x, y, z)\text{"}.$$

As far as our external commitments are concerned, we could restrict ourselves to the introduction of a single private variable, *"np"* say, and the invariant relation

P1: $(suc, end, start) = $ convex hull of the first np points of (x, y, z)

and a block

    "($suc, end, start$) **vir** *hull* := convex hull of (x, y, z)":
    begin glocon x, y, z; **virvar** $suc, end, start$; **privar** np;
    "initialize *P1* for small value of np";
      do $np \neq x.hib \rightarrow$ "increase np by *1* under invariance of *P1*" **od**
    end

but this is not sufficient for two reasons. Firstly, inside the repeatable statement we want to reuse holes, and therefore we should introduce the variable yh for the youngest hole. Secondly, the increase of np implies scanning the (faces along) edges of the convex hull. We could introduce in the repeatable statement an array that each time could be initialized with a special value for each edge, meaning "not yet confronted with the new point". Logically, this would be perfectly correct, but it seems more efficient to bring that array outside the repeatable statement and to see to it that, as the scanning proceeds, it ends up with the same neutral values with which it started. We shall call this array "*set*" and choose the neutral value $= 0$. Summing up, we introduce the invariant relation

P2:   (*suc, end, start*) = convex hull of the first *np* points of (x, y, z)
        and *yh* = youngest hole
        and (*i* is a hole $\neq 0$) $\Rightarrow$ *suc*(*i*) is the next oldest hole
        and (*i* is an edge of (*suc, end, start*)) $\Rightarrow$ *set*(*i*) = 0

and the version from which I propose to proceed is

    "(*suc, end, start*) **vir** *hull* := convex hull of (x, y, z)":
    begin glocon *x, y, z*; **virvar** *suc, end, start*; **privar** *np, yh, set*;
        "initialize *P2* for small value of *np*";
        do *np* $\neq$ *x.hib* $\longrightarrow$ "increase *np* by *1* under invariance of *P2*" **od**
    end

The initialization is very simple as soon as we realize that it suffices to do so for *np* = 3, just a triangle with two faces:

    "initialize *P2* for small value of *np*":
    begin virvar *suc, end, start, np, yh, set*;
        suc **vir** *int* **array** := $(-3, -2, -1, -3, 0, 2, 3, 1)$;
        end **vir** *int* **array** := $(-3, 1, 3, 2, 0, 3, 1, 2)$;
        start **vir** *int* := *1*; *np* **vir** *int* := *3*; *yh* **vir** *int* := *0*;
        set **vir** *int* **array** := $(-3, 0, 0, 0, 0, 0, 0, 0)$
    end

The refinement of "increase *np* by *1* under invariance of *P2*"—the only thing left to be done— is more complicated. The increase of *np* and the choice of point *np* as the new point (*npx, npy,* and *npz* will be introduced as its coordinates) is easy. The next steps are to determine the boundary and, if any, to adjust the hull. In the first step we shall use values *set*(*i*) = ± 1 to indicate "half-inspected" edges, i.e.

    set(*i*) = +*1* means: the face along edge *i* has been established light, the
                  face along edge $-i$ has not yet been confronted with
                  the current new point
    set(*i*) = −*1* means: the face along edge *i* has been established dark, the
                  face along edge $-i$ has not yet been confronted with
                  the current new point
    set(*i*) = +*2* means: the edge *i* has been established to belong to the
                  clockwise boundary of the light cap.

For edges of the convex hull not belonging to any of the above categories, we shall have *set*(*i*) = *0* during the search for the boundary. When this search has been completed, all edges i that have had $set(i) = \pm 1$ will have $set(i)$ reset to 0 or to 2.

Besides recording the boundary as "the edges with $set(i) = 2$", it is helpful to have a list of these edge numbers in cyclic order, because that comes in handy when the edges to and from the new point have to be added. Because the optimization that switches to a linear search as soon as the first edge of the boundary has been found finds the edges in cyclic order, our version will produce that list as well. We propose to record the numbers of the edges of the boundary in cyclic order in an array, "b" say; $b.dom = 0$ can then be taken as an indication that no boundary has been found. Our coarsest design becomes:

> "increase np by 1 under invariance of $P2$":
> **begin glocon** x, y, z; **glovar** suc, end, $start$, np, yh, set;
>   **pricon** npx, npy, npz; **privar** b;
> $np := np + 1$;
> npx **vir** int, npy **vir** int, npz **vir** int := $x(np)$, $y(np)$, $z(np)$;
> b **vir** int **array** := (0);
>   "establish boundary in set and b";
>   **if** $b.dom = 0 \rightarrow skip$
>   ⫿ $b.dom > 0 \rightarrow$ "adjust the hull"
>   **fi**
> **end**

To establish the boundary in "set" and "b" would require two steps: in the first step all faces are confronted with the new point and the boundary is established in "set", and in the second step we would have to trace the boundary and place its edges in cyclic order in the list "b". Although it was my original intention to do so, and to leave the transition to the more linear search as soon as the first edge of the boundary has been found as an exercise in optimization to my readers, I now change my mind, because I have discovered a hitherto unsuspected problem: the first inspection of a face that reveals an edge of the boundary may reveal more than one boundary edge. If the faces are triangles, they will be adjacent boundary edges, but the absence of faces with more than three edges is only due to the restriction that we would not have four points in a plane. I did not intend to allow this restriction to play a very central role and as a result I refuse to exploit this more or less accidental adjacency of the boundary edges that may be revealed at the inspection of a new face. And the potential "simultaneous" discovery of nonadjacent boundary edges was something I had not foreseen; adjacency plays a role if we want to discover boundary edges in cyclic order, i.e. place their edge numbers in cyclic order in array b (with "$b:hiext$"). The moral of the story seems to be to separate the "discovery" of a boundary edge —while scanning the edges of the newly inspected face— from the building up of the value of "b". Because the discovered boundary edges have to be separated in those "processed", i.e. stored as a function value of b, and those still unprocessed, some more information needs to be stored in the array "set". I propose:

$set(i) = 1$ and $set(-i) = 0$	the face along edge i has been established light, the face along edge $-i$ has not yet been confronted with the current new point
$set(i) = -1$ and $set(-i) = 0$	the face along edge i has been established dark, the face along edge $-i$ has not yet been confronted with the current new point
$set(i) = 1$ and $set(-i) = -1$	edge i is an unprocessed edge of the clockwise boundary of the light cap
$set(i) = 2$ and $set(-i) = 0$	edge i is a processed edge of the clockwise boundary of the light cap
$set(i) = 0$ and $set(-i) = 0$	the faces along i and $-i$ are both uninspected or have been established to have the same colour.

We stick to our original principle only to inspect (after the first time) a face along (the inverse of) a half-inspected edge, say along $-xx$ (i.e. $set(xx) = \pm 1$ and $set(-xx) = 0$); we can then use the value $xx = 0$ to indicate that no more inspection is necessary. The relation "$b.dom = 0$" can be used to indicate that up till now no boundary edges have been discovered; the first boundary edge to be discovered will just be placed in b (thereby causing $b.dom = 1$), the remaining boundary edges will then be placed by careful extension of b. A first sketch (at this level still too rough) is

```
"establish boundary in set and b":
  begin glocon x, y, z, suc, end, start, npx, npy, npz;
    glovar set, b; privar xx; xx vir int := start;
    do xx ≠ 0 →
        "inspect face along −xx";
        if b.dom > 0 → "extend b and refresh xx"
        ▯ b.dom = 0 → "reassign xx"
        fi
    od
  end
```

(The different names "refresh xx" and "reassign xx" have been used in order to indicate that rather different strategies are involved.)

I have called this sketch too rough: "reassign xx" has to assign to xx the number of a half-inspected edge (if it can find one, otherwise zero). It would be very awkward indeed if this implied a search over the current hull, which would imply again an administration to prevent the algorithm from visiting the same edge twice during that search! Therefore we introduce an array c (short for "candidates") and will guarantee that

> if i is the number of a half-inspected edge, then either i
> occurs among the function values of c, or $i = xx$.

(Note that function values of c —which will always be edge numbers— may also equal the number of an edge that, in the meantime, has been totally inspected.) In view of the fact that zero is the last xx-value to be produced, it will turn out to be handy to store the value zero at the low end of c upon initialization (it is as if we introduce a "virtual edge" with number zero; this is a standard coding trick). Our new version becomes:

> "establish boundary in *set* and *b*":
> **begin glocon** $x, y, z, suc, end, start, npx, npy, npz$;
>   **glovar** *set*, b; **privar** xx, c;
> xx **vir** *int* $:= start$; c **vir** *int* **array** $:= (0, 0)$;
>   **do** $xx \neq 0 \rightarrow$ "inspect face along $-xx$";
>   **if** $b.dom > 0 \rightarrow$ "extend b and refresh xx"
>   ❒ $b.dom = 0 \rightarrow$ "reassign xx"
>   **fi**
>   **od**
> **end**

Because for "reassign xx" initially edge xx is not half-inspected (for the face along $-xx$ has just been inspected!) and

$$abs(set(xx)) = 1 \text{ and } set(-xx) = 0$$

is the condition for being half-inspected, the last subalgorithm is coded quite easily:

> "reassign xx":
> **do** $xx \neq 0$ **and non** $(abs(set(xx)) = 1 \text{ and } set(-xx) = 0) \rightarrow$
> xx,c: *hipop*
> **od**

The algorithm for "extend b and refresh xx" is more complicated. If we focus our attention on the search for the edge with which we would like to extend b, we realize that we are looking for an edge, xx say, such that

P1:   it begins, where edge $b.high$ ends, i.e. $end(b.high) = end(-xx)$

P2:   the face along xx has been established to be light

P3:   the face along $-xx$ has been established to be dark.

Because $xx:= suc(b.high)$ establishes the first two, we take *P1* **and** *P2* as invariant relation. We can now distinguish four —and the largeness of four explains why this algorithm is more complicated— different cases.

1. $set(xx) = 1$ **and** $set(-xx) = -1$: in that case, xx is the next edge of the clockwise boundary of the light cap to be processed; it can be processed and after that $xx:= suc(xx)$ then re-establishes *P1* **and** *P2*.
2. $set(xx) = 0$ **and** $set(-xx) = 0$: in that case, because the face along edge xx has been established light, also the face along $-xx$ has been established light; therefore $xx:= suc(-xx)$ gives a new xx satisfying *P1* **and** *P2*.

Operation (*1*) can only happen a finite number of times because there are only a finite number of edges of the clockwise boundary of the light cap to be processed. Operation (*2*) can only be repeated a finite number of times, because $end(-xx)$ is a vertex of a face that has been established to be dark. When none of the two can take place, we have one of the following two cases:

3. $set(xx) = 1$ **and** $set(-xx) = 0$: in this case the face along $-xx$ has not been inspected yet and xx has an acceptable value for controlling the next face inspection.
4. $set(xx) = 2$ **and** $set(-xx) = 0$: in this case xx is a processed edge of the boundary and the loop must have been closed: we *must* have $xx = b.low$, and the search is completed, i.e. $xx = 0$ is the only acceptable final value for xx. We must, however, see to it that no edges i with $set(i) = \pm 1$ remain.

In the following program, for safety's sake guards have been made stronger than strictly necessary.

```
"extend b and refresh xx":
xx:= suc(b.high);
do set(xx) = 1 and set(-xx) = -1 →
        set: (xx)= 2; set: (-xx)= 0; b: hiext(xx); xx:= suc(xx)
▯ set(xx) = 0 and set(-xx) = 0 → xx:= suc(-xx)
od;
if set(xx) = 1 and set(-xx) = 0 → skip
▯ set(xx) = 2 and set(-xx) = 0 and xx = b.low →
    xx, c: hipop;
    do xx ≠ 0 →
            do abs(set(xx)) = 1 → set: (xx)= 0 od;
            xx, c: hipop
    od
fi
```

Under the assumption that "compute *lumen*" will initialize *lumen* = +*1* if the face along −*xx* is light and = −*1* if it is dark, the coding of "inspect face along −*xx*" is now fairly straightforward.

```
"inspect face along −xx":
begin glocon x, y, z, suc, end, npx, npy, npz, xx;
    glovar set, b, c; pricon lumen; privar yy, round;
    "compute lumen";
    yy vir int := −xx; round vir bool := false;
    do non round →
        if set(−yy) = 0 → set: (yy)= lumen; c: hiext(yy)
        ▯ set(−yy) = lumen → set: (−yy)= 0
        ▯ set(−yy) = −lumen →
            set: (yy)= lumen;
            do b.dom = 0 → b: hiext(lumen * yy) od
        fi;
        yy:= suc(yy); round:= (yy = −xx)
    od
end
```

The programming of the computation of "*lumen*" is not difficult, but it is tedious: it boils down to the computation of the signed volume of the tetrahedron with the vertices *np*, *end*(−*xx*), *end*(*suc*(−*xx*)) and *end*(*suc*(*suc*(−*xx*))). In passing we choose a sense of rotation for our clock.

```
"compute lumen":
begin glocon x, y, z, suc, end, npx, npy, npz, xx;
    vircon lumen; privar pt;
    pricon vol, x1, y1, z1, x2, y2, z2, x3, y3, z3;
    pt vir int := end(−xx);
    x1 vir int, y1 vir int, z1 vir int :=
        x(pt) − npx, y(pt) − npy, z(pt) − npz;
    pt:= end(suc(−xx));
    x2 vir int, y2 vir int, z2 vir int :=
        x(pt) − npx, y(pt) − npy, z(pt) − npz;
    pt:= end(suc(suc(−xx)));
    x3 vir int, y3 vir int, z3 vir int :=
        x(pt) − npx, y(pt) − npy, z(pt) − npz;
    vol vir int := x1 *(y2 * z3 − y3 * z2) +
                   x2 *(y3 * z1 − y1 * z3) +
                   x3 *(y1 * z2 − y2 * z1);
    if vol > 0 → lumen vir int := −1
    ▯ vol < 0 → lumen vir int := +1
    fi
end
```

We are left with the task of refining "adjust the hull", where the edges of
B, the clockwise boundary of the light cap, are given in two ways:

1. In cyclic order as the function value of the array b: this representation
facilitates tracing the boundary, doing something for all edges of B, etc.
2. $set(i) = 2$ holds if and only if edge i belongs to B; this facilitates answer-
ing the question "Does edge i belong to B?"

Because the number of edges that have to disappear (i.e. the inner edges
of the light cap) and the number of edges that have to be added (i.e. the
edges connecting the new point with the vertices on the clockwise boundary)
are totally unrelated, it seems best to separate the two activities:

"adjust the hull":

"removal of edges";

"addition of edges"

In the first one it does not seem too attractive to merge identification of
the inner edges with their removal: during the identification process the
light cap of the current hull has to be scanned, and I would rather not mess
with that structure by removing edges before the scanning has been carried
out completely. (This does not mean to imply that it could not be done, it
just says that I am currently no longer in the mood to investigate the possibility.)

Because, on account of our "holes", inner edge i and inner edge $-i$ have
to be removed simultaneously, it suffices for the removal to build up a list of
"undirected" edge numbers, i.e. the value i will be used to indicate that both
edge i and edge $-i$ should disappear. Calling that list rm, we are led to

```
"removal of edges":
begin glocon b; glovar suc, yh, set; privar rm;
   "initialize rm with list of inner edges";
   "removal of edges listed in rm"
end
```

In accordance with our earlier conventions about holes, the second one
is now coded quite easily

```
"removal of edges listed in rm":
do rm.dom > 0 → suc: (rm.high)= yh; yh, rm: hipop od
```

The initialization of rm is, after our earlier analysis, no longer difficult.
The relation $set(i) = set(-i) = 3$ will be used to represent "i and $-i$ have
been detected as inner edges" and enables us to test whether edge i belongs
to what we have called V (boundary + inner edges) by $set(i) \geq 2$. Again we
use an array variable, called "c", to list the candidates.

"initialize *rm* with list of inner edges":
begin glocon *b, suc;* **glovar** *set;* **virvar** *rm;* **privar** *c, k;*
  c **vir** *int* **array** := *(0); k* **vir** *int* := *b.lob;*
  do *c.dom* ≠ *b.dom* → *c: hiext(b(k)); k:= k + 1* **od;**
  rm **vir** *int* **array** := *(0);*
  do *c.dom* > *0* →
      begin glocon *suc;* **glovar** *set, rm, c;* **pricon** *h;*
      h **vir** *int:= suc(c.high); c: hirem;*
      if *set(h)* ≥ *2* → *skip*
      ⫿ *set(h)* = *0* → *set: (h)= 3; set: (−h)= 3; rm: hiext(h);*
                          c: hiext(h); c: hiext(−h)
      fi
      end
    od
  end

Finally, we have to refine "addition of edges". If we deal with one edge of the boundary at a time, connecting its end to the new point, then we have some difficulty with the first triangle: the number of the edge connecting its begin with the new point has not yet been decided. To start with, we can proceed as if this was the virtual edge, *nr.* zero, and initialize *t* (for "trail") accordingly and close the loop at the end. Before the local constant *e* is initialized with the number of the youngest hole, the algorithm checks whether there is such a hole, otherwise one is made by extending the arrays concerned at both ends. At the end of the algorithm it is assured that the value of "*start*" again is the number of an edge of the convex hull. (This is typically the kind of statement to forget; I had done so, as a matter of fact, for originally it was my intention to include this resetting in "removal of edges" because that is the action that may cause "*start*" to become equal to the number of an edge that is no longer part of the convex hull. My attention was drawn to that omission when I investigated the environment of "addition of edges", which is the environment of "adjust the hull" and there I found *start* among the global *variables*! Too lazy to make a change in the already typed-out part of my manuscript, I am seduced to a typical program patch!)

"addition of edges":
begin glovar *suc, end, start, yh, set;* **glocon** *np, b;*
  privar *t, k;*
  t **vir** *int, k* **vir** *int* := *0, b.lob;*
  do *k* ≤ *b.hib* →
      begin glovar *suc, end, yh, set, t, k;* **glocon** *np, b;*
      pricon *e;*

```
        do yh = 0 ⟶ suc: hiext(0); suc: loext(0);
                    end: hiext(0); end: loext(0);
                    set: hiext(0); set: loext(0);
                    yh:= suc.hib
        od;
        e vir int := yh; yh:= suc(e);
        suc: (b(k))= e; set: (b(k))= 0;
        suc: (e)= t; end: (e)= np; set: (e)= 0;
        suc: (t)= b(k); end: (t)= end(−b(k)); set: (t)= 0;
        t:= −e; k:= k + 1
      end
    od;
    suc: (suc(b.low))= t;
    suc: (t)= b.low; end: (t)= end(−b.low); set: (t)= 0;
    suc: (0)= 0; end: (0)= 0; set: (0)= 0;
    start:= b.low
  end
```

The above completes the historical description of the first algorithm I have made that should construct the convex hull in three dimensions. It is only my first effort and the algorithm I arrived at does not seem to be a very efficient one; its "quality" is certainly no justification for its publication. (To try to develop more efficient algorithms is an exercise that I gladly leave to my readers. I stop here, for, after all, this book is not a treatise on convex hull algorithms.) This chapter is included for other reasons.

The first reason has been stated at the beginning of this chapter: to forestall the criticism that I only deal with easy, little problems.

The second reason was that I wanted to show how such algorithms can be arrived at by means of a process of step-wise refinement. To be quite honest, I wanted to show more, viz. that the method of step-wise refinement seems one of the most promising ways of developing programs of —ultimately — considerable yet mastered complexity. I hope that with this example I have succeeded in doing so. I think that this example deserves to be called "of considerable yet mastered complexity" because the ultimate program consists of thirteen named chunks of code, whose (what we might call) "substitution hierarchy" is five layers deep! It is displayed in the following indented table:

```
0)      (suc, end, start) vir hull:= convex hull of (x, y, z)
1)          initialize P2 for small value of np
1)          increase np by 1 under invariance of P2
2)              establish boundary in set and b
3)                  inspect face along −xx
```

4)	compute *lumen*
3)	extend *b* and refresh *xx*
3)	reassign *xx*
2)	adjust the hull
3)	removal of edges
4)	initialize *rm* with list of inner edges
4)	removal of edges listed in *rm*
3)	addition of edges

The method of step-wise refinement was developed in a conscious effort to do justice to the smallness of our human skulls. This implies that when we have to design an algorithm that ultimately will be represented by a large text, we just *have* to invent the concepts that will enable us to describe the algorithm at such a level of abstraction that that description comes out short enough to be intellectually manageable. And as far as that goal is concerned, the method of step-wise refinement seems adequate. It is of course no guarantee for an in all respects high-quality program!

The third reason to include this chapter was that I wanted to be as fair and, thereby, as convincing as possible. The first example that I have used to demonstrate the method of step-wise refinement was the development of a program generating a table of the first thousand prime numbers. Although this was in many ways a very nice and compact example, its convincing power was somewhat impaired by everyone's knowledge that I already knew how to generate the first thousand prime numbers before I started to write that essay. Therefore I wrote this chapter, not having the foggiest notion how it would end when I started it. Whenever a few pages were written, I typed them out before proceeding.

Note 1. After the above had been typed out, we found by inspection three errors in the program text: a semicolon was missing, in "removal of edges listed in *rm*" I had written "*suc*: (*yh*)= *rm.high*", and in "initialize *rm* with list of inner edges" the line "*c*: *hiext*(*h*); *c*: *hiext*(−*h*)" had been dropped. It is worth noticing that only the most trivial one of these could have been detected by a syntactical checker. It is also worth noticing that the other two occurred in sections of which I had announced that they were "now coded quite easily" and "no longer difficult" respectively!

(End of note 1.)

Note 2. It is far from excluded that the efficiency of my program can be improved considerably, even without introducing strategies based upon expectation values of numbers of points inside given volumes: if the point lies already inside the convex hull, one does not need to confront it with all faces; if it lies outside, there should be (on the average, bah!) cheaper ways of finding a first boundary edge of the light cap. If, for instance, the convex hull has more than five points, there exists at least one pair whose shortest connection goes through the interior and we could try to locate the intersection of the convex hull with the plane through the new point and the two points of such a pair. Our searches would then be linear.

(*End of note 2.*)

Note 3.   In the program as published above, Mark Bebie has found an error. In order to maintain the convention

"*set(i)* = 2 **and** *set(−i)* = 0   edge *i* is a processed edge of the clockwise boundary of the light cap"

the values of *set(i)* and *set(−i)* have to be adjusted when edge *i* is processed, i.e. *b:hiext(i)* takes places. In "extend *b* and refresh *xx*" this has been done (in the third line), in "inspect face along −*xx*", however, it has erroneously been omitted. Its tenth line

do *b.dom* = 0 → *b:hiext(lumen * yy)* **od**

should therefore be replaced by

do *b.dom* = 0 → *b:hiext(lumen * yy);*
          set:(b.high) = 2; *set:(−b.high)* = 0
     od

(*End of note 3.*)

25 FINDING THE MAXIMAL STRONG COMPONENTS IN A DIRECTED GRAPH

Given a directed graph, i.e. a set of vertices and a set of directed edges, each leading from one vertex to another, it is requested to partition the vertices into so-called "maximal strong components". A strong component is a set of vertices such that the edges between them provide a directed path from any vertex of the set to any vertex of the set and vice versa. A single vertex is a special case of a strong component; then the path can be empty. A maximal strong component is a strong component to which no further vertices can be added.

In order to establish this partitioning, we have to be able to make two kinds of assertions: the assertion that vertices belong to the same strong component, but also —because we have to find *maximal* strong components— the assertion that vertices do *not* belong to the same strong component.

For the first type of assertion, we may use the following

THEOREM 1. Cyclically connected vertices belong to the same strong component.

Besides (directed) connections between individual vertices, we can talk about directed connections between different strong components; we say that there is a connection from a strong component A to a strong component B if there exists a directed edge from a vertex of A to a vertex of B. Because A and B are strong components, there is then a path from any vertex of A to any vertex of B. And as a result, Theorem 1 can be generalized into

THEOREM 1A. Vertices of cyclically connected strong components belong to the same strong component.

COROLLARY *1*. A nonempty graph has at least one maximal strong component without outgoing edges.

So much for theorems asserting that vertices belong to the same strong component. Because for different points to be in the same strong component there must be paths between them in both ways, assertions that vertices do not belong to the same strong component can be made on account of:

THEOREM 2. If the vertices are subdivided into two sets *svA* and *svB* such that there exist no edges originating in a vertex of *svA* and terminating in a vertex of *svB*, then

firstly: the set of maximal strong components does not depend on the presence or absence of edges originating in a vertex of *svB* and terminating in a vertex of *svA*, and
secondly: no strong component comprises vertices from both sets.

From Theorem 2 it follows that as soon as a strong component without outgoing edges has been found, we can take its vertices as set *svA* and conclude that this strong component is a maximal strong component and that all ingoing edges of *svA* can further be ignored. We conclude:

THEOREM 2A. A strong component whose outgoing edges, if any, are all ingoing edges of maximal strong components is itself a maximal strong component.

Or, to put it in another way, once the first maximal strong component without outgoing edges —the existence of which is guaranteed by Corollary 1— has been found (identified as such by being a strong component without outgoing edges), the remaining maximal strong components can be found by solving the problem for the graph consisting of the remaining vertices and only the given edges between them. Or, to put it in still another way, the maximal strong components of a graph can be ordered according to "age", such that each maximal strong component has outgoing edges only to "older" ones.

In order to be able to be a little bit more precise, we denote by

$$sv:$$ the given set of vertices (a constant)
$$se:$$ the given set of edges (a constant)
$$pv:$$ a partitioning of the vertices of *sv*.

The final relation to be established can then be written as

$$R: \qquad\qquad pv = \text{MSC}(se)$$

in which for the fixed set *sv* the function MSC, i.e. the partitioning in Maximal Strong Components, is regarded as a function of the set of edges *se*.

The corresponding invariant relation is suggested by the standard technique of replacing a constant by a variable, *se1* say, whose value will always be a subset of *se*:

P: $pv = \text{MSC}(se1)$

Relation P is easily initialized for empty *se1*, i.e. each vertex of *sv* is a maximal strong component all by itself. Because *se1* is bounded in size by *se*, monotonically increasing *se1* guarantees termination; if we can accomplish this under invariance of P, relation R has been established by the time that $se1 = se$. In our discussions it will be convenient also to have a name, *se2* say, for the remaining edges, i.e. $se = se1 \mp se2$.

Our task is clearly to discover the most convenient order in which edges are to be added to *se1*, where "convenience" is related to the ease with which the invariance of relation P is maintained. This, as we know, can also be phrased as: what is our general intermediate state, what types of *pv*-values do we admit? In order to describe such a general intermediate state, it seems practical to group the vertices of *sv* also in disjoint subsets (as we have done for the edges *se1* and *se2*). After all, we are interested in partitioning vertices!

The general intermediate state should be a generalization of both initial state and final state. At the beginning, it has not been established for any of the vertices to which maximal strong component in MSC(*se*) they belong, eventually it has been established for all vertices. Analogous to *se1* we can introduce (initially empty and finally comprising all vertices) *sv1*, where

sv1   contains all vertices of *sv*, for which the maximal strong component in MSC(*se*) to which they belong has been identified.

We intend to use Theorem 2A for deciding that a strong component is a maximal one; that is after having established something about *all* its outgoing edges. When we now identify:

se1   with the set of all processed edges, and

se2   with the set of all unprocessed edges, i.e. edges whose presence has not yet been taken into account,
then we see that

$P1$:   all outgoing edges of vertices in *sv1* are in *se1*

It is, however, too crude to group all remaining vertices in a single set *sv2*. The way in which *sv1* is defined implies that, each time a new maximal strong component of MSC(*se*) has been identified, all the vertices of that maximal strong component have to be transferred *together* to *sv1*. Between two such transfers, in general a number of edges have to be processed (i.e. transferred from *se2* to *se1*), and for the description of the intermediate states that have to be taken into account with respect to "processing one edge at a time", the remaining vertices have to be separated a little bit more subtly, viz. into two disjoint subsets, $sv2$ and $sv3$ say (with $sv = sv1 \mp sv2 \mp sv3$), where $sv3$ contains the totally unprocessed vertices,

P2:   no edge in $se1$ begins or ends at a vertex in $sv3$

($sv3$ is initially equal to sv and finally empty).

Transfer from $sv3$ to $sv1$ can then take place in two steps: from $sv3$ to $sv2$ (one at a time) and from $sv2$ to $sv1$ (together with all other vertices from the same definite maximal strong component).

In other words, among the vertices of $sv2$ we shall try to build up (by enlarging $se1$) the next maximal strong component of MSC(se) to be transferred to $sv1$. The maximal strong components in MSC($se1$) —note the argument!— are such that they comprise either vertices from $sv1$ only, or vertices from $sv2$ only, or a (single) vertex from $sv3$. We propose a limitation on the connections that the edges of $se1$ provide between the maximal strong components in MSC($se1$) that contain nodes from $sv2$ only: between those maximal strong components the edges of $se1$ shall provide no more and no less than a single directed path, leading from the "oldest" to the "youngest" one. We call these maximal strong components "the elements of the chain". This choice is suggested by the following considerations.

Firstly, we are looking for a cyclic path that would allow us to apply Theorem 1 or 1A in order to decide that different vertices belong to the same maximal strong component. Under the assumption that we are free to prescribe which edge will be the next one to be added to $se1$, there does not seem to be much advantage in introducing disconnected maximal strong components in MSC($se1$) among those built up from vertices of $sv2$.

Secondly, the directed path from the "oldest" to the "youngest" component in the chain —as "cycle in statu nascendi"— is easily maintained, as is shown by the following analysis.

Suppose that $se2$ contains an edge that is outgoing from one of the vertices of the youngest maximal strong component in the chain. Such an edge "e" is then transferred from $se2$ to $se1$, and the state of affairs is easily maintained:

1. If e leads to a vertex from $sv1$, it can be ignored on account of Theorem 2.
2. If e leads to a vertex from $sv2$, the youngest element of the chain can be combined with zero or more next older elements to form the new youngest element of the chain. More precisely, if e leads to a vertex in the youngest element, it can be ignored; if it leads to an older element in the chain, a cycle between strong components has been detected and then Theorem 1A tells us that a number of the younger elements of the chain have to be combined into a single one, thus reducing the length of the chain, measured in number of elements.

3. If e leads to a vertex from $sv3$, that latter vertex is transferred to $sv2$ and as new youngest element (a maximal strong component in MSC($se1$) all by itself) it is appended to the chain, whose length is increased by one.

If there exists no such edge "e", there are two possibilities. Either the chain is nonempty, but then Theorem 2A tells us that this maximal strong component of MSC($se1$) is a maximal strong component of MSC(se) as well: the youngest element is removed from the chain and its vertices are transferred from $sv2$ to $sv1$. Or the chain is empty: if $sv3$ is not empty, an arbitrary element of $sv3$ can be transferred to $sv2$, otherwise the computation is finished.

In the above degree of detail we can describe our algorithm as follows:

$se1, se2, sv1, sv2, sv3 := empty, se, empty, empty, sv$;
do $sv3 \neq empty \rightarrow$ {the chain is empty}
    transfer a vertex v from $sv3$ to $sv2$ and initialize the chain with $\{v\}$;
    do $sv2 \neq empty \rightarrow$ {the chain is nonempty}
        do $se2$ contains an edge starting in a vertex of the youngest
            element of the chain $\rightarrow$
            transfer such an edge e from $se2$ to $se1$;
            if e leads to a vertex v in $sv1 \rightarrow$ *skip*
            ◻ e leads to a vertex v in $sv2 \rightarrow$ compaction
            ◻ e leads to a vertex v in $sv3 \rightarrow$ extend chain and trans-
                              fer v from $sv3$ to $sv2$
        fi
        od; {the chain is nonempty}
        remove youngest element and transfer its vertices from $sv2$ to $sv1$
    od {the chain is again empty}
od

Note 1. As soon as vertices are transferred from $sv2$ to $sv1$, their incoming edges (if any) that are still in $se2$ could be transferred simultaneously from $se2$ to $se1$, but the price for this "advanced" processing (the gain of which is doubtful) is that we have to be able to select for a given vertex the set of its incoming edges. As the algorithm is described, we only need to find for each vertex its outgoing edges. Hence the above arrangement.
                                  (*End of note 1.*)

Note 2. Termination of the innermost repetition is guaranteed by decrease of the number of edges in $se2$; termination of the next embracing repetition is guaranteed by decrease of the number of vertices in $sv2 +$ $sv3$; termination of the outer repetition is guaranteed by decrease of the number of vertices in $sv3$. The mixed reasoning, sometimes in terms of edges and sometimes in terms of vertices, is a symptom of the nontriviality of the algorithm we are developing. (*End of note 2.*)

To the degree of detail in which we have described our algorithm, each edge is transferred once from *se2* to *se1* and each vertex is transferred once from *sv3* via *sv2* to *sv1*: as such our algorithm implies an amount of work linear in the number of edges and vertices. In our next refinement we should try not to spoil that pleasant property, as we would do if, for instance, the test whether v is in *sv1*, *sv2*, or *sv3* (which occurs within the innermost repetition!) implied a search with a computation time proportional to the number of vertices. The restricted way in which our vertex sets are manipulated, in particular the fact that the vertices enter and leave the chain in last-in–first-out fashion, can be exploited for this purpose.

We consider our vertices consecutively numbered and tabulate the function "$rank(v)$", where v ranges over all vertex numbers; we assume NV to denote the number of vertices:

$$rank(v) = 0 \text{ means: vertex } nr. \ v \text{ is in } sv3$$

$$rank(v) > 0 \text{ means: vertex } nr. \ v \text{ is in } sv1 \mp sv2$$

(The sets *sv2* and *sv1* are, to start with, combined: one of the possible forms of compaction is a skip!)

If *nvc* equals the "number of vertices in the chain", i.e. the number of vertices in *sv2*, then

$$1 \leq rank(v) \leq nvc \text{ means: vertex } v \text{ is in } sv2$$

$$rank(v) \geq NV + 1 \text{ means: vertex } v \text{ is in } sv1$$

All vertices in *sv2* will have different *rank*-values, and as far as *rank* and *nvc* are concerned, transferring vertex v from *sv3* to *sv2* will be coded by

$$\text{"}nvc := nvc + 1; \ rank:(v) = nvc\text{"}$$

i.e. the vertices in the chain are "ranked" in the order of decreasing "age in the chain". The latter convention allows us to represent how the vertices of *sv2* are partitioned in strong components quite efficiently: vertices belonging to the same element of the chain have consecutive values of *rank*; and for the elements themselves, the rank of their oldest vertex is a decreasing function of the element age. Using $cc(i)$ to denote the rank of the oldest vertex of the *i*th oldest element of the chain (we have then *cc.dom* = the number of elements in the chain), as far as *rank*, *nvc*, and *cc* are concerned, we can code the alternative construct (combining the first two alternatives) as follows:

if $rank(v) > 0 \rightarrow$ **do** $cc.high > rank(v) \rightarrow cc:hirem$ **od**
⫿ $rank(v) = 0 \rightarrow nvc := nvc + 1; rank:(v) = nvc; cc:hiext(nvc)$
fi

In the meantime we have somewhat lost trace of the identity of the vertices in the chain. If, for instance, we would like to transfer the vertices of the youngest element of the chain from $sv2$ to $sv1$, our current tabulations would force us to scan the function rank for all values of v, such as to find those satisfying $cc.high \leq rank(v) \leq nvc$. We would not like to do that, but thanks to the fact that at least for the vertices in $sv2$, all values of $rank(v)$ are different, we can also store the inverse function:

for $\qquad 1 \leq r \leq nvc$: $\qquad rank(v) = r \Leftrightarrow knar(r) = v$

So much for keeping track of the vertices; let us now turn our attention to the edges. The most crucial question with regard to the edges is, of course, the guard of the innermost repetitive construct: "$se2$ contains an edge starting in a vertex of the youngest element of the chain". That guard is evaluated easily with the aid of a list of edges from $se2$ outgoing from the vertices of the youngest element of the chain. One of the ways in which the youngest in the chain may change, however, is compaction; in order to maintain that list we, therefore, also need the corresponding lists for the older elements of the chain. Because for those edges we are interested only in the identity of their "target vertex", we introduce as the next part of our chain administration two further array variables —with domain = 0 when the chain is empty— called "tv" (for "target vertices") and "tvb" (for "tv-bounds").

The domain of tvb will have one point for each element of the chain: its value equals the number of outgoing edges of $se2$ from vertices of older elements in the chain (the domain of tvb is all the time equal to that of cc, which also stores one value for each chain element). Each time a new vertex v is transferred from $sv3$ to $sv2$, the array tvb is extended at the high end with the value of $tv.dom$, whereafter tv is extended at the high end with the target vertices of the outgoing edges of v. Denoting that latter operation with "extend tv with target of v" the whole inner repetition now becomes (taking $knar$, tv, and tvb into account as well)

```
"inner loop":
do tv.dom > tvb.high →
    v, tv:hipop;
    if rank(v) > 0 →
        do cc.high > rank(v) → cc:hirem; tvb:hirem od
    ▯ rank(v) = 0 →
        nvc:= nvc + 1; rank:(v) = nvc; knar:hiext(v);
        cc:hiext(nvc); tvb:hiext(tv.dom);
        "extend tv with targets of v"
    fi
od
```

We had introduced for vertices v in $sv1$ the convention: $rank(v) > NV$. We can make a stronger convention by numbering the maximal strong components from 1 onwards (in the order in which they are detected) and introducing the convention that for a vertex v in $sv1$ we will have

$$rank(v) = NV + v\text{'s maximal strong component number}$$

With the variable "$strno$" (initially $= 0$), we can now code the

```
"middle loop":
do cc.dom > 0 →
    "inner loop";
    strno:= strno + 1;
    do nvc ≥ cc.high →
        nvc:= nvc − 1; rank:(knar.high) = NV + strno;
        knar:hirem; sv1count:= sv1count + 1
    od;
    cc:hirem; tvb:hirem
od
```

(The variable $sv1count$, initially $= 0$, counts the number of vertices in $sv1$; then $sv1count = NV$ will be the criterion for completion of the task.)

We assume the vertices numbered from 1 through NV, and the edges to be given by means of two array constants "$edge$" and "$edgeb$", such that for $1 \leq i \leq NV$ the values of $edge(j)$ for $edgeb(i) \leq j < edgeb(i + 1)$ give the numbers of the vertices to which the edges outgoing from vertex $nr.$ i lead. We can then code

```
"extend tv with targets of v":
begin glocon edge, edgeb, v; glovar tv; privar j;
    j vir int:= edgeb(v + 1);
    do j > edgeb(v) → j:= j − 1; tv:hiext(edge(i)) od
end
```

The last problem to be solved is the selection of an arbitrary vertex v from $sv3$ for the initialization of the chain. If each time the search would start at vertex $nr.$ 1, computation time could be proportional to NV^2, but again this can be avoided by taking a relation outside the repetition and introducing at the outer level a variable "$cand$" (initially $= 1$) with the property:

$$sv3 \text{ contains no vertex } v \text{ with } v < cand$$

```
begin glocon edge, edgeb, NV; virvar rank; privar svlcount, cand, strno;
    rank vir int array:= (1); do rank.dom ≠ NV → rank:hiext(0) od;
    svlcount vir int, cand vir int, strno vir int:= 0, 1, 0;
    do svlcount ≠ NV →
        begin glocon edge, edgeb, NV; glovar rank, svlcount, cand, strno;
            privar v, cc, tv, tvb, knar, nvc;
            do rank(cand) ≠ 0 → cand:= cand + 1 od; v vir int:= cand;
            nvc vir int:= 1; rank:(v) = 1; knar vir int array:= (1, v);
            cc vir int array:= (1, 1); tvb vir int array:= (1, 0);
            tv vir int array:= (1);
            "extend tv with targets of v";
            "middle loop"
        end
    od
end
```

Note 1. A very similar algorithm has been developed independently by Robert Tarjan. *(End of note 1.)*

Note 2. In retrospect we see that the variable *"nvc"* is superfluous, because *nvc = knar.dom*. *(End of note 2.)*

Note 3. The operation "extend *tv* with the targets of *v*" is used twice. *(End of note 3.)*

Remark 1. The reader will have noticed that in this example the actual code development took place in a different order than in the development of the program for the convex hull in three dimensions. The reason is, I think, the following. In the case of the convex hull, the representation had already been investigated very carefully as part of the logical analysis of the problem. In this example the logical analysis had been largely completed when we faced the task of selecting a representation that would admit an efficient execution of the algorithm we had in mind. It is then natural to focus one's attention on the most crucial part first, i.e. the innermost loop. *(End of remark 1.)*

Remark 2. It is worth noticing the various steps in which we arrived at our solution. In the first stage our main concern has been to process each edge only once, forgetting for the time being about the dependence of the computation time on the number of vertices. This is fully correct, because, in general, the number of edges can be expected to be an order of magnitude larger than the number of vertices. (As a matter of fact, my first solution for this problem —not recorded in this chapter— was linear in the number of edges but quadratic in the number of vertices.) It was only in the second stage that we started to worry about linear dependence on the number of vertices as well. How effective this "separation of concerns" has been is strikingly illustrated by the fact that in that second stage graph theory did no longer enter our considerations at all! *(End of remark 2.)*

26 ON MANUALS AND IMPLEMENTATIONS

In the fifties I wrote for a number of machines of Dutch design what I called "a functional description" —the type of document that I should encounter later under the name "reference manual"— and I still remember vividly the pains I took to see that these functional descriptions were unambiguous, complete, and accurate: I regarded it as my duty to describe the machines as far as their properties were of importance for the programmer. Since then my appreciation of the relation between machine and manual, however, has undergone a change.

Eventually, there are two "machines". On the one hand there is the physical machine that is installed in the computer room, can go wrong, requires power, air conditioning, and maintenance and is shown to visitors. On the other hand there is the abstract machine as defined in the manual, the "thinkable" machine for which the programmer programs and with respect to which the question of program correctness is settled.

Originally I viewed it as the function of the abstract machine to provide a truthful picture of the physical reality. Later, however, I learned to consider the abstract machine as the "true" one, because that is the only one we can "think"; it is the physical machine's purpose to supply "a working model", a (hopefully!) sufficiently accurate physical simulation of the true, abstract machine.

This change in attitude was accompanied by a change in terminology: instead of "computer science" the term "computing science" came into use and we no longer gave courses in "Programming for Electronic Computers" —we could not care less whether the physical machine worked electronically, pneumatically or by magic! But it was of course more than a mere play with words; it was the symptom that slowly the programming profession was becoming of age. It used to be the program's purpose to instruct our computers; it became the computer's purpose to execute our programs.

The full force of an interface was emerging, and a discrepancy between abstract and physical machine was no longer interpreted as an inaccuracy in the manual, but as the physical machine not working according to specifications. This presupposes, of course, that these specifications were not only completely unambiguous, but also so "understandable" —and orders of magnitude more simple than the engineering documentation of the machine— that everybody could agree that they described what was intended. I remember the time that with respect to hardware specification such interfaces were achieved with a clarity that satisfied everybody's needs: the hardware designers knew what they had to achieve and the programmer had complete control over his tool without the need for "experimental" programs for discovering its properties. This rigorous and indispensible clarity did not only extend itself over the hardware, but also over the basic software, such as loaders, input and output routines, etc., no more than a few hundred, perhaps a thousand instructions anyhow. (If I remember correctly, the ominous term "software" had still to be invented.)

Sad remark.   Since then we have witnessed the proliferation of baroque, ill-defined and, therefore, unstable software systems. Instead of working with a formal tool, which their task requires, many programmers now live in a limbo of folklore, in a vague and slippery world, in which they are never quite sure what the system will do to their programs. Under such regretful circumstances the whole notion of a correct program —let alone a program that has been proved to be correct— becomes void. What the proliferation of such systems has done to the morale of the computing community is more than I can describe.   (*End of sad remark.*)

In the preceding chapters we have introduced predicates for the characterization of sets of states and have shown how program texts could be interpreted as codes for predicate transformers, establishing a relation between what we called "final and initial states". In accordance with that approach we have presented the programming task as the construction of (a code for) a predicate transformer establishing a desired relation between those two states.

When introducing the various ways of constructing new predicate transformers from existing ones —semicolon, alternative, and repetitive constructs — we have given hints as to how these could be implemented. We would like to stress, however, that, although these possibilities have certainly acted as a source of inspiration, they have no defining function whatsoever. The fact that our program texts admit the alternative interpretation of "executable code" has played a role in our motivations, but plays no role in the definition of the semantics of our programming language: our semantic definitions are not based upon any "model of computation".

Note 1. We have aimed at a semantic definition independent of computational history with a very specific purpose in mind, viz. a separation of concerns that strikes me as vital in the whole programming activity. The concerns to be separated could be called "the mathematical concerns" and "the engineering concerns". With the mathematical concerns I refer to the program's correctness; with the engineering concerns I refer mainly to the various cost aspects —such as storage space and computation time — associated with program execution. These cost aspects are only defined with respect to an implementation, and, conversely, the implementation (or, stronger, the interpretation of the program text as executable code) need only be taken into account when cost aspects are in discussion. As long as we are interested in program correctness, it suffices to interpret the text as a code for a predicate transformer and nothing is gained by simultaneously remembering that the text can also be interpreted as executable code. On the contrary! Hence our preference for an axiomatic system for the semantics that is independent of any computational model and that does not define the final state as "the output" of a computational process with the initial state as "the input". (*End of note 1.*)

Note 2. The simplicity of the formal system presented, together with the circumstance that to some extent it could be forged into a tool for the formal derivation of programs of a certain type, is for me its greatest attraction. The question of how much (or how little) of what should (or could) be done with automatic computers can be captured in this way falls outside the scope of this monograph. For the time being the part that could be captured seems rich enough to justify exploration.

(*End of note 2.*)

Having defined semantics independent of any computational model raises the question of to what extent we may hope that our programming language can be implemented at all. From a very etheric point of view, we could dismiss the question, saying that this is none of our business, that this is the implementer's concern, and that as long as we don't want our programs to be executed the question is irrelevant anyhow. But to dismiss this question is not my intention.

Actual machines have stores of a finite capacity and, left to themselves, they behave in principle like finite state automata which after a sufficient large number of steps must return to a state in which they have been before. (If, in addition, the machine is deterministic, history will from then on repeat itself.) For the overall behaviour of today's modern computers, the theory of finite state automata is, however, of limited significance, because their number of possible states is so incredibly huge that they could go on working for years without returning to a state in which they have been before. As an alternative we can study "the infinite state automaton" and drop the restriction of a finite store capacity. This, apparently, is what we have done: we have introduced a finite number of variables, but, having introduced variables of type "integer", there is no bound on their number of possible values and, therefore, no bound on the number of possible states. We have written programs for the Unbounded Machine "UM", and this is clearly something no engineer can build for us!

He can, however, build a Sufficiently Large Machine "SLM" that, when loaded with the same program S as the UM, will simulate the latter's behaviour successfully when UM embarks upon the execution of the program S started at an initial state satisfying wp(S, T). Thanks to the fact that for each initial state satisfying wp(S, T) both nondeterminacy and the number of computational steps are bounded, the collection of integer values possibly manipulated by the UM is finite and, therefore, they all fall within a finite range. Provided that the SLM can manipulate integers in that finite range, it can simulate the UM's behaviour on that computation (hopefully fast enough to make the simulation interesting).

Note 3.   Since Turing it is customary for mathematicians to regard the SLM, i.e. the machine performing with a finite speed computational steps in a bounded state space, as "feasible". It is in this connection wise to remember that the engineer must simulate the SLM by analogue means and that most theoretical physicists seem to believe that the probability of erroneous simulation of the SLM differs from zero and increases with the speed of operation. (*End of note 3.*)

The implementation of the nondeterminacy requires some special attention. When we consider the program part

S: **do** *go on* $\longrightarrow$ *x*:= *x* + *1*
                 ▯ *go on* $\longrightarrow$ *go on*:= *false*
            od

our formalism gives for all $k \geq 0$: $H_k(T) = $ **non** *go on* and, therefore,

$$wp(S, T) = \textbf{non } go\ on$$

We imagine that the hypothetical machine UM will execute the repetitive contruct by evaluating all the guards, terminating if they are all false, otherwise selecting one of the alternatives with a true guard for execution, and then, i.e. after successful completion of the latter, repeating the process. When initially **non** *go on* holds, i.e. *go on* = *false*, our formalism tells us that initially wp(S, T) is satisfied and this is in full accordance with our desire that termination is guaranteed: as a matter of fact, the UM will immediately stop repeating. If, however, initially *go on* = *true*, wp(S, T) is initially not satisfied, and if we wish to stick to our interpretation of wp(S, T) as the *weakest* precondition guaranteeing termination, we must reject any would-be UM in which the freedom of choosing would be exercised so "fairly" with respect to the various alternatives that each possible alternative will be selected sooner or later. We could think of a gambling device, such as tossing a coin, heads for the first and tails for the second alternative. As no unbiased coin is obliged sooner or later to turn up with "tails", it would satisfy our requirement. But in a sense we are now over-specifying the UM. The trouble is that the then natural assumption of an unbiased coin would tempt us to conclude that, although termination is not exactly guaranteed, the probability of nontermination is 0 and that the expectation value for the amount by which x will be increased equals 1. Such probabilistic studies can very soon become very difficult, but, luckily, we should not embark on them, for there is something wrong in the whole approach: we allowed nondeterminacy in those cases that we did not care which way the UM would choose, but after that we should not start caring! The most effective way out is to assume the UM not equipped with an unbiased coin, but with a totally erratic daemon; such a daemon makes all these probabilistic questions a priori void. (And we can live with such a daemon in the machine; whenever, at second thought, we do care which of the alternatives will be chosen and when, we had better strengthen the guards.)

It might be thought that the simulation of the UM with its erratic daemon presents some serious problems to the engineer who has to design the simulating SLM. It would, indeed, be difficult, if it required the generation of truly erratic choices—whatever that may be. But as the daemon is only a metaphor embodying our ignorance, its implementation should not present the slightest problem. If we know that our engineer of the SLM has ten different "quasi-daemons" on the shelf, we give him complete freedom in his choice which quasi-daemon he plugs in when we want to use the SLM and we solemnly declare that we shall even not complain when he plugs in an eleventh one that he may have concocted in the meantime. As long as we don't know and refuse to know its properties, everything is all right.

We have now reached the stage that, given a program and given the initial state, we could, at least in principle, select a sufficiently large machine SLM, but such a course of action is somewhat unrealistic for two reasons. Firstly, it is highly unusual to have a whole sequence of SLM's of increasing size on the shelf; secondly, it is in general quite a job to determine for an arbitrary program and a given initial state a priori the size of the SLM that would do it. It is easier "to try".

The more realistic situation is that, instead of a sequence of SLM's, we have one "hopefully sufficiently large machine" HSLM. The HSLM is two things, merged into one. Besides acting as the largest SLM we can afford, it checks, when called to execute a program, as the computation proceeds, whether this SLM is large enough for the current computation. If so, it proceeds with the simulation of the UM's behaviour, otherwise it refuses to continue. The HSLM enables us "to try", i.e. to do the experiment, whether the SLM it embodies is really sufficiently large for the current computation.

If the HSLM carries the computation out to the end, we can deduce from the nonoccurrence of the refusal that the embodied SLM has been large enough.

From the above it is clear that explicit refusal by the HSLM, whenever asked to do something exceeding its capacity, is a vital feature of the HSLM: it is necessary for our ability of doing the experiment. There exist, regretfully enough, machines in which the continuous check that the simulation of the behaviour of the UM is not beyond their capacity is so time-consuming, that this check is suppressed for the supposed sake of efficiency: whenever the capacity would be exceeded by a correct execution, they just continue —for the supposed sake of convenience— incorrectly. It is very difficult to use such a machine as a reliable tool, for the justification of our belief in the correctness of the answers produced requires in addition to the proof of the *program's* correctness a proof that the *computation* is not beyond the capacity of the machine, and, compared to the first one, this second proof is a rather formidable obligation. We would need an (axiomatic) definition of the possible *happenings* in the UM, while up till now it sufficed to prescribe the net effects; besides that, the precise constraints imposed by the actual machine's finiteness are often very hard to formulate. We therefore consider such machines that do not check whether simulating the UM exceeds their capacity as unfit for use and ignore them in the sequel.

Thanks to its explicit refusal to continue, recognizable as such, the HSLM is a safe tool, but it would not be a very useful one if it refused too often! In practice, a programmer does not only want to make a program that would instruct the UM to produce the desired result, he also wants to reduce the probability (or even to exclude the possibility) that the HSLM refuses to simulate the UM. If, for a given HSLM, this desire to reduce the probability of refusal entails very awkward obligations for the programmer (or, also, if the programmer has a hard time in estimating how effective measures that he considers to take will turn out to be) this HSLM is just awkward to use.

We now return to the notion of a so-called "liberal" pre-condition, which has been discussed at the end of the chapter "The Characterization of Semantics". A liberal pre-condition guarantees that a post-condition will be satisfied provided that the computation has terminated properly, but does not guarantee the proper termination itself. In the intervening chapters we had no use for this notion, because we defined the semantics as a relation between initial and final state, independent of program execution, and it is only in connection with execution that the notion becomes meaningful. The possibility of program execution only entered the picture when we introduced the unbounded machine UM. But of the UM we have only required that it would execute our programs, i.e. that it would bring for any (unmentioned) post-condition R itself in a state satisfying R provided that we started it in an initial state satisfying $wp(S, R)$; in particular, we only insisted upon proper termination, provided that the initial state satisfied $wp(S, T)$. For initial states not satisfying $wp(S, T)$ we have not cared to prescribe a behaviour of the

UM and to the UM the notion of a liberal pre-condition is therefore not applicable. But we do introduce the notion with respect to the HSLM, by requiring the latter to refuse would-be continuation when its capacity is exceeded. In other words, we accept an HSLM that is only able to simulate properly a subset of the computations that are guaranteed to terminate properly when executed by the UM.

Note 4.   The notion of the liberal pre-condition is introduced here in recognition of the fact that the HSLM is so bounded. This is in sharp contrast to the very similar notion of "partial correctness", which has been introduced in connection with unbounded machines (such as Turing machines) because of the undecidability of the Halting Problem.

(*End of note 4.*)

One may raise the question —but I shall not answer it— of what the UM will do when started at an initial state for which we don't know whether it satisfies wp(S, T) or not. I take the position (from a philosophical point of view probably very shaky) that as long as we have not *proved* that the initial state satisfies wp(S, T), the UM may do as it likes, in the sense that we have no right to complain. (We can imagine the following setup. In order to start the UM, the user must push the start button, but in order to be able to do so, he must be in the computer room. For reasons of protection of the air conditioning, the UM can only be started provided that all doors of the computer room are closed and for safety's sake, the UM (which has no stop button!) will keep the doors locked while in operation. This environment shows how deadly dangerous it can be to start a machine without having proved termination!)

This refusal to commit the UM to a well-defined behaviour if it has not been proved that wp(S, T) is initially satisfied, has the consequence that we cannot draw any conclusion from the fact of termination itself. We could try to use a machine to search for a refutation of Goldbach's Conjecture that each natural number $n \geq 2$ is the average of two primes, but would the following program do?

```
begin privar n, refuted;
    n vir int:= 1; refuted vir bool:= false;
    do non refuted →
        begin glovar n, refuted; privar x, y;
            n:= n + 1;
            x vir int, y vir int:= 2, 2 * n;
            do x < y and x + y < 2 * n →
                    x:= smallest prime larger than (x)
            ▯ x < y and x + y > 2 * n →
                    y:= largest prime smaller than (y)
            od;
            refuted:= (x + y ≠ 2 * n)
        end
```

         od;
         printbool(refuted)
      end

Because I have not proved that Goldbach's Conjecture is false, I have not proved that $wp(S, T)$ is initially true; therefore, the UM may act as it pleases and I am, therefore, not allowed to conclude that Goldbach's Conjecture is wrong when it prints *"true"* and stops. I would be allowed to draw that surprising conclusion, however, if the third line had been changed into

$$\text{``\textbf{do non} \textit{refuted} \textbf{and} } n < 1\ 000\ 000 \rightarrow\text{''}$$

and, at second thought, I even prefer the modified program, because it is more honest than the original version: no one starts with a computation without an upper bound for the time he is willing to wait for the answer.

27 IN RETROSPECT

Once the automatic computer was there, it was not only a new tool, it was also a new challenge and, if the tool was without precedent, so was the challenge. The challenge was —and still is— a two-fold one.

Firstly we are faced with the challenge of discovering new (desirable) applications, and this is not easy, because the applications could be as revolutionary as the tool itself. Ask the average computing scientist: "If I were to put a ten-megabuck machine at your disposal, to be installed for the benefit of mankind, how and to what problem would you apply it?", and you will discover that it will take him a long time to come up with a sensible answer. This is a serious problem that puts great demands on our fantasy and on our powers of imagination. This challenge is mentioned for the sake of completeness; this monograph does not address it.

Secondly, once an (hopefully desirable!) application has been discovered, we are faced with the programming task, i.e. with the problem of bending the general tool to our specific purpose. For the relatively small and slow machines of the earlier days the programming problem was not too serious, but when machines at least a thousand times as powerful became generally available, society's ambition in applying them grew in proportion and the programming task emerged as an intellectual challenge without precedent. The latter challenge was the incentive to write this monograph.

On the one hand the mathematical basis of programming is very simple. Only a finite number of zeros and ones are to be subjected to a finite number of simple operations, and in a certain sense programming should be trivial. On the other hand, stores with a capacity of many millions of bits are so unimaginably huge and processing these bits can now occur at so unimaginably high speeds that the computational processes that may take place —and that, therefore, we are invited to invent— have outgrown the level of triviality by several orders of magnitude. It is the unique combination of basic simplicity and ultimate sophistication which is characteristic for the programming task.

We realize what this combination implies when we compare the programmer with, say, a surgeon who does an advanced operation. Both should exercise the utmost care, but the surgeon has fulfilled his obligations in this respect when he has taken the known precautions and is then allowed to hope that circumstances outside his control will not ruin his work. Nor is the surgeon blamed for the incompleteness of his control: the unfathomed complexity of the human body is an accepted fact of life. But the programmer can hardly exonerate himself by appealing to the unfathomed complexity of his program, for the latter is his own construction! With the possibility of complete control, he also gets the obligation: it is the consequence of the basic simplicity.

One consequence of the power of modern computers must be mentioned here. In hierarchical systems, something considered as an undivided, unanalyzed entity at one level is considered as something composite at the next lower level of greater detail; as a result the natural grain of time or space that is appropriate for each level decreases by an order of magnitude each time we shift our attention from one level to the next lower one. As a consequence, the maximum number of levels that can be distinguished meaningfully in a hierarchical system is more or less proportional to the logarithm of the ratio between the largest and the smallest grain, and, therefore, we cannot expect many levels unless this ratio is very large. In computer programming our basic building block, the instruction, takes less than a microsecond, but our program may require hours of computation time. I do not know of any other technology than programming that is invited to cover a grain ratio of 10^{10} or more. The automatic computer, by virtue of its fantastic speed, was the first to provide an environment with enough "room" for highly hierarchical artifacts. And in this respect the challenge of the programming task seems indeed without precedent. For anyone interested in the human ability to think difficult thoughts (by avoiding unmastered complexity) the programming task provides an ideal proving ground.

When asked to explain to the layman what computing scientists call "modularization", the easiest analogy to use is probably the way in which the scientific world has parcelled out its combined knowledge and skills over the various scientific disciplines. Scientific disciplines have a certain "size" that is determined by human constants: the amount of knowledge needed must fit into a human head, the number of skills needed may not be more than a person can learn and maintain. On the other hand, a scientific discipline may not be too small, too narrow either, for it should last a lifetime at least without becoming barren. But not any odd collection of scraps of knowledge and an equally odd collection of skills, even of the right size, constitute a viable scientific discipline! There are two other requirements. The internal requirement is one of coherence: the skills must be able to improve the knowledge and the knowledge must be able to refine the skills. And finally there is the external requirement —we would call it "a narrow interface"— that the subject matter can be studied in a reasonably high degree of isolation, not at any moment critically dependent on developments in other areas.

The analogy is not only useful to explain "modularization" to the layman, conversely it gives us a clue as to how we should try to arrange our thoughts when programming. When programming we are faced with similar problems of size and diversity. (Even when programming at the best of our ability, we can sometimes not avoid that program texts become so long that their sheer length causes (for instance, clerical) problems. The possible computations may be so long or so varied that we have difficulty in imagining them. We may have conflicting goals such as high throughput and short reaction times, etc.) But we cannot solve them by just splitting the program to be made into "modules".

To my taste the main characteristic of intelligent thinking is that one is willing and able to study in depth an aspect of one's subject matter in isolation, for the sake of its own consistency, all the time knowing that one is occupying oneself with only one of the aspects. The other aspects have to wait their turn, because our heads are so small that we cannot deal with them simultaneously without getting confused. This is what I mean by "focussing one's attention upon a certain aspect"; it does not mean completely ignoring the other ones, but temporarily forgetting them to the extent that they are irrelevant for the current topic. Such separation, even if not perfectly possible, is yet the only available technique for effective ordering of one's thoughts that I know of.

I usually refer to it as "a separation of concerns", because one tries to deal with the difficulties, the obligations, the desires, and the constraints one by one. When this can be achieved successfully, we have more or less partitioned the reasoning that had to be done —and this partitioning may find its reflection in the resulting partitioning of the program into "modules" — but I would like to point out that this partitioning of the reasoning to be done is only the result, and not the purpose. The purpose of thinking is to reduce the detailed reasoning needed to a doable amount, and a separation of concerns is the way in which we hope to achieve this reduction.

The crucial choice is, of course, what aspects to study "in isolation", how to disentangle the original amorphous knot of obligations, constraints, and goals into a set of "concerns" that admit a reasonably effective separation. To arrive at a successful separation of concerns for a new, difficult problem area will nearly always take a long time of hard work; it seems unrealistic to expect it to be otherwise. But even without five rules of thumb for doing so (after all, we are not writing a brochure on "How to Think Big Thoughts in Ten Easy Lessons"), the knowledge of the goal of "separation of concerns" is a useful one: we are at least beginning to understand what we are aiming at.

Not that we don't have a rule of thumb! It says: don't lump concerns together that were perfectly separated to start with! This rule was applied before we started this monograph. The original worry was that we would end up with unreliable systems that either would produce the wrong result that could be taken for the correct one, or would even fail to function at all. If such a system consists of a combination of hardware and software, then, ideally, the software would be correct and the hardware would function flawlessly and the system's performance would be perfect. If it does not, either the software is wrong or the hardware has malfunctioned, or both. These two different sources of errors may have nearly identical effects: if, due to a transient error, an instruction in store has been corrupted or if, due to a permanent malfunctioning, a certain instruction is permanently misinterpreted, the net effect is very similar to that of a program bug. Yet the origins of these two failures are very different. Even a perfect piece of hardware, because it is subject to wear and tear, needs maintenance; software either needs correction, but then it has been wrong from the beginning, or modification because, at second thought, we want a different program. Our rule of thumb tells us not to mix the two concerns. On the one hand we may ponder about increasing the confidence level of our programs (as it were, under the assumption of execution by a perfect machine). On the other hand we may think about execution by not fully reliable machines, but during that stage of our investigations we had better assume our programs to be perfect. This monograph deals with the first of the two concerns.

In this case, our rule of thumb seems to have been valid: without the separation of hardware and software concerns, we would have been forced to a statistical approach, probably using the concept MTBF (= "Mean Time Between Failures", where "Mean Time Between Manifested Errors" would have been more truthful), and the theory described in this monograph could never have been developed.

Before embarking upon this monograph, a further separation of concerns was carried through. I quote from a letter from one of my colleagues:

"There is a third concern in programming: after the preparation of "the program text as a static, rather formal, mathematical object", and after the engineering considerations of the computational processes intended to be evoked by it under a specific implementation, I personally find hardest actually achieving this execution: converting the human-readable text, with its slips which are not seen by the eye which "sees what it wishes to see", into machine-readable text, and then achieving the elusive confidence that nothing has been lost during this conversion."

(From the fact that my colleague calls the third concern the "hardest" we may conclude that he is a very competent programmer; also an honest one! I can add the perhaps irrelevant information that his handwriting is, however, rather poor.) This third concern is not dealt with in this monograph, not because it is of no importance, but because it can (and, therefore, should) be separated from the others, and is dealt with by very different, specific precautions (proof reading, duplication, triplication, or other forms of redundancy). I mentioned this third concern because I found another colleague —he is an engineer by training— so utterly obsessed by it that he could not bring himself to consider the other two concerns in isolation from it and, consequently, dismissed the whole idea of proving a program to be correct as irrelevant. We should be aware of the fact, independent of whether we try to explain or understand the phenomenon, that the act of separating concerns tends to evoke resistance, often voiced by the remark that "one is not solving the real problems". This resistance is by no means confined to pragmatic engineers, as is shown by Bertrand Russell's verdict: "The advantages of the method of postulation are great; they are the same as the advantages of theft over honest toil.".

The next separations of concerns are carried through in the book itself: it is the separation between the mathematical concerns about correctness and the engineering concerns about execution. And we have carried this separation through to the extent that we have given an axiomatic definition of the semantics of our programming languages which allows us, if we so desire, to ignore the possibility of execution. This is done in the book itself for the simple reason that, historically speaking, this separation has not been suggested by our rule of thumb; the operational approach, characterized by "The semantics itself is given by an interpreter that describes how the state vector changes as the computation progresses." (John McCarthy, 1965) was the predominant one during most of the sixties, from which R.W. Floyd (1967) and C.A.R. Hoare (1969) were among the first to depart.

Such a separation takes much more time, for even after having the inkling that it might be possible and desirable, there are many ways in which one can go. Depending on one's temperament, one's capacities, and one's evaluation of the difficulties ahead, one can either be very ambitious and tackle the problem for as universal a programming language as possible, or one can be cautious and search consciously for the most effective constraints. I have clearly opted for the second alternative, and not including procedures (sec, or also as parameters or even as results) seemed an effective simplification, so drastic, as a matter of fact, that some of my readers may lose interest in the "trivial" stuff that remains.

The remaining main questions to decide were the following ones:

1. whether to derive a weakest pre-condition from a desired post-condition or to derive a strongest post-condition from a given pre-condition;
2. whether to focus on weakest pre-conditions —as we have done— or on weakest liberal pre-conditions;
3. whether or not to include nondeterminacy;
4. whether the "daemon" should be erratic or in some sense "fair".

How does one settle them? The fact that the derivation of the weakest pre-conditions instead of strongest post-conditions seemed to give a smoother formalism may be obvious to others, I had to discover it by trying both. When starting from the desired post-condition seemed more convenient, that settled the matter in my mind, as it also seemed to do more justice to the fact that programming is a goal-directed activity.

The decision to concentrate on just pre-conditions rather than liberal pre-conditions took longer. I wished to do so, because as long as predicate transformers deriving weakest liberal pre-conditions are the only carrier for our definition of the semantics, we shall never be able to guarantee termination: such a system seemed too weak to be attractive. The matter was settled by the possibility of defining the wp(DO, R) in terms of the wp(IF, R).

The decision to incorporate nondeterminacy was only taken gradually. After the analogy between synchronizing conditions in multiprogramming and the sequencing conditions in sequential programming had suggested the guarded command sets and had prepared me for the inclusion of nondeterminacy in sequential programs as well, my growing dislike for the asymmetric "if B then *S1* else *S2* fi", which treats *S2* as the default —and defaults I have learned to mistrust— did the rest. The symmetry and elegance of

$$\textbf{if } x \geq y \rightarrow m := x \, \square \, y \geq x \rightarrow m := y \textbf{ fi}$$

and the fact that I could derive this program systematically settled this question.

For one day —and this was a direct consequence of my experience with multiprogramming, where "individual starvation" is usually to be avoided— I thought it wise to postulate that the daemon should select "in fair random order", i.e. without permanent neglect of one of the permissible alternatives. This fair random order was postulated at the stage when I had only given an operational description of how I thought to implement the repetitive construct. The next day, when I considered a formal definition of its semantics, I saw my mistake and the daemon was declared to be totally erratic.

In short, of course after the necessary exploratory experiments, questions (*1*) through (*4*) have mainly been settled by the same yardstick: formal simplicity.

My interest in formal correctness proofs was, and mainly still is, a derived one. I had witnessed many discussions about programming languages and programming style that were depressingly inconclusive. The cause of the difficulty to come to a consensus was the absence of a few effective yardsticks in whose relevance we could all believe. (Too much we tried to settle in the name of convenience for the user, but too often we confused "convenient" with "conventional", and that latter criterion is too much dependent on each person's own past.) During that muddle, the suggestion that what we called "elegant" was nearly always what admitted a nice, short proof came as a gift from heaven; it was immediately accepted as a reasonable hypothesis and its effectiveness made it into a cherished criterion. And, above all, length of a formal proof is an objective criterion: this objectivity has probably been more effective in reaching a comfortable consensus than anything else, certainly more effective than eloquence could ever have been. The primary interest was not in formal correctness proofs, but in a discipline that would assist us in keeping our programs intelligible, understandable, and intellectually manageable.

I have dealt with the examples in different degrees of formality. This variation was intended, as I would not like to give my readers the impression that a certain, fixed degree of formality is "the right one". I prefer to view formal methods as tools, the use of which might be helpful.

I have tried to present programming rather as a discipline than as a craft. Since centuries we know two main techniques for transmitting knowledge and skills to the next generation. The one technique is characteristic for the guilds: the young apprentice works for seven years with a master, all knowledge is transferred implicitly, the apprentice absorbs, by osmosis so to speak, until he may call himself a master too. (This implicit transfer makes the knowledge vulnerable: old crafts have been lost!) The other technique has been promoted by the universities, whose rise coincided (not accidentally!) with the rise of the printing press; here we try to formulate our knowledge and, by doing so, try to bring it into the public domain. (Our actual teaching at the universities often occupies an in-between position: in mathematics, for instance, mathematical *results* are published and taught quite explicitly, the teaching of how to *do* mathematics is often largely left to the osmosis, not necessarily because we are unwilling to be more explicit, but because we feel ourselves unable to teach the "how" above the level of motherhood statements.)

While dealing with the examples I have been as explicit as I could (although, of course, I have not always been able to buffer the shock of invention); the examples were no more than a vehicle for that goal of explicitness.

We have formulated a number of theorems about alternative and repetitive constructs. That was the easy part, as it concerns knowledge. With the aid of examples we have tried to show how a conscious effort to apply this knowledge can assist the programming process, and that was the hard part, for it concerns skill. (I am thinking, for instance, of the way in which the knowledge of the Linear Search Theorem assisted us in solving the problem of the next permutation.) We have tried to make a few strategies explicit, such as the Search for the Small Superset, and a few techniques for "massaging" programs, such as bringing a relation outside a repetitive construct. But these are techniques that are rather closely tied to (our form of) programming.

Between the lines the reader may have caught a few more general messages. The first message is that it does not suffice to design a mechanism of which we hope that it will meet its requirements, but that we must design it in such a form that we can convince ourselves —and anyone else for that matter— that it will, indeed, meet its requirements. And, therefore, instead of first designing the program and then trying to prove its correctness, we develop correctness proof and program hand in hand. (In actual fact, the correctness proof is developed slightly ahead of the program: after having chosen the form of the correctness proof we make the program so that it satisfies the proof's requirements.) This, when carried out successfully, implies that the design remains "intellectually manageable". The second message is that, if this constructive approach to the problem of program correctness is to be our plan, we had better see to it that the intellectual labour involved does not exceed our limited powers, and quite a few design decisions fell under that heading. In the problem of the Dutch national flag, for instance, we have been warned for the case analysis in which the number of cases to be distinguished between is built up multiplicatively: as soon as we admit that, we are quickly faced with a case analysis exceeding our abilities. In the problem of the shortest subspanning tree, we have seen how a restriction of the class of admissible intermediate states (here, the "red" branches always forming a tree) could simplify the analysis considerably. But most helpful of all —it can be regarded as a separation of concerns— has been the stepwise approach, in which we try to deal with our various objectives one after the other. In the problem of the shortest subspanning tree, we found by the time that we started to worry about computation time, the N^2-algorithm as an improvement of the N^3-algorithm. In the problem of the maximal strong components, we first found an algorithm linear in the number of edges, and only the next refinement guaranteed a fixed maximum amount of processing per vertex as well. In the problem of the most isolated villages, our crude solution was independently subjected to two very different optimizations, and, after they had been established, it was not difficult to combine them.

As remarked above, the purpose of thinking is to reduce the detailed reasoning needed to a doable amount. The burning question is: can "thinking" in this sense be taught? If I answer "No" to this question, one may well ask why I have written this book in the first place; if I answer "Yes" to this question, I would make a fool of myself, and the only answer left to me is "Up to a point . . .". It seems vain to hope —to put it mildly— that a book could be written that we could give to young people, saying "Read this, and afterwards you will be able to think effectively", and replacing the book by a beautiful, interactive system for Computer-Aided Instruction ("CAI" for the intimi) will not make this hope less vain.

But insofar as people try to understand (at first subconsciously), strive after clarity, and attempt to avoid unmastered complexity, I believe in the possibility of assisting them significantly by making them aware of the human inability "to talk of many things" (at any one moment, at least), by making them alert to how complexity is introduced. To the extent that a professor of music at a conservatoire can assist his students in becoming familiar with the patterns of harmony and rhythm, and with how they combine, it must be possible to assist students in becoming sensitive to patterns of reasoning and to how they combine. The analogy is not far-fetched at all: a clear argument can make one catch one's breath, like a Mozart adagio can.